Praise for the first edition of Anne Michaud's *Why They Stay*

"Skillful prose makes the dishy profiles an engaging read."
— *Kirkus Review*

"Anne Michaud breathes life into headlines that I thought I knew so well with fresh details about well-known political spouses like Hillary Clinton, Silda Wall Spitzer and Huma Abedin. Her thorough reporting helped cast them into an entirely new light and see how their personal struggles reflect the internal struggles women have faced for centuries."
— **Christine Haughney, Senior Editor,** *NBC News*

It's about time that a book such as *Why They Stay* should appear to comment on the wives of politicians and why they remain in place despite reports of infidelity and bad behaviors. Not only does this apply to the highest political offices past and present, but its message and analysis will reach many a marriage where friends may wonder about the reasons why a wife stays in the home after misconduct is uncovered. This is not to say that the two environments (political and personal) are identical and hold the same commitments and conundrums — far from it. As *Why They Stay* points out, political pressures and purposes are similar to traditional marriages in some aspects and far different in others. It's a gripping production especially recommended for any interested in women's issues and political scandals and their aftermath.
— **Diane Donovan,** *Midwest Book Review*

No one could have written this book better than Anne Michaud, a columnist who has covered politicians for decades. Her observations are sharp and compelling and her prose shines with her unique signature for phraseology, crispness, and excellent diction. *Why They Stay: Sex Scandals, Deals, and Hidden Agendas of Nine Political Wives* is a very informative, engaging, and entertaining work.

— **Christian Siam,** *Readers' Favorite*

"Marriage is a mysterious thing and political unions are even more so. In the engrossing and important *Why They Stay*, Anne Michaud peers into the heart of some of the most famously troubled political marriages of the past 100 years in an attempt to understand why accomplished women ranging from Hillary Clinton to Silda Spitzer put up with men many others would have quickly kicked to the curb. Her answers will no doubt influence how we think about these scandals going forward – not to mention the ones still to come."

— **Helaine Olen, author of** *Pound Foolish*

Anyone interested in politics or the dynamics of couples in public positions would definitely find this book of interest. *Why They Stay: Sex Scandals, Deals and Hidden Agendas of Nine Political Wives* by Anne Michaud is a poignant look at modern political partnerships whose message not only speaks to the validity of marriage in leadership positions but also to the principles and morals of our leaders themselves.

— **Kimberly Luyckx,** *Reader Views*

"It's a story we've heard often: Prominent politicians suddenly find themselves ensnared in humiliatingly public sex scandals, but their wives decide to stay with them. With a prodigious amount of research and deft storytelling skill, Anne Michaud goes beyond the headlines and explores the stories of both spouses, on both sides of the Atlantic, revealing the pain, the loyalty, and the calculations behind the wives' decisions. Every political couple should read it."
— **Bob Keeler, author and Pulitzer Prize-winning journalist**

"I found it really interesting, meticulously researched, and well-documented. *Why They Stay* doesn't revert to sensationalism but really goes to the question of why they stay in the marriage."
— **Stephen F. Medici, author of *The Girls in Pleated Skirts***

Why They Stay is definitely not a flippant read, but a memorable one, and one from which few of the characters at the heart of the stories come out particularly well. Readers will find scandal, shock and a deep sense of discomfort at times, and many will not like the pretext, but the question is a valid one. Why did they stay? The reasons vary, naturally, but this tells the real-life tales, and gives a sense of how each scenario came to be.
— **James Hendicott, *IndieReader***

Why They Stay

Sex Scandals, Deals, and Hidden Agendas of Eight Political Wives

Second Edition

Anne Michaud

Ogunquit-NY Press

‡

Why They Stay: Sex Scandals, Deals, and Hidden Agendas
of Nine Political Wives. Second Edition /Anne Michaud
ISBN 13: 978-0-9976633-4-1
ISBN 10: 0997663340
Library of Congress Control Number 2016914885
Second Edition, June, 2021
Cover designer: Janet Michaud
Cover photographer: C.J. Burton
Editor: Bonnie Britt
Photos:
Eleanor and Franklin Roosevelt, Library of Congress
Jacqueline and John F. Kennedy, Toni Frissell/Library of
Congress
Marion Stein and Jeremy Thorpe, PA Images/Alamy
Silda Wall & Eliot Spitzer, Shutterstock
Wendy & David Vitter, Reuters/Lee Celano/Alamy
Bill & Hillary Clinton, Joseph Sohm/Shutterstock
Huma Abedin & Anthony Weiner, Sky Cinema/Shutterstock
Donald and Melania Trump, Mark Reinstein/Shutterstock

Publisher: Ogunquit-NY Press
P.O. Box 1520, Huntington NY 11743-2714
www.annemichaud.com
For inquiries, contact: OgunquitPress@gmail.com

Dedication

For Daniel, Isabelle, and Charlotte for believing.

Contents

Prologue

The White Queen Relationship

In October 2016, with two days to go until the second presidential debate, *The Washington Post* published a video of Donald Trump bragging about sexually assaulting women — "when you're a star, they let you do it," he told the program host of *Access Hollywood*.

The hit to Trump's campaign was immediate and disastrous. Women claiming he had assaulted them spoke to the media: Trump's campaign had to think fast. And it did. By the time Republican Donald Trump faced Democrat Hillary Clinton on stage at Washington University in St. Louis, his campaign had rounded up three women who accused Hillary's husband of sexual assault, and a fourth who said Senator Clinton had harmed her by defending her rapist in court. With their presence and words, the women sent the message that candidate Hillary Clinton had been complicit in silencing them.

The Trump campaign intended to fight fire with fire by nullifying accusations against him by raising them against Senator Clinton.

In 2017, when the first edition of *Why They Stay* was published on the subject of women who stay with male politicians who betray their marriage vows, I was ready to move on. The topic, however, burst with new energy after Donald Trump became president and the First Lady brushed aside alleged infidelities — in some of the same ways women had in the earlier profiles. The topic of sexual assault became front and center: Melania Trump ignored the accusations in favor of standing by her man.

The first year Trump was in office, millions of women raised their voices. Many of them posted the hashtag #MeToo on social media to indicate they too had been harassed and assaulted by well-known men.

I decided to put the Trump marriage through the *Why They Stay* lens, which led to this second edition to include this couple and other updates. What we witness playing out in the relationships of our public figures we risk finding acceptable in our private lives. Feminists have connected women's sexual subordination to their unequal status in society, and have strived to transform women's expectations in their private lives. Private dignity at home equates to dignity in the workplace and the public sphere.

The 2016 presidential battleground moved the public conversation. In the past, questions about a male politician's adultery were an inquiry about morality. Did he have the character to represent people in office? One answer — the one Hillary Clinton gave in the 1990s — was that if the wife forgave him, then the public could, too. She was essentially vouching for his private contrition and deep-down goodness, his fitness for office.

This generation's questions are not about adultery, but they are still about morality, from sexual assault to demands for sex to promote careers. How would Melania respond by her example?

When the Trumps first entered the White House, the public was trying to figure out this relatively unknown First Lady. Social media mavens wanted to like Melania and so viewed her as a captive. They tweeted #FreeMelania and shared videos of her swatting away Donald's hand-holding gestures. She made some early moves to comport with tradition, by hosting a luncheon in honor of International Women's Day in 2017 and presiding over the rolling of Easter eggs across the South Lawn of the White House.

By the end of the four-year term, Americans hold a bifurcated view of Mrs. Trump. Many Republicans, especially women, revere her as elegant, graceful, beautiful and wronged by the press. A pastor in Missouri held up Melania as a wifely model to which other women should aspire — or risk losing their men.

At the same time some southern preachers referred to then-Senator and presidential candidate Kamala Harris as Jezebel, the Bible's most nefarious woman and archetype of female cunning. There could be no surer sign that the life stories of prominent women affect the lives of private women than when pastors hold them up as positive or negative role models.

To be sure, Democrats similarly vilify Melania Trump. They point out that she took advantage of immigration rules to win citizenship for herself and her parents.

Marriages like that of Melania and Donald Trump fascinate me. I began to think that perhaps this sort of marriage, at the top echelons of Washington and international society, is made from different rules than I had agreed to when I married. Fidelity, honesty — perhaps these were quaint ideas better suited to less ambitious people. When one had the heights of the free world practically in one's grasp, maybe the bargain at the altar became more pragmatic. Certainly, if that were Melania's calculation — that with her brains and his brass, they could conquer the world — she has many predecessors as role models. Jacqueline Kennedy, Maria Shriver, Wendy Vitter, Silda Wall Spitzer, Hillary Clinton. Did their decisions to prop up their politically ambitious husbands send the message that sacrificing marital intimacy for political power might be a worthwhile bargain? Like the strategy of Mellie Grant, the character of the president's wife in the television series *Scandal,* every choice in the marriage — even to conceiving a child — was grounded in cold political calculation.

The people at the center of these stories of power couples mostly choose to see their own motives as selfless. In Elizabeth Edwards' autobiography *Resilience,* she wrote of her marriage to John, U.S. senator from North Carolina, "We were lovers, life companions, crusaders, side by side, for a vision of what the country could be."

When she found out he was cheating on her, the crusading together became "the glue" that kept them together. "I grabbed hold of it. I needed to," Edwards wrote. "Although I no longer knew what I could trust between the two of us, I knew I could trust in our work together." She wanted "an intact family fighting for causes more important that any one of us."

Another difference affecting marriages of such public figures is that they are subject to so much scrutiny: every wart is inevitably exposed and magnified. The couples learn to distrust what is said about them and to turn inward toward each other in times of crisis. Dina Matos McGreevey is the former wife of New Jersey Gov. Jim McGreevey who, in 2004, resigned his office, declaring himself "a gay American." In her memoir *Silent Partner*, she wrote about ignoring press reports. "Yes, I'd once or twice heard the rumor that Jim was gay, but I dismissed it just as I dismissed many other stories, most of which I knew not to be true." Living in a bubble, powerful, public couples sift every report through the lens of what they know to be behind-the-scenes reality. This forces them into an extreme inward focus in which the spouse is often the only trusted confidante. The couple forms a hard shell against embarrassment and criticism. With years of experience in the political trenches, they are conditioned to fight back when trouble comes.

Hillary Clinton summoned political aides to a war room to defend her husband, legally and in the media, against scandal when news of his affair with a 22-year-old White House intern broke. Wendy Vitter, a steely former prosecutor, tried to shame a Louisiana crowd of reporters in July 2007. Her husband Senator David Vitter had been revealed as a client of "D.C. Madam" Deborah Jeane Palfrey. After a week's hibernation, the Vitters called a press conference where Wendy Vitter said, "You know, in most any other marriage, this would have been a private issue between a husband and a wife, very private. Obviously, it's not here."

It wasn't always that way for the wives of powerful men. Prior to the 1960s, the press generally kept mum about the sex lives of politicians. When Eleanor Roosevelt discovered her husband's affair by reading a love letter, she kept it to herself — and used it to gain the upper hand in her marriage, which had the additional benefit of setting her free to pursue writing and social activism. Today's wives of philandering politicians do some of that. They also receive sympathy for being publicly martyred. "Look at her," people may say. "What a rock she is. He doesn't deserve her." Hillary Clinton arguably gained a measure of sympathy by keeping her family together after Bill's affairs, which may have been helpful in her victory as a U.S. senator from New York.

The media's role also changed dramatically from Eleanor's day to Melania's. The modern spotlight on private affairs inflates political couples' sense of themselves, making a public admission of defeat — ending the marriage — that much harder. Being a leading power couple means not only submitting to media scrutiny but also commanding coverage. To leave the marriage behind is to step out of the spotlight. It means fading into normalcy, returning to ordinary life, perhaps an impossible admission for women who have built their egos on being one member of a powerful team. To divorce might be to admit defeat for women who have come to see themselves as extraordinary and who circulate with other famous and history-making figures.

I've researched some of the most high-profile couples who stayed together after a sex scandal — Eleanor and Franklin Roosevelt, Jackie and Jack Kennedy, Marion Stein and Jeremy Thorpe, Hillary Rodham Clinton and Bill Clinton, Silda Wall Spitzer and Eliot Spitzer, Huma Abedin and Anthony Weiner, Wendy and David Vitter, Melania and Donald Trump. In these pages, I have defined staying in the marriage not only as 'til death do us part,' but also as a determined effort to resurrect the political fortunes of their husbands and restore their vision of their life together. I found a set of common characteristics and motivations among the women profiled here. Intriguingly, it is a feminine dynamic that dates back centuries. One historical figure, in particular, represents the idea of rising to prominence through marriage. Elizabeth Woodville, a 15th century commoner in England's War of the Roses, came to be known as the White Queen. The War of the Roses was a medieval war for the throne by two competing family lineages, one that adopted the metaphor of a red rose and the other, a white rose.

Woodville was a widow when she met the man who would become Edward IV. They married for love — unheard of for a royal at the time. Her fortuitous match led to the rise of her 10 siblings at court, who then became the objects of royal favors and grants. Edward IV had many mistresses but as queen, Elizabeth Woodville ignored Edward IV's promiscuity in favor of wielding power. When her husband died a premature death at age 40, Elizabeth conspired with another powerful matriarch, Margaret Beaufort, to install Beaufort's son, Henry Tudor, on the English throne as Henry VII. Their marriage united the competing Red and White Rose family lineages for the throne of England. Woodville's eldest daughter, Elizabeth of York, became queen by marrying him. Their marriage produced the history-making monarchies of Henry VIII and then Elizabeth I.

The traits of the White Queen that resemble those of contemporary women who stay married to powerful but unfaithful men are:

1. The degree to which she is the family's emotional caretaker;

2. How she follows patriarchal rules prescribed for women;

3. Her wish to build a legacy for her generation and the next;

4. Her motivation for financial and emotional security;

5. How much she's moved by a sense of patriotism or desire to see the country move in directions she believes in.

I was inspired to compare modern women with those of medieval England in part because the contrast seems so improbable. Centuries ago, a woman's only means of rising above the circumstances of her birth was through marriage.

Today, modern women in politics and leadership have choices. They can earn a living, support a family, run for office — or choose to walk away and live a private life. Given women's gains in legal and practical rights over the last 50 years — in dramatic contrast to medieval times — I wondered why some political women choose to stay in marriages where they are publicly humiliated.

If their White Queen compromises seem a mystery to the average woman, who might not permit such humiliation in her life, assuming she is financially independent, we must allow for some unusual pressures of history and ambition on powerful, public couples. Not every one of the women profiled in these chapters displays all five of the White Queen traits. Generally, however, their stories offer five common motives and calculations.

Trait One: Submitting to Tradition

Modern White Queens were prepared from early life to accept the limits and burdens of marrying men with great political ambitions. Marriage as a goal in itself — and especially marriage to an important, wealthy man — is an aspiration for which women have trained for centuries. It is a patriarchal mindset. In the medieval era, there was a literal patriarchy: men ruled and women did not inherit property. Today, a remnant of this power hierarchy exists in our minds — and to some degree, in the political and corporate worlds — especially among people of privilege and social rank.

Politics reinforces this mindset because it is a tradition-bound world. Political leaders exist in a bright spotlight where they are expected to respect time-tested rituals, hierarchies, decorum, and unwritten maxims. Politicians pay a good deal of money to advisers to counsel them and their

14

wives about how to behave to appeal to the largest voting bloc. For example, when Bill Clinton ran for president for the first time in 1992, campaign advisers told him that voters were uneasy about the idea of him and Hillary serving as co-presidents — a suggestion he had made while stumping in New Hampshire. "While voters genuinely admire Hillary Clinton's intelligence and tenacity, they are uncomfortable with these traits in a woman," wrote advisers Celinda Lake and Stan Greenberg. "She needs to project a softer side... the role of First Lady appears to be one of the last bastions of tradition."

Couples who enter the political world are at least comfortable with its underlying culture and assumptions, and that comfort deepens over the years they remain in politics. Men who aspire to high office seem to choose partners who fit the patriarchal image of what a wife should be: supportive, home-focused, feminine, gracious and self-sacrificing. Political wives who do not by nature conform to this mold are forced to come to uneasy terms with it. Think of candidate's wife Hillary Clinton competing in an election-year cookie bake-off against First Lady Barbara Bush, or Silda Wall, years into her marriage, finally taking the last name Spitzer to accommodate her husband's run for New York attorney general.

Although women are becoming more of an active force in U.S. politics, they remain a minority among elected officials at the federal level where patriarchal norms still dominate. American voters are conflicted about women and power. In two studies published in the *Journal of Personality and Social Psychology* in 2010, researchers found that female politicians who openly expressed a desire for power in America were viewed as less competent, less caring, and less sensitive than other women. Power-seeking behavior even sparked voters' feelings of moral outrage. Male politicians, on the other hand, did not suffer negative consequences for public expressions of ambition — and, in fact, the respondents' perceptions of them improved. The studies' authors concluded that a female politician's career progress could be hindered by the perception that she wants power, because this desire violates expectations for women.

Nevertheless, in 2020, voters sent more women to the House and Senate in greater numbers than ever before. As a result, in 2021, one quarter of the Senate is female and more than 25% of the House is female. The growing popularity of electing women to political office has not been without aggressive hostility among right-leaning people, especially men. Their anger has famously been directed toward House Speaker Nancy Pelosi, Vice President Kamala Harris, Rep. Alexandria Ocasio-Cortez, and Stacey Abrams, who is credited with establishing the infrastructure that brought many new voters to the polls in 2020 in Georgia.

However, white male bitterness is not always expressed in words. Some are alleged to have made action plans. In December 2020, six men were indicted for conspiring to kidnap Michigan Gov. Gretchen Whitmer. Prosecutors said the men are anti-government extremists who were angry over Whitmer's coronavirus policies. Eight other men were also charged with providing material support for terrorist acts. Some of them are accused of taking part in the alleged plot against Whitmer.

Until recently, for the three quarters of federal politicians who are male, getting married and staying together — projecting a "family man" image — was the usual way a male politician could close the deal with voters. Joan and Ted

Kennedy hit the campaign trail together for his 1980 presidential bid, even though it meant Joan had to smile bravely and brush back questions about her battles with alcoholism and her husband's infidelities. It meant she faced questions about Mary Jo Kopechne, who died in Ted's car after a night of partying, as it sank off Chappaquiddick Island. The Kennedys were no doubt mindful that divorce cost Nelson Rockefeller the presidential nomination in 1964. The divorce taboo has played a significant role in women choosing the White Queen path — even though today, that prohibition is loosening. Ronald Reagan had been divorced for 30 years before becoming president in 1980. Newt Gingrich, John McCain, Andrew Cuomo, Michael Bloomberg — all paved significant political paths following the breakup of their marriages. Former Gov. Mark Sanford was elected to Congress from South Carolina even after a very public liaison with an Argentine lover.

Political couples shun divorce for another reason: class. Divorce is stigmatizing in circles where parents are ambitious about providing the most favorable environment for their children. Eleanor and Franklin Roosevelt thought that staying married to each other would be best for the health and fortunes of their five children. Even today, there remains a gap in divorce rates between those who are highly educated, and those without college degrees, according to a 2010 study by the National Marriage Project at the University of Virginia. Among college-educated couples, rates of divorce or separation within the first 10 years of marriage are lower now than they were 40 years ago, dropping from 15 percent to 11 percent. Divorce and separation among the less educated have risen during the same period.

Tradition among the upper classes holds that wives turn a blind eye to their husbands' extra-marital affairs. Prince Charles of England married Princess Diana even as he continued his affair with Camilla Bowles, whose husband, Andrew Parker Bowles, was said to be "the man who lay down his wife for the country."

For all of the feminist waves that have washed through Western society, we still undervalue women's experience. From the stories of political families in these pages, it becomes obvious that patriarchal assumptions play into the reasons why highly accomplished women stay with spouses who stray.

Trait Two: Longing for Security

Many of the women profiled here, like Elizabeth Woodville, had insecure early lives that led them to seek stability as adults. Woodville was in a precarious position as a widow in her mid-20s with two children by a recently deceased member of the lower nobility. Her second marriage enriched her siblings and children.

From the outside, Eleanor Roosevelt's parents appeared to be leading a life of comfort and culture. However, her father was an alcoholic who was absent from her young life. Her socialite mother mocked Eleanor's plain looks and bookish demeanor, calling her "Granny" when she was a little girl. Both parents died before her 10th birthday. Another modern White Queen, concert pianist and British arts patron Marion Stein, fled the Nazis with her family from Austria, only to have her father imprisoned by the British government on the absurd suspicion that he was a spy. Hillary Clinton's father was overbearing, stingy to the point of cruelty, and stoically, he withheld praise from his bright, accomplished daughter.

For each of these women, the fear of the unknown — of leaving a marriage and casting off alone — may have bound them to a marriage where there is insensitivity, neglect, or even outright abuse. People learn intimacy at home, and when those early standards are set too low, a wife may second-guess her judgment about when and whether she should leave.

This is true as well when a husband is sleeping around. Numbers are hard to come by concerning infidelity, but recent surveys estimated that six in 10 married couples have had at least one unfaithful partner, according to Yale University psychologist Janis Abrahms Spring. Most women won't leave a marriage just because of infidelity; 80 percent of married couples in the United States survive such affairs. And when people grow up in a home where extramarital sex is condoned, they're much less likely to regard it as a deal-breaker. Jacqueline Bouvier's father, "Black Jack," confided in her about his female conquests, even going so far as to play a game with Jackie when he visited her at boarding school. She would point to a classmate's mother, and Jack would respond, "Yes" or "Not yet" — answering the silent question, had he slept with that one? Similarly, Jackie's future husband Jack Kennedy grew up with the idea that powerful men didn't need to be faithful to their wives. His father Joe's many affairs — especially with the glamorous Gloria Swanson — were publicized in newspaper gossip columns. Yet Joe Kennedy's wife Rose ignored it all, choosing family togetherness, social status, stately houses and money over confrontation.

Many of the modern White Queens had reason to suspect before they married that their intended husbands would cheat on them: Marion Stein, Hillary Clinton, Huma Abedin, Melania Trump.

Did they believe, because that's how they were raised, that men are natural-born cheaters? Did they think the trade-offs were worth it — that what they lost in trust and intimacy, they gained in security, excitement, and prestige?

Philandering may make a man appear stronger and more powerful. Anne Sinclair, former wife of French politician Dominique Strauss-Kahn, was asked in a magazine interview what she thought of her husband's reputation as a seducer. She replied that she is "rather proud. It's important for a politician to be able to seduce."

Former New Jersey first lady Dina Matos McGreevey rejected the White Queen bargain and left her marriage. She's been accused of making a cynical deal when she married. "Many journalists were convinced that I'd known all along that Jim was gay and that my marriage had been a contrived political arrangement," Matos McGreevey wrote in *Silent Partner.* "Some took gratuitous swipes at Hillary Clinton while taking swipes at me, saying that, like her, I was an opportunist, and that I'd married Jim knowing he was gay because I wanted to be First Lady and wanted to advance my own political future. Reading those stupid speculations made me angrier and even more depressed." She hadn't known Jim was gay, she wrote, and married him because she loved him and believed he would make a good father.

The expansion of work opportunities for middle class women has contributed to power shifting toward women. Yet as desirable as this may seem, new pressures and problems emerge, according to clinical psychologist Joan

Lachkar, author of *The Many Faces of Abuse: Treating the Emotional Abuse of High-Functioning Women*. For one, the women can become isolated in their do-it-all roles while men may feel displaced. A successful woman "becomes the target of man's competitive and rivalrous nature, and thus subject to even more aggression and abuse. Do men, unconsciously or not, project their hostility onto the women who usurped their positions?"

Among some, this may explain the judgment of, and lack of compassion toward betrayed political wives — as well as the outright hostility. Hillary Clinton has likened the wild, baseless conspiracy theories about her — satanic rituals, child murderer — to a larger culture of sexism and misogyny. "This is rooted in ancient scapegoating of women, of doing everything to undermine women in the public arena, women with their own voices, women who speak up against power and the patriarchy," she told *The New York Times*. "This is a Salem Witch Trials line of argument against independent, outspoken, pushy women. And it began to metastasize around me."

Trait Three: A Personal Sense of Patriotism

As can be observed from Elizabeth Edwards' *Resilience*, another trait of power couples is having a sense of personal or patriotic destiny to work for a cause greater than themselves. Elizabeth Woodville was a benefactor of two institutions of higher education that were in theory open to everyone: Cambridge's Queens' College and Eton College.

One might not expect this of Eleanor Roosevelt, who grew up among privilege — with a pony, a maid, and a

French governess. But as a teenager she ventured to New York City's Lower East Side to teach dance and exercise to poor girls. Later, she championed the presidential policies of Franklin D. Roosevelt for racial equality, job programs for unemployed youth, and women's rights. She was crucial to drafting the United Nations' Universal Declaration of Human Rights.

As a teenager, Hillary Clinton babysat for the children of Mexican migrant workers, an experience that helped form her views on immigration. She began her law career fighting for the legal rights of children, and she is a frequent speaker for women's rights. Silda Wall Spitzer's family was active in charitable causes in her North Carolina community. She founded an organization called Children for Children and championed environmental conservation and education as New York's first lady.

Sometimes, it is only after a great disappointment in marriage that these women come into their own, and their sense of civic duty blossoms. After her husband's tryst with a White House intern and his impeachment, Hillary Clinton ran for office for the first time and won a U.S. Senate seat from New York. When Eleanor Roosevelt discovered her husband's affair with Lucy Mercer, she began writing a six-day-a-week newspaper column to cheer Americans during the Great Depression. Silda Spitzer left her marriage six years after her husband's resignation over patronizing high-priced call girls. Today, Silda is a sought-after fundraiser for Democratic women candidates for office.

Trait Four: Responsibility for the Family's Emotional Health

Another White Queen trait is taking on responsibility for the emotional health of the family — especially in a crisis. Franklin Roosevelt was just 39 when his legs were paralyzed by polio. His need for Eleanor burgeoned overnight, and she responded, helping him dress and move into his wheelchair, managing finances, and taking on the hundreds of daily tasks he could no longer do. She became mother and father to their children, discovering resources in herself she hadn't known she possessed. All of this was after she had discovered his first affair. Huma Abedin, wife of sexting former Congress member Anthony Weiner, has said she would not be able to face the couple's young son, Jordan, if she abandoned his father when he most needed her.

Without exception, the modern White Queens guard their families' emotional health.

Ethicist and psychologist Carol Gilligan argues that women's psychological makeup — our biological heritage — is to subscribe to an ethic of care. That is, spouses of adulterous politicians struggle to draw the line at where giving of oneself for the sake of union is loving, and where it is self-destructive. Gilligan writes *In a Different Voice: Psychological Theory and Women's Development*: "Relationship... requires a kind of courage and emotional stamina which has long been a strength of women, insufficiently noted and valued."

Women demonstrate a moral perspective that develops from feeling interconnected with others — what feminist philosopher Sara Ruddick first termed maternal thinking — in her contribution to the book *Women and Moral Theory*.

Rather than stressing rights and rules, maternal thinking is characterized by nurturance and an emphasis on responsibility to others. The image comes to mind of a spouse diligently and patiently working through marital issues rather than packing a suitcase and walking out the door.

After Eliot Spitzer resigned as New York's governor after he was caught frequenting high-priced hookers, his wife took partial responsibility. She said in an interview, "The wife is supposed to take care of the sex. This is my failing; I wasn't adequate." Elizabeth Edwards, whose presidential candidate husband John fathered a child with another woman, asked in *Resilience,* "How had I failed as a wife?"

Research in Finland with dozens of women who had considered divorce but chose to stay in their marriages found that maternal thinking played an essential role. Vanessa May, the study's author, said that the women defined themselves first as mothers. They positioned themselves as responsible for the continued existence of the whole family and, most importantly, saw it as their task to secure their children's wellbeing. If the father was a good parent, the mother felt she must ensure that the father remained a part of the family even though, on another level, she may wish to end the relationship. Marriage for these women was more than the relationship between themselves and their husband — it was the foundation for a web of relationships that connect and create family.

"A feminist ethic of care directs analytical focus to take into account crucial issues such as gender and the balancing act of providing care for others and caring for oneself, particularly when children are involved," May wrote. "For [the wives], there are other, often more important reasons for keeping the marriage intact even after the pure relationship between husband and wife has withered. ... Many... argue for their decision to stay in their marriage within a family context — it is not only the marital relationship that matters, it is also the whole family that they have taken into account. Thus they see their marital relationship not as a dyadic relationship, but as the basis for a larger web of relationships. And it is in order to maintain this web of relationships that they stay married."

Betrayed wives grapple with their own wounds even while tending to their children's feelings. Depending on age, a young child may withdraw socially or have temper tantrums. An older child may become involved in substance abuse, sexual promiscuity, or other self-destructive behavior as a way to bury the hurt or demonstrate unacknowledged feelings about their parents' actions.

The CBS series *The Good Wife,* which debuted in 2009 and ended in 2016, revolved around Alicia Florrick and her two children as they coped with the crisis of their district attorney father going to jail on corruption charges. Peter Florrick's troubles began, like those of former Gov. Eliot Spitzer, after he paid a hooker for sex. *Good Wife* creators Michelle and Robert King, who are husband and wife, say they drew inspiration from imagining Silda's life after Eliot's downfall. Like Alicia, Silda had given up work as an Ivy League-educated lawyer earlier in the marriage to raise their children.

As Alicia sells their beautiful suburban home, downsizes to an urban apartment and begins work at a law firm, her reasons for staying married to Peter unfold. First, there's his assumption that once he beats the corruption charges, their life will go "back to normal." His mother, who helps the family care for their young teens, tells Alicia, "he's hurting, and he needs you to forgive him." Naturally, the children want their father to return and their family to be reunited. When Peter finally leaves jail and again runs for office, his astute political adviser tells Alicia he has no chance of winning without her Good Housekeeping stamp of approval. In other words, she can choose to stand by him or deny him his redemption. As the writers of this show have it, Alicia acts out of concern for everyone around her.

Jenny Sanford — who ultimately rejected the White Queen role — also considered duty as she and her husband, Mark, the former governor of South Carolina, spent months working through his infidelity: "I was under no illusion that Mark would change overnight, so I steeled myself to be gentle and patient. I prayed for the strength to be so." She questioned which decision would be best for their four boys — an intact marriage and a present father? Or, would her forgiveness of his philandering give them permission to do the same when they became men? In the end, Jenny's decision to leave came not from anger so much as from her own moral reckoning. "I have lived these married years as loyally, as honestly, as lovingly and as committed as I could."

Trait Five: Ambition to Build and Bequeath a Legacy

A final signifier of a White Queen relationship is the desire to build a legacy for one's partner and children. This is perhaps the signature accomplishment of Elizabeth Woodville. From a lowly court position, she negotiated a valuable alliance with the Tudors that led to her grandson, Henry VIII, becoming one of the most influential British monarchs of all time. Her daughter, Elizabeth of York, was the mother not only of Henry VIII but of Margaret, later wife of the king of Scotland, and Mary, later married to the king of France. Woodville's great-granddaughters include Queen Mary I and the enormously significant Queen Elizabeth I.

In a similar spirit, days after JFK's assassination, Jackie Kennedy invited their friend Theodore White, a journalist and historian, to the White House and proposed that Jack's administration had been like Camelot. "In time the Camelot metaphor would be used to epitomize the entire Kennedy presidency, as if that brief, turbulent era, so full of intrigue and vendetta, was one thousand days of unmitigated beauty and light," Jackie's cousin John H. Davis has written. She was building a legacy as she worked to establish the John F. Kennedy Memorial Library in Boston. Jackie invited friends who had worked closely with Jack to her home to speak to her children about their father, so they would know the perspective of his allies such as Arthur Schlesinger Jr., Theodore Sorensen, and Robert McNamara.

England's Marion Stein fought legacy battles twice. First, in refusing to leave her royal first husband for many years while he was in love with another woman, she held out for a deal that would allow her three sons to inherit titles and fortunes. Jeremy Thorpe, her second husband, developed Parkinson's disease a couple of years after his trial and public disgrace. The disease brings on tremors, loss of motor skills and balance, and deterioration of speech until it is almost incomprehensible. Marion translated for her husband for the remainder of their lives, another 30 years, which allowed him to continue to participate in social life, including his beloved North Devon Liberal Democrat party, of which he was the honorary president from 1988 until his death in 2014.

Hillary Clinton not only defended her husband from charges of infidelity, but raised a strong and proud daughter in the shadow of what could have been debilitating shame.

Chelsea Clinton works with her father in the Clinton Foundation raising money and awareness for women and children's health and economic betterment worldwide. Hillary's contribution was the basis for an extraordinary family legacy.

Living through a sexual scandal is hard on children because of the breach of faith. *In Parents Who Cheat: How Children and Adults Are Affected When Their Parents Are Unfaithful,* veteran therapist and author Ana Nogales writes: "Most children still want and expect their parents to be a faithful couple. Children are more likely to thrive when their parents are stable and focused on the family rather than on an outside romantic relationship."

Nogales surveyed 822 people whose parents had been unfaithful and describes this fallout for the children: loss of trust, including fear of rejection and abandonment; low self-esteem; shame for being part of a family in which at least one parent has betrayed life's most valued commitment; confusion about the meaning of love and marriage.

In 2010, when ex-California Gov. Arnold Schwarzenegger revealed that he had fathered a son with the family's longtime housekeeper, 17-year-old Patrick Schwarzenegger publicly changed his surname on his Twitter page to Shriver. His mother is Maria Shriver, now Arnold's ex-wife. It was as though Patrick were saying, "My father's a shit and my mother has nothing to do with it," said psychologist Don-David Lusterman, author of *Infidelity: A Survival Guide.*

Nogales said of Patrick's name change, "There is a strong sense of shame about what has happened, especially in adolescents because their identity is developing."

Popular wisdom holds that children of cheaters will end up being unfaithful themselves. If their sympathies lie with the betrayed parent, it is possible they may become attracted to someone who will cheat on them, as an unconscious way to work through their feelings about their parents' relationship. Or, they may choose partners with whom they can be the betrayer, and thus act out a kind of revenge against the cheating parent. If they identify with the betrayer, they might feel that cheating is okay, and that it is just a matter of not getting caught. Some feel they must be unfaithful in order to avoid becoming a victim of infidelity. It is also possible that promiscuity is a biological trait. Researchers from the State University of New York in Binghamton announced in 2010 that a certain type of dopamine receptor gene, DRD4, is associated with infidelity and one-night stands. However, scientists are still exploring how these genes affect behavior.

A heritage of infidelity isn't absolute. Many children create psychic distance from their parents' adultery, said Laurie Appelbaum, a psychiatrist who heads the outpatient child and adolescent clinic at Allegheny University Hospitals/ MCP. She was interviewed in August 1998, as Bill Clinton's scandals engulfed the Clinton family, and Chelsea was an 18-year-old entering her sophomore year at Stanford University. According to Appelbaum, some adolescents can say, "that's them, and I'm me. I don't like what my father did, but he's still important to me, and I can look at the good."

Eliot Spitzer's daughters were also teens when *The New York Times* broke the story in March 2008 that he had patronized a high-priced prostitution service called Emperors Club VIP. The two eldest Spitzer girls — Elyssa, 18, and Sarabeth, 15, — went to school, as usual, the following morning, to Horace Mann in Riverdale. Later that day, their father resigned as New York's governor. Though the Spitzer girls put on brave faces, they were likely "devastated," said Lusterman, a psychologist who specializes in helping children and adults cope with infidelity. "Children regard their father, especially when he's a respected public figure such as Spitzer, as their ultimate model and moral authority," Lusterman told the *New York Daily News*. "They will be devastated, because they will start questioning every aspect of their past family life and fear they have been 'taken in.' "

Much of the girls' emotional recovery, he said, would depend on the health of their relationship with their mother and how she reacts to the situation with them.

As the children gauge their mothers' reactions, the public watches closely, as well. As they stand on the podium with the cheating husband, modern White Queens receive a good deal of public scorn, even though it was the husband who strayed outside of marriage and is more deserving of condemnation. For all of the egalitarian feminist advances since the Middle Ages, contemporary women who survive in these relationships do so because of a deep imprint from patriarchal culture.

Patriarchy's influence often lives in the minds of women who were raised in a certain way and who aspire to a certain type of greatness — as one half of a powerful, leading couple. They act from behind the scenes, from behind a husband, because their goals and dreams, their stature in the world, is achieved most effectively through the influence of men — or so they believe. Without their husbands, they seem to doubt that they can fully express themselves.

The motives of women in power political couples may be foreign to women in private life, but we should consider that the women who hold or aspire to great power have unique pressures and uncompromising standards. Does that compromise make sense when the couple can do so much good in the world, accomplish their political and policy goals, and build a platform and legacy for their children and grandchildren? Political women struggle with these questions.

Eleanor & FDR

Living Separate Lives Together

The marriage between Eleanor and Franklin Roosevelt has served as a template for political couples who search for a way to stay together through the husband's serial infidelity. As the story has come down to us, the Roosevelts suffered a rift over his affair and then went on to live separate, successful, and very public lives under the same roof. But a closer look shows that their reality was very painful, messy, and human.

The less messy version of the Roosevelts' story — that they lived successful, happy and separate lives together — has endured because, for nearly 50 years after the first rupture over Franklin's affair, outside of the few people involved, the details were known only as rumor and supposition. No public recriminations for this couple, no chastened wife standing at a podium while her husband confessed; they lived in an age when the press ignored adulterous rumors. The public wouldn't know about Eleanor's heartbreak or their marital accommodation until after both had died. Even though Eleanor wrote extensively about her life, including a six-day-a-week newspaper column, "My Day," and three autobiographies, she never included her feelings or any details about this sensitive personal subject.

In 1918 Eleanor discovered a packet of love letters written to Franklin from Lucy Mercer, a young, single woman who had been Eleanor's social secretary and, eventually, a member of the family's inner circle of friends. The letters were the first undeniable evidence of the affair, which Eleanor had suspected for many months, and which had become an open secret in Washington circles. On discovering the letters, Eleanor finally confronted Franklin.

By staying in the marriage, Eleanor believed she was doing right for their five children and for her husband. Just as she was experiencing her own shattering sense of betrayal, she was called on to rally behind Franklin as he stepped onto the national stage as the Democrats' vice-presidential candidate in 1920. She traveled on his whistle-stop tour, monitored his press coverage, and gave him advice on his speeches. Her patriotic devotion to the public ideals the couple stood for revealed itself in her own design for a fulfilling life outside her empty marriage. Using her position first as the wife of New

York's governor and then as first lady, she advocated for safe housing, laws against child labor, wider voter registration, birth control, and civil rights. Her determination to rise above personal pain gave the world one of its great leaders.

The Roosevelts didn't discuss the Lucy affair with their children, even though the aftermath permeated the remaining days of the couple's relationship like an "armed truce," according to their oldest son, James. Instead, bits of the story slipped out over the years, until one of Franklin's former aides, Jonathan Daniels, published the details in a book in 1966. Then in 1973, Elliott, the acknowledged rebel of the Roosevelt children, penned his own account of his parents' marriage, complete with the conjecture that Franklin had another long affair, this one with his aide Missy LeHand. She'd helped build back Franklin's confidence to take his place as a public figure and to run for office again, after polio crippled him in 1921.

Though the intimate rift between Eleanor and Franklin wouldn't be made public during their lifetime, the undercurrents in their marriage were surely felt by their children. The five Roosevelt children had 17 marriages among them. One daughter-in-law slashed her wrists during a family Thanksgiving and was rushed to a hospital, one in a series of ugly encounters that persuaded Eleanor to give up on family reunions. After their divorces, two ex-wives of Roosevelt children moved in together in Majorca; two others committed suicide.

Eleanor was laden with guilt over her role as mother. "Where was the guidance you should have had from Father and equally from me?" Eleanor asked her son Elliott. "Nobody was willing to devote time to provide you with a proper upbringing."

In his memoir, Elliott Roosevelt wrote of his parents, "Probably aware that they had not presented a picture of a contented marriage when we were children, and that they had in addition moved about and neglected us, they may have felt partly responsible that we found it difficult to settle down ourselves."

Eleanor's White Queen Quotient: 8

Eleanor's training in patriarchal values was perhaps the strongest of any of the modern White Queens. She grew up in a rarified world of families that emigrated in the 17th century from Europe to settle in America and build vast fortunes in mercantile trade, banking and real estate. By her generation, they formed an exclusive circle of "the 400" prominent families who claimed for themselves the right to wealth and influence. Though we admire their lives today, Teddy and Franklin Roosevelt scandalized their set by entering the déclassé world of politics. Eleanor's Uncle Teddy and husband Franklin brought a sense of mission to government she found compelling.

Eleanor's need for emotional security was strong. Though financial security was not an issue, she grew up in a troubled household, unsure of her worth. One bright spot was the father-daughter bond. She idealized her father, which served to strengthen the patriarchal values of Eleanor's extended family and social plane. But her father was largely unreliable. In choosing a mate, Eleanor unwittingly found someone just like him: a man who seemed to offer security, love, and attachment, but who would abandon her emotionally.

Eleanor turned her great heart to the outside world for validation and for refuge, and to exercise her gifts for public mission. As a young woman, she broke with family norms to work with immigrant children in New York City tenements. Two traumas in her life pushed her further in this direction: first the devastation of Franklin's infidelity and then his crippling illness. Raised in the upper class at a time when divorce was unacceptable, Eleanor rebelled at Franklin's affair but cloaked her feelings to appear dutiful. She didn't leave the marriage, but gained enough of an upper hand that she could focus on her own interests. Franklin was too guilt-ridden to object. Later, after he lost the use of his legs, Eleanor moved aggressively into national and world matters on his behalf.

Sadly, the caretaking she performed to create a legacy for her loved ones — for her children and to honor her predecessors, and even to support her straying husband — ended up bewildering the next generation. One son in particular, Elliott, portrayed her in *Mother R.: Eleanor Roosevelt's Untold Story* as a distant parent who cared more for strangers — i.e., her social crusades — than for her own children. Her refusal to draw close to her husband toward the end of his life, even when he asked for another chance, created bitterness. Their only daughter, Anna, facilitated secret meetings between Franklin and Lucy Mercer. Emotionally, for this family, the puzzle pieces didn't fit. Just as Eleanor married a man much like her father, the children of Franklin and Eleanor, in turn, reenacted their parents' drama in trying to heal their own childhood wounds.

I give Eleanor an 8 on a scale of 1 to 10, as described in the Prologue, for a White Queen Quotient. She submitted to tradition, longed for security, established her patriotism, and took care of her family's legacy. However, her emotional caretaking for her family was inept. Discouraged, she bonded with a small number of very close friends who, toward the end of her life, became her surrogate family.

Seeking Security in a World of Privilege and Dissolution

Eleanor and Franklin were distant cousins. Their shared forbearers were among the first to settle in America. Claes Martenszen van Rosenvelt came from Holland in 1649, when New York was still Nieuw Amsterdam and there were fewer than 1,000 people in the settlement. The family made its way as merchants and traders. Claes' grandsons, Jacobus and Johannes, created the two branches of the family by establishing themselves to the north and east of New York City. Jacobus, who Americanized his name to James, moved north to Hyde Park in Dutchess County where Franklin grew up. Johannes, who became John, settled in Oyster Bay, the eventual home to Theodore Roosevelt and his niece, Eleanor.

The Hyde Park Roosevelts became Democrats, and the Oyster Bay, Republicans. The geographical split set up a family rivalry, with Franklin admitting in later years that his ambition was to outdo Teddy. At one point when Franklin ran for vice president on the Democratic ticket, Teddy Jr. was dispatched to trail him at whistle stops and inform the crowd that this wasn't the same Roosevelt family.

If Eleanor regretted her abilities as a mother to her children, she had no role model. Her father Elliott was Teddy's brother. Elliott was never healthy; he suffered from painful headaches and dizzy spells, which drove him to drink and take opiates. He tried to work a little, for relatives who were realtors or brokers, but he didn't care for work. He built a mansion at Hempstead, Long Island, where he gave parties, played polo, and "rode to the hounds."

At 19, Elliott married the beautiful socialite Anna Hall who had fixed ideas about the proper life. "My mother belonged to that New York City society which thought itself all-important," Eleanor said. "In that society, you were to be kind to the poor; you did not neglect your philanthropic duties in whatever community you lived; you assisted the hospitals and did something for the needy. You accepted invitations to dine and to dance with the right people only; you lived where you would be in their midst. You thought seriously about your children's education; you read the books that everybody read; you were familiar with good literature. In short, you conformed to the conventional pattern."

At first, Anna enjoyed the social whirl of Elliott's play-boy set, but she soon tired of it, and accused him of wasting his life. They argued, and Elliot threatened suicide. At one point, he vanished for several months. Later, he impregnated one of Anna's servants; she blackmailed him until Teddy bought her silence.

Anna was disappointed with her marriage and ridiculed her plain, serious daughter, so different from herself. Mean-spiritedly, Anna called her daughter "Granny" and Eleanor retreated into a shell to obsess over her buckteeth and curved spine for which she wore a brace. Eleanor was rescued when her doting father returned home from his travels but the reunions were unpredictable, deepening Eleanor's insecurity.

Anna died suddenly of diphtheria when Eleanor was 8. Later, she said her mother's death "meant nothing to her except that she hoped it would bring her father back to her." Instead, Elliott made handfuls of promises he didn't keep. He told her he loved her and someday, when she was older, they could make a home together and she could care for him. He left again, but wrote to Eleanor occasionally. She wrote to him often, pleading to live with him.

But Elliott continued to decline. Two years after his

wife's death, at 34, he threw himself out of a window in a suicide attempt. He survived the initial fall but suffered a seizure and died a few days later. Eleanor was an orphan at the age of 10.

She went to live with her maternal Grandma Hall, a bitter and biblically strict woman who nonetheless struggled to control her children. Eleanor had to endure some uncles who drank to excess and possibly abused her. For protection, her grandmother or an aunt installed three heavy locks on Eleanor's bedroom door. A girlfriend who slept over asked Eleanor about the locks. She said they were "to keep my uncles out."

At 15, Eleanor was sent to boarding school at Allenswood, just outside of London. Headmistress Marie Souvestre acknowledged Eleanor's providential background. When guests came to the school — including Beatrice Chamberlain, the sister of future Prime Minister Neville Chamberlain — Eleanor was invited to stay and talk with the headmistress and her guests.

Marie Souvestre taught her students to use their talents and to dedicate themselves to helping people in need. Eleanor began to see herself as more than an "ugly duckling" and to believe she might have something to offer the world. She tended to her grooming, experimented in the arts, and read widely with the result that she began to see how others saw life. She developed her own opinions. Returning home, and much to the distaste of her family, she volunteered with immigrant children at a settlement house on Manhattan's Lower East Side. Later she introduced Franklin to areas of poverty, opening his eyes to the struggles of the poor and uneducated.

Schooled in a Proud Patriarchal Legacy

For security and affection, Franklin's childhood couldn't have been more different than Eleanor's. His parents, James Roosevelt and Sara Delano, were separately connected by marriage to high-society czarina Mrs. William Astor. When the couple decided to marry, they stayed securely within "the 400" socially prominent American families. The newlyweds honeymooned in Europe for nearly a year.

Sara came to the marriage with an inheritance of more than $1 million, which her father Warren had made in the Chinese opium trade. For a time, Sara lived with her parents and six brothers and sisters in Hong Kong, so that when they finally settled into life along the Hudson River, she felt herself "a person apart." Few of her contemporaries or neighbors had seen so much of the world. She never let her son or her grandchildren forget that they were "special people, inheritors of a grand name and proud tradition, and a part of high society."

Fifteen months after the wedding, in January 1882, Franklin was born. In keeping with upper class American custom, Franklin saw more of the help than he did his parents, who continued their active social lives. Before his fifteenth birthday, he had traveled eight times to Europe. James and Sara employed several servants: a housekeeper, a cook, a butler, a gardener, an equestrian, multiple maids and laborers as work required.

Even so, Sara doted on Franklin. When he had scarlet fever and she was not permitted into his room, "Sara scaled a rickety ladder so she could sit and talk to him through his upstairs window." Boys normally entered boarding school at Groton at age 12 and stayed for six years, but Sara couldn't part with Franklin so young, and had him tutored at home until he was 14.

After Groton, Franklin enrolled at Harvard University where he lived in a large apartment along Mt. Auburn Street, the 'Gold Coast' of student quarters for boys from wealthy families. In his third year at Harvard, Franklin had his first successes, being named head of the student newspaper, the *Crimson,* and permanent chairman of the senior class committee. By this time, he and Eleanor had met at family social gatherings and were writing letters. Franklin could have graduated from Harvard after three years, but Eleanor encouraged him to return for a fourth year and take advantage of his new leadership positions. She wrote how proud she was of him and how much she hoped for his future.

How did two such different people come to be married? One theory is that Franklin thought it would be an advantage to marry the niece of the U.S. president. In fact, Franklin patterned his career after Teddy's from an early age, telling fellow law clerks in 1907 that he intended to run for office at the first opportunity, and that he thought he had a very real chance to be president.

However, there seems little doubt that Eleanor and Franklin were in love. This is the family lore they passed on to their children: When he proposed, she is supposed to have said, "Why me? I am plain. I have little to bring you." And, he is supposed to have replied, "With your help, I will amount to something." Their son James has written that this story sounds like them. "She believed in father and encouraged him," James wrote. "Intelligent and thoughtful, she could contribute to him and to his ideas."

For Eleanor after her itinerant childhood, the thought of a having a loyal brood of Delano-Roosevelts was no doubt

41

comforting. They stuck together in a way that Eleanor's family never had. "They were a clan," Eleanor wrote. "And if misfortune befell one of them, the others rallied at once... The Delanos might disapprove of one another, and if so, they were not slow to express their disapproval, but let someone outside as much as hint at criticism, and the clan was ready to tear him limb from limb."

From their wedding day in 1905, held at the Upper East Side Manhattan brownstone of Eleanor's cousin Susie Parish, the couple's married life took a backseat to politics. President William McKinley had been assassinated four years earlier, and the Secret Service was taking no chances on losing Uncle Teddy. Officers cordoned off the entire neighborhood and stopped guests to interrogate them. In patriarchal tradition, Teddy stood in for his brother, Elliott, Eleanor's father in "giving her" to her new husband. Teddy teased the couple afterward, "Well, Franklin, there's nothing like keeping the name in the family!"

Teddy also stole the show. Most of the guests were most interested in seeing and listening to the president, Eleanor wrote, "and in a very short time this young married couple were standing alone." She surely hoped that her new husband would speak up, but he was as smitten as the rest: "I cannot remember that even Franklin seemed to mind."

To Washington, and Temptation

To be near Eleanor after Harvard graduation, Franklin enrolled at Columbia University Law School. He passed the New York bar exam in 1907 and joined the firm of Carter, Ledyard, and Millburn in New York City. Away from work, Franklin mingled with the people his elite background told him would help him make a successful start in life. He sailed at the Yacht Club and ate lunch at the Knickerbocker Club. In the city, he golfed in Westchester County, and at home in Hyde Park, he played the Dutchess County courses. He gave the appearance of a young man pursuing the comforts and status expected of someone of his class.

But Franklin had other ambitions: entering politics. A family friend had disparaged Teddy's first run for political office, saying that world was "grubby, low, and rough," and that politicians were not the kind of people with whom a gentlemen associated. Teddy replied that if the governing class were such, then he planned to do his part to change the nature of the governing class. And so, Franklin followed suit — sort of.

Franklin ran as a Democrat in New York, doubling down on the disapproval from his family. At least Teddy had been a Republican. New York Democrats were associated with one of the most corrupt, crony political organizations in American history: Tammany Hall. Franklin ran in 1911 and won a seat in the New York State Senate. Two years later, as Democrats swept into the White House under the new Woodrow Wilson administration, Franklin was named Assistant Secretary of the Navy. Serving in both of these positions — as a New York State legislator and then as the Navy's assistant secretary — he strode exactly in the footprints left by his famous cousin Teddy.

By the time Franklin was offered the Washington position, Eleanor and their growing family had been moving with the seasons among their three homes — in New York City, Hyde Park, and Campobello Island off the Maine coast — and she was pregnant with their fifth child. Her work of bearing and raising children was lightened by the employment of at least five servants, and occasionally more. She had additional help parenting from her mother-in-law Sara, whose heavy hand was never far from the young family's affairs.

Washington presented unfamiliar social territory to the Roosevelts, and Eleanor felt she needed a guide. She hired Lucy Mercer to help her navigate the social intricacies. Eleanor called on naval officers' wives, paying as many as 60 visits in a week. At dinner parties, she spoke with cabinet members, senators, justices, and lobbyists. Lucy kept Eleanor's schedule, handled paperwork and paid the bills. Soon, Lucy, with her charming manner and refined background, began to become part of the Roosevelts' social circle for dinners. She had a sparkle that matched Franklin's high spirits but that contrasted with Eleanor's gravity. Eleanor appreciated Lucy's help, but the two were in many ways opposites, and the relationship was not warm.

Besides, Eleanor had begun to notice Franklin light up when Lucy entered the room. Eleanor's lifelong insecurity about her appearance, combined with the many pregnancies, left her feeling old and ugly. Lucy's presence didn't help matters — and Franklin seemed to grow more distinguished and handsome each year. Eleanor felt she was losing Franklin, but rather than draw nearer to him, she reacted in the way that the painful abandonments from her childhood had taught her: she closed off emotionally. Meanwhile, Franklin's own childhood had accustomed him to living at the center of the universe. As his wife pulled away, his need for Lucy's companionship intensified.

Summers when Eleanor and the children left for Campobello, Franklin began drawing out his departure from Washington. His letters to Eleanor during this time were lighthearted, often mentioning Lucy. Eleanor's replies were stiff or scolding: "I don't think you read my letters for you never

answer a question and nothing I ask for appears!"
Eleanor's cousin Alice, Teddy's daughter, encouraged the affair by inviting Franklin and Lucy to dinners together. Alice's own marriage was disintegrating, and her antipathy toward her cousin Eleanor had intensified when they both ended up living in Washington. Alice — beautiful, personable and outgoing — often teased Eleanor for being too serious. She complained that Eleanor dampened parties with her tendency to launch into philosophical discussions, like "whether contentment and happiness were the same thing."

By 1916, Franklin and Lucy found time for riding, driving, and sailing. Son Elliott recalled this period as a "cold war" between his parents. The two fought, not directly over the affair, which remained unspoken, but over other matters.

Franklin's duties for the Navy during World War I took him to France and Britain on an inspection tour. This gave Lucy a reason to write to him regularly for the first time. When he returned from overseas, Franklin had intended to unpack his bags himself, but he fell into bed sick with pneumonia, and as he drifted in and out of consciousness, Eleanor discovered Lucy's letters. "The bottom dropped out of my own particular world," she told her friend Joseph Lash years later. "And I faced myself, my surroundings, my world, honestly for the first time."

Why She Stayed

It's a measure of how deeply Eleanor felt this betrayal that she never put her feelings in writing. She published the first of her three autobiographies, *This is My Story*, in 1937. In it, she wrote about Franklin's mission to Europe for the Navy, her 18-hour shifts volunteering at the Red Cross canteen in Washington, and her sick husband returning from overseas and being carried into his mother's house — but not a word about the near-destruction of her marriage. She went so far as to destroy the tender letters she had sent him during their courtship.

Little is known about the couple's initial confrontation. Their story picks up in the library in the house at Hyde Park, where Eleanor and Franklin met with his mother Sara to discuss what they would do. According to an aunt, and to versions of the story their children absorbed over the years, Eleanor offered Franklin his freedom to divorce and pursue his feelings for Lucy.

This would have freed Eleanor from a situation that had become emotionally unbearable. She had been betrayed by two people close to her — Lucy and Franklin. She was humiliated in the eyes of Washington society where people had become accustomed to seeing Franklin and Lucy together. In an age of ubiquitous camera phones and social media, Eleanor couldn't have denied the affair as long as she had — for more than four years.

Weighing against a divorce for Eleanor was that it was virtually unheard of in their day. No one in either branch of the Roosevelt family had ever divorced. The children would face life disgraced by a broken home. And, how would a divorced Franklin support the family? No divorced man had succeeded in politics, nor built a respectable career in law or business, at least not in the Roosevelts' circle.

For her part, Sara made a powerful appeal to Franklin's wallet. "If divorce were the answer, she would cut off father's money as punishment for his offense," Elliott wrote. In Sara's world, affairs could be concealed and even tolerated, but divorce was a calamity. She used her financial heft to sway Franklin's decision.

The annual income from Eleanor's trust, $8,000, and

Franklin's own $5,000 could support an upper-middle-class life, but not the life the Roosevelts led. The upkeep on their homes, the servants' salaries, his memberships in the most exclusive clubs in New York and Washington, the children's tuition at the best private school, the first-class cabins for travel abroad — this was a lifestyle well beyond their means without Sara's money. Within the previous year, Franklin had written to thank Sara for paying his doctor bills and to remind her that a payment was due on his boat and his life insurance premium.

Franklin also asked for divorce advice from Louis Howe, his political mentor. Howe was a friend from college who had nurtured Franklin's White House dreams, and he argued that Franklin must mend his marriage if he wanted a future in politics. To divorce in New York at the time, a couple had to show that one or the other had committed adultery. If that information appeared in court documents — and subsequently in the press — Franklin surely would have lost his foothold on the political ladder. Josephus Daniels, Franklin's boss in the Department of the Navy, was a puritanical man who had gone so far as to rescind the issuance of condoms for sailors on shore leave, saying that young men should remain abstinent.

And so, Eleanor and Franklin came to an agreement, a White Queen-style political calculation. They would stay together for their financial lifestyle, their political futures, and the legacy they still intended to build for themselves and their children. Franklin acquiesced to ending his relationship with Lucy — a promise he would break repeatedly. Eleanor and Franklin agreed to move into separate bedrooms and end their physical relationship. Eleanor was just 34, with five children ranging in age from 2 to 12. She established a separate residence for herself, Val-Kill, in Hyde Park, New York. The bargain with her husband left her depressed and even more insecure. Photos of her at this time reveal a woman unable to look directly at the camera, as if concealing a private shame. Her weight dropped alarmingly.

"Apparently, after everyone had their say, father and mother sat down and agreed to go on for the sake of appearances, the children and the future, but as business partners, not as husband and wife," James Roosevelt wrote. "After that, father and mother had an armed truce that endured to the day he died."

A few months later, in January 1919, President Woodrow Wilson asked Eleanor and Franklin to attend the peace conference at Versailles. Women openly flirted with Franklin, and Eleanor became upset. In mid-February, she wrote in her diary, "I do not think I ever felt so strangely as in the past year… All of my self-confidence is gone." The couple succumbed to long arguments, and Franklin walked out repeatedly to avoid the drama.

As Eleanor began to remake herself outside Franklin's orbit, her depression eventually lifted. She rediscovered her passion for social justice as the couple pursued the path for which they had made their pact: Franklin's growth as a political leader.

Eleanor's Commitment to Duty Tested

For the time being, though, as luck would have it, just as the Roosevelts' marriage was withstanding its greatest challenge from within, the couple was confronted from without by Franklin's most devastating political setback: the Newport sex scandal. In March 1919, word reached the Navy office in Washington that there was a homosexual subculture in Newport, R.I., that centered on the Army and Navy YMCA and the Newport Art Club, where civilians and naval personnel met. Franklin asked the attorney general to undertake an investigation, but the man botched it. He chose undercover investigators who were young and good-looking, presumably to lure attention — and they did. Some participated in the sex and described their activities on the witness stand during a military court-martial. Scandalized, Congress established a committee to review the investigation; in 1921, the Senate censured both Franklin and his boss Josephus Daniels for involving Navy personnel in "a deplorable, disgraceful, and most unnatural proceeding."

Even before Congress finished its work, Franklin was moving to his next political opportunity: accepting the Democratic Party's nomination for vice president in the summer of 1920.

Franklin ran on the ticket with Ohio Gov. James M. Cox, a pair that had no chance at all of winning against Republican Warren G. Harding in a race that proved to be a national backlash against Woodrow Wilson's progressivism. Still, Franklin pursued this opportunity in the national spotlight for all it was worth, and in August 1921 he set out on a month-long tour by train across the country. Candidates' wives didn't always accompany their husbands on political tours, but Franklin invited Eleanor, in part figuring that her presence would help him in this first election where women were allowed to vote. In that way, ironically enough, the Roosevelts brought balance to the ticket. They were widely perceived as a devoted couple, while Cox had been divorced. Harvard's former president Charles W. Eliot, for one, withheld his support from Cox for that reason.

Eleanor's sense of duty — and perhaps her lingering suspicions of her husband's fidelity — prompted her to join him. She was the sole woman in the entourage. The candidates, their assistants, and the reporters who covered them smoked cigars and ran round-the-clock card games on the whistle-stop tour. For the first part of the trip, Eleanor had little to do but knit, read — often a book a day — write letters, and look out the window.

Franklin's adviser and old Harvard classmate Louis Howe noticed Eleanor's withdrawal. He decided to introduce her to the press people, and speaking with them sparked her interest in politics. Howe and company shared ideas and believed they were important, and this nourished Eleanor's self-confidence. That campaign tour marked the resurgence of Eleanor's activism, which had its roots in her early settlement house and Red Cross work, and would ultimately see her emerge as an independent political figure in the 1920s.

Traits that began to shine through Eleanor's activism revealed many of the same inner qualities that persuaded her to stay married to Franklin. They included commitment; self-sacrifice for his career and for the children's financial and emotional security; rising above personal discomfort and past her class prejudices to develop compassion for the poor, the wounded, the jobless, and those who were excluded from the class she grew up in: African-Americans and Jews.

When the Cox-Roosevelt ticket lost in a landslide, Eleanor was freed from the duties of political wife and resettled her family in New York. She took practical courses to remove the mystery from everyday tasks that had always been performed for her by a staff of servants: typing, shorthand, and cooking. Her biographer Blanche Wiesen Cook wrote that mastering such practical tasks allowed Eleanor to feel less dependent and more in control. She joined the board of the League of Women Voters of New York State, and the leadership invited her to write monthly reports on national legislation.

The quiet Hyde Park hiatus wouldn't last for long. In the summer of 1921, when the family was vacationing at Campobello Island, Franklin contracted polio and lost the use of his legs. Eleanor describes his convalescence as a time when she felt wonderfully needed by him, but also as a great deal of hard work: with her becoming halftime father in addition to full-time mother to their children.

The burden proved too much, and soon Eleanor began to distance herself from Franklin's care as he sought the healing of Warm Springs, Georgia, as an alternative to the cold Atlantic waters off Campobello. After her first visit, Eleanor hated Warm Springs and turned over the duties of caring for Franklin to his aide Marguerite "Missy" LeHand.

"Rather than a cause for jealousy, Missy's presence at Warm Springs provided Eleanor with a guilt-free ticket out of this abhorred place allowing her to get on with her own life," wrote historian Joseph E. Persico. Emotionally for Franklin, these were "wilderness years" when he wondered whether he would regain the strength to pursue his political ambitions again and whether the voting public would accept him. "Whether during periods of stubborn optimism or patches of despair, it was Missy at his side, while the increasingly occupied Eleanor made speeches for the League of Women Voters, attended lunches with college deans, and read magazines to tired workers in the evening at the Women's Trade Union League. She wrote Franklin chatty, wifely letters almost daily."

Fashioning a New Kind of First Lady

Franklin, of course, did rebound. In 1928, he was elected governor of New York, and in 1932, president. By this time, Eleanor had carved out such a cherished independent life for herself that she lamented leaving it for Washington again. She little guessed what an enormous impact she would have in her new role.

As First Lady, Eleanor traveled so much around the country that one *Washington Post* headline announced, "Mrs. Roosevelt spends night at White House." She met miners in Morgantown, West Virginia; she visited city slums and impoverished farms. She reminded the men and women who were in despair that the government was aware and concerned — and she brought their stories back home to the White House.

In 1935, she accepted a contract to write 500-word columns six days a week. The column conveyed to millions of Americans that the White House shared their concerns. Eleanor's top priority, in both her writing and politics, was to include those who had been on the outside looking in at American prosperity: African-Americans, women, and children.

Eleanor pressed Franklin to advocate for the Costigan-Wagner Anti-Lynching Bill, which was being filibustered in the Senate. Franklin was cautious, not wanting to alienate Democratic southerners. At the time, African-American reporters were not even allowed to attend the president's press conferences. When the Daughters of the American Revolution refused to allow black opera singer Marian Anderson to perform at Washington's Constitution Hall, the largest auditorium in the city, Eleanor resigned from the DAR and saw to it that the concert was held in the open air in front of the Lincoln Memorial.

In 1935, she became concerned that 3 million unemployed young Americans were losing faith in democracy to meet their needs. "I have moments of real terror when I think we may be losing this generation. We have got to bring these young people into the active life of the community and make them feel that they are necessary," she wrote. Eleanor worked with the Works Project Administration to conceive of a 2-year volunteer program, the National Youth Administration, which cost millions.

Along with other New Deal programs, such activity alienated Franklin from the people he had spent his life among. "Regardless of party and regardless of religion," Henry Luce's *Time* magazine asserted in April 1936, "today, with few exceptions, members of the so-called Upper Class frankly hate Franklin Roosevelt."

Franklin died in office in 1945, at age 64. Eleanor was 61. The FDR administration had presided over the Great Depression, World War II, and a vast expansion of social welfare programs like Social Security. It's not possible to overstate Eleanor's role in dreaming up and petitioning for the New Deal. She also argued for the United States to join the newly forming United Nations, and after Franklin's death, she served as one of the first U.S. delegates, helping to write a document that would become a beacon of decency after the horrors of Nazi Germany, the Universal Declaration of Human Rights. She was the only woman in the U.S. delegation to the United Nations. She said of her United Nations work, "There must be a great deal of Uncle Ted in me, because I enjoy a good fight."

After her husband's death, Eleanor pared her life down to a simpler scale, getting rid of the servants, the wardrobe, and the entertainment budget that went along with being First Lady. She financed her newly modest lifestyle through writing and speaking. At 75, she traveled to the Boston suburb of Waltham twice a month to teach international law and organization at Brandeis University. Democratic presidential candidate John F. Kennedy courted her support and appointed her to chair the Presidential Commission on the Status of Women. She wrote him long letters of advice about the White House and public policy.

Eleanor died in November 1962 at age 78, having overcome her agonizing childhood, the narrow prejudices of her social class, and the continuous disappointments in her marriage to become the most recognizable woman in the world standing for women's rights and human dignity.

Infidelity's Legacy for the Five Roosevelt Children

With parents who had made such a success of public life, great things were expected of the Roosevelt children. But they would struggle to find security in love and career, and the relationships among the children and their mother often dissolved into angry détentes. Elliott, the third of the five children, co-authored a series of family biographies, as well as mystery novels starring a fictional Eleanor as detective. Yet his portrayal of her in real life was so bleak that James, the eldest son, felt he had to respond with *My Parents: A Differing View,* which takes pains to restore Eleanor as a warmhearted friend and mother. He dedicated it to "the Rebel" — Elliott.

It seems old-fashioned now to place the responsibility for the emotional life of a family so exclusively in a mother's lap. Her efforts to build a fulfilling life for herself outside the marriage are viewed by these biographer sons as detracting from her role as a parent. And yet, where is Franklin in these accounts? When the children were ages 5 to 15, he succumbed to polio, and for eight years, he was struggling to recover physically and politically, eventually winning election as governor of New York. When he entered the White House in 1933, the five children ranged in age from 17 to 27, and he remained president for the rest of their lives, dying in office in 1945. Anna, the oldest, reminds us, "He was a very busy guy."

Yet the manner in which Franklin dealt with his marriage and his own needs for intimacy reverberates throughout the lives of his children. Their first marriages were to spouses with the right pedigree. Infidelities abounded. Partners who failed to fulfill their needs were discarded in favor of others. Worldly success often took precedence over happiness at home. In their lives, the children of Eleanor and Franklin tried to work through the issues their parents left unresolved in their marriage.

"At first, each of us married into moneyed families. Not because we needed money, but because we were exposed to moneyed people," James wrote. "Eventually, we made other marriages. Some of us married outside the social register... Hopeless romantics, we Roosevelt children married again and again."

The eldest, Anna, briefly attended college at Cornell University but quit in 1926 to marry Curtis Dall, a successful stockbroker. She said she married to "get out of the life I was leading," a reference to the difficult family situation in the aftermath of Franklin's affair with Lucy Mercer.

Anna and Curtis separated as Franklin entered the White House in 1932, and Anna moved there with her two children. She met and married a reporter, John Boettiger; it was a second marriage for both. Eleanor felt Anna and John entered this marriage having learned from their sufferings and mistakes, and she commented to a friend in a letter that marriages should not be preserved for the sake of the children.

"Never for a minute would I advocate that people who no longer love each other should live together because it does not bring the right atmosphere into a home," she wrote. She added that it was sad when a couple was unable to make a success of marriage, "but I feel it is equally unwise for people to bring up children in homes where love no longer exists."

Anna and John moved to Seattle, where he had been offered the job of publisher of the *Post-Intelligencer*, and Anna would edit the "women's pages." The paper's owner, William Randolph Hearst, was an early FDR supporter. But Hearst and John soon crossed swords over Franklin's New Deal programs, which Hearst deplored.

After Franklin died in 1945, John quit as publisher. He and Anna bought a small weekly newspaper in Arizona, planning to bring a liberal voice to this conservative region. After two erratic years, the effort failed, and John was devastated. He began seeing other women, and took off, leaving Anna holding the financial debts of their business. They divorced in 1949, and the following year, John killed himself.

Eleanor and Franklin's second child, James, married Betsey Cushing, the daughter of a socially prominent Cleveland physician. Like Anna and Elliott, James married young; he was just 23. It would be the first of four marriages for him, including one to a woman who nursed him while he was having surgery, another to a receptionist from his office, and yet another to his son's teacher. He ran for governor of California in 1950 but couldn't concentrate on the campaign because of marital problems; he lost. In 1959, he moved to Switzerland to accept a job with the Investors Overseas Service. He stayed out late one night, and when he returned, his third wife stabbed him in the back with a souvenir from his service in World War II, a marine knife.

The first of Elliott's five marriages was in 1932 to Betty Donner, heiress to a steel fortune. Her family disapproved of FDR and, so too of Elliott. Their marriage ended in divorce in 1933 — the first White House child in history to divorce, setting off criticism around the country. Elliott wanted to marry Ruth Goggins, of Texas, and Eleanor pleaded with him not to rush into a second marriage so quickly, especially since he didn't have a job. But Elliott flew to Reno to divorce Betty, changed planes in Chicago, and headed straight to Iowa to marry Ruth. Ruth and Elliott's marriage drowned in a sea of debt. His third wife, actor Faye Emerson, slashed her wrists at a Roosevelt Thanksgiving at Val-Kill and had to be rushed to a hospital; Elliott committed his fourth wife to a sanitarium and approved electroshock therapy for her. He then tried to get control of her assets through a conservatorship, and when she discovered what he was doing, she ended the marriage. Eleanor asked Elliott to try to mend this relationship: "All of us have feelings, you know, but in time a husband and wife get to make allowances for the other's faults as long as they refuse to be selfish."

But Elliott had a fifth replacement wife in waiting: Patricia Peabody, a 38-year-old divorcee with four children. He tried to introduce her at dinner at Eleanor's Manhattan apartment, which James and John refused to attend. Anna and Franklin Jr. showed but were unfriendly. After drinks, Franklin Jr. propositioned Patty as "the only sister-in-law I haven't had." On her deathbed, Eleanor refused to see Elliott or Patty.

Unsurprisingly, given his extramarital suggestion to his new sister-in-law, Franklin Jr. was also divorced several times.

John, the youngest of the Roosevelt children, married a Massachusetts debutante, Anne Sturgess Clark, while he was at Harvard. Their marriage lasted a long time, and John took pride for many years in being the only sibling who hadn't divorced. When they did finally part, Anne went to live in Majorca with Elliott's third wife, Faye Emerson.

To be sure, not every marriage that ends in divorce should be considered a failure. But it does seem that the Roosevelt children, as a group, had an unusually difficult time finding peace and happiness in their intimate relationships. If Eleanor and Franklin stayed together for the children, their accommodation for years did little more than paper over their emotional distance. Eleanor seemingly struggled throughout the rest of her life with her decision, alternatively encouraging Elliott to "make allowances" for his wife, and admitting on the occasion of Anna's remarriage that people who no longer love each other bring the wrong atmosphere into a home.

Eleanor and Franklin's marital deal resulted in an enormously successful public life for them, but it created a painful, tense, and chilly home life for their children. That pain never seemed to leave the Roosevelt progeny as they tried, and often failed, to form marital relationships of their own. In the end, Eleanor and Franklin fashioned a pact that allowed them to flourish politically but detracted from the heart and intimacy that sustains a healthy family. As a political force, the Roosevelt legacy is large and intact. But its heirs inherited emotional brokenness.

Jackie & JFK

A Legacy of Adultery

When her husband was assassinated in Dallas on Nov. 22, 1963, Jackie Kennedy could have been forgiven for withdrawing into her own grief. Raised to marry for money and social standing, Jackie had exceeded all of her parents' expectations by becoming not only wealthy but the most glamorous First Lady in American history. Her marriage to the compulsively womanizing Jack Kennedy had cost her emotionally — and she was left to cope in the wake of his brutal death.

Raising Caroline and John Jr., ages 5 and 2, kept Jackie moving forward. After the family left the White House, Jackie took to inviting her late husband's close friends and colleagues to their new home to tell the children stories about their father. Among them were historian Arthur Schlesinger Jr., speechwriter Theodore Sorensen and Defense Secretary

Robert McNamara. These private conversations — seminars, really — continued for years. Jackie also had her children meet regularly with developmental psychoanalyst Erik Erikson. He served as their therapist in an era when Americans didn't usually acknowledge children's emotional pain, much less offer them help. Jackie stepped outside the norm to make sure her kids were well cared for.

At the same time, she was concerned with managing the Kennedy legacy. Jackie began mythologizing JFK's short reign within two weeks of his death. She invited the pro-Kennedy journalist and historian Theodore White to tape an interview, in which she suggested that Jack's thousand days in the White House were akin to the enlightened, noble times of the fictional *Camelot* — a popular musical then playing on Broadway. The magic of her husband's presidency, Jackie suggested, was "an interlude marked by grand intentions, soaring rhetoric, and high style." In White's hands, the Arthurian metaphor would capture the American popular imagination. Early in her courtship and marriage, Jackie resented the Kennedy clan's love for the right sort of publicity although, like a pro, she learned to turn it to her family's advantage.

In many other ways, Jackie worked tirelessly to burnish her husband's legacy. She sweet-talked President Lyndon Johnson into renaming Cape Canaveral for JFK and raised millions of dollars to build the I.M. Pei-designed presidential library in Boston. New York City Mayor Robert F. Wagner Jr. rechristened the Idlewild International Airport for JFK, and Congress changed the name of the planned national cultural center in Washington to the John F. Kennedy Center for the Performing Arts, appropriating $15.5 million in funds to match private donations.

Unfortunately for Jackie's White Queen legacy building, her efforts didn't serve as a complete bulwark against the seamier side of the Kennedy White House years. In 1981, Jackie was working as an editor at Doubleday when she remarked to a rising novelist, Edward Klein, that she was concerned that her children were being influenced by warped accounts of JFK's presidency and her relationship with their father. "Once a mythical figure, Kennedy was being portrayed as a coarse, shallow, morally deficient, power-hungry man," Klein wrote. Jackie "was often depicted in books and in the supermarket tabloids as the snooty, spiteful, greedy, needy Jackie, the original material girl."

Jackie's White Queen Quotient: 7

And with some justification. Jacqueline Kennedy, like Eleanor Roosevelt, was raised to marry at a certain level. Whereas Eleanor's choice of Franklin grew out of the assumptions of her class and her times, Jackie's was a more studied and calculated contract. Born to a mother who hid her lower-class Irish ancestry and a father whose once-wealthy family was in financial decline, Jacqueline was actively tutored to marry a patriarchal figure who would rescue her — and secure the social niche her family hoped to inhabit. It was a time of great social mobility in America. Joe Kennedy, Jack's father, had amassed a powerful fortune after his forebears had fled poverty and oppression in Ireland. From birth, Jackie Kennedy was cast into the role of a beautiful debutant with a mission.

At the same time, she had much in common with Eleanor that drove her to seek security: a heartbreaking childhood, a glamorous and manipulative father, and a heritage of infidelity and betrayal in her parents' generation. Like

Eleanor, Jacqueline struggled with her disappointment in marriage and found ingenious ways to assert her identity, integrity, and patriotic influence on American culture. As a young mother as well as First Lady, Jackie taught the country's women to see themselves in a new light. Just as popular culture was proselytizing that American women's proper role was keeping a home, Jackie elevated this function by presenting a new image of homemakers as consumer experts and arbiters of taste.

While Eleanor's patriotism focused outward as she championed the poor and marginalized, Jackie held herself apart from, and above the crowd. She was pillbox hats and oversized sunglasses, a woman to admire and envy. Always concerned with staying model thin, Jackie nurtured favored clothing designers and interior decorators, and she reveled in international tabloid attention. Once, when she tired of Jack's philandering, she allowed the press to witness her openly traveling with a beau in England, so much so that her father-in-law felt forced to rein her in with a promise of money — reportedly millions, as we shall see later in this chapter. After JFK's death, Jackie was supposed to play the part of the tragic American heroine — but she shocked her admirers and the world by marrying jet-setting shipping magnate Aristotle Onassis. Hardly a patriotic choice, and for this, Jackie forfeits White Queen points.

However, as an emotional caretaker of her family, Jackie was extraordinary. Even before her husband's assassination, during their White House years, she fought to create a normal life for her two children, despite having to raise them in the political limelight. She took them out of the White House to play in the countryside, and she protected them from too much publicity. With the same determination, she propped up her husband as his image suffered one political defeat after another, as evidenced in the coming pages.

Superficial portraits of Jackie Kennedy usually discount her noble qualities. For her patriarchal views, her need for security, and her care for her family's emotional health and legacy, Jackie gets high marks. However, her patriotism to a cause larger than herself suffered after JFK's assassination. For those reasons, I rate Jackie Kennedy a White Queen Quotient of "7."

The Kennedys and Fitzgeralds: Stepping Up from 'Second Class'

The story of Jack and Jackie Kennedy's marriage is best understood in the context of what it meant at the time to be a descendant of Irish immigrants in America. Indeed, Jack's mother Rose Kennedy made each of her 29 grandchildren read Leon Uris's *Trinity,* the saga of Catholic rebellion in Ireland against the Protestant reign. Of course, by the time most of Rose's grandchildren were reading this tale of oppression and flight, the Kennedy family had risen to the highest reaches America could offer: Her husband Joe, a millionaire many times over, had arranged trust funds worth more than $10 million apiece for his wife and eight children. Their second son, Jack, had served in the highest elective office in the land.

Theirs was a remarkable history of progress for a family that had left Ireland in poverty just three generations earlier. Patrick Kennedy, Joe's grandfather, lived under strict penal laws imposed by the Protestant British on the Roman Catholic Irish majority, which essentially prevented Catholics from bettering themselves socially or economically.

Catholics could not sit in Parliament, join the armed forces, be employed in government service, or join the legal profession. They weren't allowed to teach or maintain schools, or to send their children abroad for education. Catholics couldn't keep firearms, own a horse worth more than five pounds, or purchase land. Land leases by Catholics were limited to 31 years.

Patrick sailed for America in 1848, arriving in Massachusetts where white Anglo-Saxon Protestants controlled banking, commerce, manufacturing, education and government. "The Irish ... were utterly despised," wrote historian John H. Davis. "The want ads in Boston newspapers read, 'None need apply but Americans,' 'Positively no Irish need apply'." Boston hired Irish labor at the cheapest rates possible, as domestic servants and in gangs laying down new highways and railroad lines.

Patrick married another Irish immigrant, Bridget, and they had four children. The years were hard on Patrick, and a decade after his voyage, he contracted cholera and died, penniless, at 35. Bridget carried on by opening a "notions shop" — a convenience store selling groceries, toiletries, and other household items. She lived with her children upstairs. Her youngest child and only son, P.J., would launch the family on its next trajectory.

The choices P.J. made tempt one to imagine that he held old British penal laws in the back of his mind. He secured ownership of a business — a saloon — and shortly afterward, he ran for public office. His leadership was such that he was seen as someone who could 'deliver' the East Boston vote. Together with a few fellow players, he parlayed his political influence into kingmaker status behind the scenes in Boston mayoral elections. With an eye on the next rung of the social ladder, P.J. sent his son Joe to the very best of the Brahmin educational enclaves: Boston Latin School and Harvard University.

Like the Kennedys, the Fitzgeralds had staked their claim in America through politics. Rose Fitzgerald's father, John, started with election to Boston's Common Council and worked his way up to become the city's first Irish Catholic mayor. He didn't approve of the romance between Joe Kennedy and his daughter. The Fitzgeralds saw themselves as a better breed of Irish immigrant. Shortly after graduation, Joe began taking risks in banking and the stock market and got himself appointed president of an East Boston bank. That impressed John, nicknamed Honey Fitz, who finally gave Rose and Joe his blessing.

The newlyweds bought a home in the upscale Boston suburb of Brookline, started a family, and spent summers at Nantasket Beach on Boston's South Shore. It was an inviting Catholic enclave, but eventually not satisfying to the ego of the increasingly wealthy and prominent Joe Kennedy. In 1927, he applied for membership at the neighboring Cohasset Country Club, and was rejected. Angrily, Joe announced that his family would move — closer to Wall Street and the stock market hub in Riverdale, New York. While Boston's social inner sanctum remained closed to the Kennedys, New York offered a world where newly minted wealth was respected.

The Bouviers:
A Façade of Financial Security

At about the same time, Jacqueline Bouvier's family grappled with social anxiety of its own. In 1815, Michel Bouvier arrived in Philadelphia equipped to continue cabinetmaking and fine furniture craftsmanship that had won his family acclaim in their native France. Michel and his sons speculated in real estate, and moved into trading stocks. By 1929, Michel's son M.C. Bouvier was worth $4 million, while his contemporary P.J. Kennedy left an estate worth just $57,000.

In the coming years, the families' financial positions flip-flopped. Joe Kennedy, the risk-taker, adroitly manipulated the stock market during the crashes of the 1930s by selling stocks short: he bet that a stock would continue to decline. It wasn't considered a gentlemanly wager, predicated as it was on others losing money, but it worked. He emerged from those tumultuous years that crushed so many fortunes richer by about $1 million. Meanwhile the Bouviers suffered catastrophic losses. By Jacqueline's generation, the family fortune was nearly exhausted. The Bouviers refused, however, to ratchet back their lifestyle to match their income, putting further pressure on the family coffers.

Keeping up appearances, John Vernou Bouvier III "looked like money, breeding and power" in 1928 when he married Jacqueline's mother. He was a 37-year-old bachelor, tall, with icy blue eyes and a swarthy magnetism that many women found irresistible. He kept himself tanned by using a sunlamp, earning him the nickname "Black Jack" — which given his womanizing was no doubt a double entendre. His wife, Janet Lee, was 15 years younger. She came from a family very similar to the Kennedys in the 1920s: an Irish-American clan on the rise financially and socially, tough and ambitious. Janet understood that to marry up, she had to pretend to be the product of a socially superior background.

She did so, but would soon learn that Black Jack's pose was also an act. The Bouviers were not, as he liked to claim, related to French nobility. Where they were once fabulous-ly wealthy, they were no longer. He was a womanizer who played around even after their daughters Jacqueline and Lee were born. The Bouviers' living arrangement made infidelity almost too easy. During the week, Janet was in East Hampton with the children while Jack spent his weekdays working on Wall Street. After work, he stopped by the Polo Bar at the Westbury Hotel and inevitably fell into the arms of some beautiful woman who he'd take back to his Park Avenue duplex. He didn't mention that the fabulous digs belonged to the father of the wife he was at that moment betraying.

Black Jack was a violent drunk, and when Janet learned of his extramarital escapades, she flew into rages as well. He beat her in front of the children, and she fought back by hurling plates and curses.

Adultery was the only grounds for divorce, at the time, in New York. Janet and her father devised a plan to trap Jack in his philandering: They arranged for a "Scandinavian blonde" to meet him, and they had him followed by a private detective. Soon, Janet had her evidence. She filed for divorce and vindictively shared the news with the New York *Daily Mirror*. "Society broker sued for divorce" read the Jan. 26, 1940 headline. Not only did the story damage Black Jack's reputation, but it also brought shame to his 10-year-old daughter Jacqueline. She put up with ugly remarks at school and became withdrawn at Bouvier gatherings. "From this point on," wrote her same-age cousin and biographer John H. Davis, "young Jacqueline was to crave one thing above all others: respectability and status."

Jackie's Mother: Schooling her Daughters to Marry Mr. Right

Janet Lee Bouvier's reaction to her divorce was extraordinarily instructive for her young daughters. She spent her time hunting for a rich husband. The girls' governess, Bertha Kimmerle, presented a sworn statement to the court in June 1939 as part of the Bouviers' custody dispute. "She was a lady that unmistakably had a will, and was generally engaged in doing what she wanted, when she wanted and where she wanted," wrote Kimmerle about Janet. "It was thus a matter if not daily at least of frequent occurrence, that Mrs. Bouvier was not home, and the children, consistently without their mother, were always in my company. She would stay out late almost every night and not get up until noon the next day, when she would quickly pull herself together for a luncheon date."

Janet was irritable and impatient with the girls, according to Kimmerle: "Mrs. Bouvier was a lady of quick temper... Mrs. Bouvier gave Jacqueline a very severe spanking because the little girl had been too noisy in her play. She would spank Jacqueline quite frequently and became often irritated with the child, but for no reason that I was able to see..."

Within three years, Janet found her new match in Hugh D. Auchincloss, a well-off stockbroker and lawyer with three children from two previous marriages. He was 54 and she was 36. They lived at Hammersmith Farm, on 75 acres over-looking Narragansett Bay, and at Merrywood in McClean, Virginia above the Potomac River. Hugh and Janet had a daughter and a son, bringing the number of Auchincloss heirs to five. As the daughters of Jack Bouvier, Jackie and Lee stood to inherit nothing from Auchincloss, whom they called "Uncle Hughdie." Their mother made it clear: You must marry well to secure your future.

This lesson came through in Janet's reaction to Jackie's first brief engagement, to John G. W. Husted Jr., the son of a prominent New York banker. Husted made an annual salary of $17,000 as a stockbroker — respectable for a young man but nowhere near Hugh's yearly earnings. When Janet discovered this, she told Jackie bluntly that she could not afford to marry him.

Not only did Janet instruct her daughters by example, but the Bouvier clan also overtly discouraged its women from pursuing careers to become self-supporting. Edith Ewing Bouvier Beale, Black Jack's sister, had a rich and powerful singing voice and an electric presence on stage. Both her father, and her husband Phelan Beale, who worked as a lawyer in her father's firm, persuaded her to give up the theater as it was an inappropriate pursuit for a woman of her class. Edith, or "Big Edie," became an eccentric recluse and the subject of a 1975 documentary, *Grey Gardens*.

At 22, Jackie revealed the narrow parameters of her dreams in a travelogue written with her sister Lee, then 18. *One Special Summer* chronicled the sisters' trip through Europe in the summer of 1951. A photomontage toward the end depicted Jackie and Lee in regal gowns and crowns above the caption "Dreams of Glory." The dreams of the two Bouvier girls were filled with images of marrying well and wealthily, and acquiring a royal title.

When Jack met Jackie, he was equally anxious for a suitable union, but for very different reasons. In 1952, Jack Kennedy had just won election to the U.S. Senate, after having served three mostly unremarkable terms in the House of Representatives. In Washington, Jack was known as a playboy who didn't work particularly hard. His status as a World War II hero and scion of one of the most astute, image-making families in America helped in his election to the Senate. The book about his wartime activities, *P.T. 109,* won a Pulitzer Prize, and his *Why England Slept,* adapted from his thesis at Harvard, helped distance him from his father's politically disastrous appeasement policies toward Germany as U.S. Ambassador to England. At 35 and as the newly elected senator from Massachusetts, Jack needed a wife if he was going to run for president.

Jacqueline Bouvier was an excellent candidate. The *New York Journal-American* had named her 1947's Debutante of the Year. The article described her as regal and having poise, intelligence, and the daintiness of Dresden porcelain. Even more acceptable to the Kennedys, Jackie was Catholic with the added stature of a French surname. Knowing that the Kennedys were insecure about their social status, she took pains to allude to her Bouvier ancestors, who had been in the New York *Social Register* continuously since 1889, and the celebrated Auchinclosses. She downplayed her Irish heritage from her mother's side, and conjured an image of wealth by inviting Jack to visit her grand homes at Merrywood and Hammersmith Farm so he wouldn't think she was after his money.

Male Privilege: Philandering
in Both Houses

Both Jack Kennedy and Jacqueline Bouvier came from families in which the male privilege of sleeping around was tolerated and sometimes celebrated, depending on which family member was consulted. Joe Kennedy worked to convince Rose to become his wife and to turn aside her father's hesitation about him. Once they were married, he left her alone to raise the children while he spent most of his hours building his financial empire; he came home just in time to sleep. Rose began to doubt her marriage and believe that maybe her father had been right. After their third child was born, Rose went to her parents' home seeking sympathy. She talked about leaving Joe but her parents wouldn't hear of it. Her father Honey Fitz told Rose she was a wife and mother in the Catholic tradition; she must return home and honor her commitments.

Perhaps it was the realization that she had no other option that made Rose stick with Joe through what was to become very public philandering. It would have been nearly impossible for Rose to ignore the rumors of her husband's infidelities, as they were printed in many newspapers, including those in Boston. In 1926, Joe became interested in Hollywood and briefly ran three studios. There he met the sultry Gloria Swanson, 11 years his junior and one of the most sought-after actresses in Hollywood. In the winter of 1928, Joe invited Swanson to Florida to share the height of the Palm Beach social season with him. In the words of her sixth husband, she was the "ultimate trophy mistress." Swanson agreed but brought along her then-husband, Henri, a minor French nobleman. Joe dispatched him on a fishing trip and afterward gave him a job in Paris as head of Pathé Studios in Europe, clearing the field for a passionate affair that Gloria described in her 1980 memoir *Swanson on Swanson.*

Rose affected the stance that Gloria was just one of Joe's business associates. In her memoir, Rose wrote, "Obviously, the best adviser-manager-financier in Hollywood was Joe Kennedy ... I do know Gloria wanted his advice and he did help to set her up as an 'independent'," as Gloria Productions Inc. In fact, Joe's poor management of Swanson's career helped sink her professionally and financially.

One method Rose used to deal with her husband's infidelity was avoidance. In the mid-1930s, she took at least 17 pleasure trips to Europe. Another method was reminding herself what she gained by remaining the non-confrontational Mrs. Joseph P. Kennedy. In 1936, after helping Franklin D. Roosevelt win re-election to a second term, Joe Kennedy was named ambassador to England — a title that would lift the family's stature and carry the delicious irony that the line of Kennedys that had fled British oppression were now being introduced at the Court of St. James. In her 1974 memoir, *Times to Remember,* Rose carefully chronicled the couple's grand introduction to the King and Queen of England.

Jackie's mother obviously coped very differently with her first husband's infidelity, confronting him in angry, dish-tossing rages and having him followed. Nonetheless, Black Jack made his sleeping around seem acceptable to his eldest daughter. He did this by confiding in her about his seductions. He told her that on his honeymoon, on his way over to England with Janet on the Aquitania, he had slipped away and slept with tobacco heiress Doris Duke. When he visited Jackie at boarding school in Farmington, Connecticut, as described in the Prologue, the two would gossip about which of Jackie's classmates' mothers Jack had bedded. He was said to be capable of sleeping with two or three women in an evening.

Little wonder that Jackie, who saw her dad as a man of great style and sophistication, responded this way when warned about her future husband's playboy ways: "All men are like that. Just look at my father." She echoed this in later years when trying to reassure her sister-in-law, Joan, who was upset by her husband Teddy's affairs. "All Kennedy men are like that," Jackie said. "You can't let it get to you because you shouldn't take it personally."

Possibly Jackie saw JFK's appeal to other women as tantalizing. They could want him, but Jackie had him. She had won. However, it's also likely that she underestimated her husband's near-constant pursuit of sexual reassurance and release. "While on one level Jackie must have known what she was getting into by marrying a thirty-six-year-old playboy, she never suspected the depth of Jack's need for other women," said Kirk LeMoyne "Lem" Billings, Jack's prep school roommate and lifelong friend. "Nor was she prepared for the humiliation she would suffer when she found herself stranded at parties while Jack would suddenly disappear with some pretty young girl."

When Jack was campaigning for the presidency in 1960, he made a campaign stopover in Las Vegas where he met his brother Teddy and their friend, Frank Sinatra. The singer introduced the brothers to Judith Campbell, a stunningly beautiful Los Angeles divorcee who had been married to an actor. The group stayed out late and had lunch the next day, after which Jack and Campbell exchanged phone numbers. A week later, from the campaign trail, he sent her a dozen roses and phoned her every day. The affair continued for a year and a half, well into JFK's White House days.

After his election to the presidency, Kennedy attended three side parties of the inaugural ball without Jackie. He was anxious to impress some of his girlfriends whom he had invited to the inauguration, including Campbell and actress Angie Dickinson, who was escorted at Jack's request by his old Navy buddy Red Fay. Here was a man, newly elected president, struggling to lead a bachelor life and a married life simultaneously. The early White House days included nude young women openly cavorting in the swimming pool and aides having to scour rooms in the family quarters for hairpins and other incriminating evidence before Jackie returned from weekends away.

Coping in Bed and All the Way to the Bank

How did Jackie cope? Sometimes she feigned ignorance, and sometimes refused to show up at official events, to communicate her displeasure and power. During the president's 45th birthday celebration at Madison Square Garden, for example, Jackie was pointedly absent. It was just the sort of vulgar display she detested, with toasts and performances from artists Jack Benny, Maria Callas, Henry Fonda, Ella Fitzgerald, Peggy Lee, and Peter Lawford. Bombshell Marilyn Monroe sang "Happy Birthday" to Jack in a dress that was so tight she had to be sewn into it.

In the months that followed, during the summer of 1962, Monroe began telling people about her affair with the president — and word got back to Jack about her indiscretion. The president's brother, Bobby, flew to California to speak to Monroe and cool her off, presidential brother-in-law Peter Lawford told author C. David Heymann. There's some evidence the Monroe affair was the last straw for Jackie, who threatened to divorce Jack. "Because of my father, I was used to infidelities, but Jack's womanizing hurt me greatly," she told her friend William Walton.

Jackie soon became one of the most absentee First Ladies in American history — recalling the strategy Rose Kennedy used to bear Joe's skirt chasing. Jackie spent three of four days a week at Glen Ora, a 400-acre estate the Kennedys rented in Middleburg, Virginia. There she rode her beloved horses. She spent most summers in Hyannis Port, and a good deal of the winter in Palm Beach. Jackie took a three-week trip to India and Pakistan, three weeks in Italy, and another long vacation in Greece, all unaccompanied by her husband.

The First Lady also tried dealing with her husband's needs more directly. She met a cardiologist, Dr. Frank Finnerty, through her brother-in-law Bobby. Finnerty was a friend and neighbor. He and Jackie struck up a telephone friendship where she called him twice a week for consolation and advice. She told him she knew what was going on with Jack, and that the Secret Service covered for him. "She was also sure that Jack felt no love or any kind of affection" for these women, Finnerty reported. He was "just getting rid of some hormonal surge" that he had "undoubtedly inherited from his father."

With the doctor, Jackie learned about foreplay and other ways she and Jack could discover more pleasure with each other in bed. The phone consultations included a script Jackie could present to her husband to raise the issue of changing their bedroom routine without offending his masculine ego. Jack's philandering didn't stop, but at least his wife could reassure herself that it wasn't because they lacked intimacy in the bedroom.

Jackie considered having affairs, perhaps as a way to get even with her husband. Her sister Lee's first marriage, to Michael Canfield, was dissolving and would be annulled in 1959 after six years. Meanwhile, Lee was conducting affairs with a number of prominent men, thumbing her nose at the bourgeois convention with which they had been raised. No longer was the pursuit of sexual adventure limited to the powerful husband. Author Sally Bedell Smith calls this time in American history a "shadowy reality — a hedonism and moral relativism that anticipated the sexual revolution of the following decades."

In a conversation with Washington journalist Ben Bradlee's wife, Tony, Jackie confided that she considered taking lovers but decided it was too risky, given her prominence. Jackie took her job very seriously, "she didn't want to make some scandal," said a friend, Benno Graziani.

However, she did allow men to serve as her escorts, particularly when she was out of the country. On one trip, Jackie went to England for the glamorous parties and shooting weekends, and word got back to the States that she was behaving like an unattached woman. Washington columnist Drew Pearson reported this, and the story was picked up by *Time* magazine.

Joe was alarmed by the reports and invited Jackie to lunch when she returned. He described their lunch discussion later to his friend, the singer Morton Downey, and Jackie told her version to her sister. Both agreed on this: Jack doesn't want to lose you, Joe told Jackie, and "it's up to a wife to keep a marriage together." The versions of what happened next differ. One story says that Joe offered to set up trusts for Jackie's future children, which would revert to her in 10 years if she remained childless. No specific amount was mentioned. Another version of the story is that Joe offered Jackie $1 million, but she held out for $10 million. More recent reports put Jackie's price of staying in the marriage at $20 million.

Turning Outward Toward Caretaking

Did Jackie stay for money? For the glamour of weeks spent riding horses in the Virginia countryside and partying with other socialites abroad? Or did she simply believe, given the times, that she had few other options outside of meeting the expectations of her position and class? She remarked in those years to a number of friends that she felt sorry for women who couldn't find fulfillment through their husbands and had to try to prove themselves in a man's arena such as business.

"My mother was brought up in an era when very few women worked outside of the home," her daughter Caroline said in an interview in 2011. "She was somewhat unusual in that she had a job after college working on a newspaper, but typical in that she quit when she got engaged. She was raised to be a traditional wife and many of the views she expresses seem hopelessly old-fashioned. As First Lady, her top priority was to help my father in any way she could, and to make his family life as happy and easy as possible. I think many First Ladies feel the same way even today when they see the strain of being President."

What she made of her situation was admirable. Jackie defied the instructions of White House social advisers to make time for raising her children in as normal a way as possible. She called on her own education, Bouvier family style, and sense of history to charm foreign audiences, and to remake the neglected White House interior into a national treasure.

In the process, Jackie served as a role model for American women. She came along at a time when women were struggling with the idea that "homemaker" was supposed to fulfill them. She presented an image of a new attention to glamour and domesticity, wrote marriage historian Stephanie Coontz. Women could be consumer experts and arbiters of taste. "First Lady Jackie Kennedy was the supreme exemplar of this role in the early 1960s," Coontz observed. Noted columnist and fashion editor Diana Vreeland has written, "Before the Kennedys 'good taste' was never the point of modern America at all."

Moving into the White House, Jackie decided to restore it to the way it was at the time of President James Monroe, who served in office from 1817 to 1825. Then, it had been decorated in the then-fashionable French style, but in subsequent years had suffered mistreatment and neglect. Looking for period pieces to restore and set off, Jackie searched through the 54 rooms and 16 bathrooms, the basement, storage bins, carpenters' shops and Fort Washington warehouses.

The project turned Jackie into a celebrity, a role that further locked her in to playing the modern White Queen. In February 1962, the First Lady took CBS television's Charles Collingwood on a tour, watched by an estimated 56 million television viewers on the CBS and NBC networks. The televised tour gave the American people beauty, elegance, and a sense of the nation's past.

Jackie also heightened Americans' image abroad when she accompanied her husband on a trip to Paris, Vienna, and London. She charmed France's then President Charles de Gaulle with her knowledge of and interest in France and her fluency in the language. The boost could not have come at a more opportune time for Jack, who had experienced a series of humiliating setbacks: the Russians' first man in space triumph, the erection of the Berlin Wall, the bungled Bay of Pigs invasion, civil rights disturbances in the South. He acknowledged his wife's triumph by quipping, "I am the man who accompanied Jacqueline Kennedy to Paris."

After Paris, Jackie had a hook into her husband that a Kennedy could most appreciate: she was now a political asset and, as such, was the one person Jack could not do without.

The First Lady's success marked change in the way Jack treated Jackie. On the eve of his nationally televised speech about the missile crisis, he asked Jackie to return to the White House from Glen Ora so he could spend some quiet evenings alone with her and their two children. "Their marriage got better," said George Smathers, who had served in the House and Senate with JFK. "When you're president, you get kicked around a lot. The wife of the president starts feeling very protective. He sees that she's loyal and that they're in this thing together. They have to pull together; they have no choice. That's what happened to Jack and Jackie."

Jackie's determination to endure Jack's extramarital adventures also probably arose from her desire to make a secure home life for their children. Shortly before the election, when Caroline was three and Jackie was pregnant with JFK Jr., she remarked in a TV interview that she needed to be with her children in the White House. "If you bungle raising your children, I don't think whatever else you do matters very much."

Shortly after the inauguration, Jack asked Angier Biddle Duke, his chief of protocol, to speak with Jackie about her new duties. She told him that she wanted to do as little as possible in the way of lunches, speeches, teas and accepting degrees. "The kids are young and I just want to do as much as I can within the bounds of my responsibility to my children," she told him. The White House staff was incensed and embarrassed as she refused one invitation after another. But after the first couple of months, after it became clear that her absence was distributed evenhandedly, she had set a precedent that would-be hosts could accept without feeling too slighted.

Instead, Jackie and the children spent their weekdays at Glen Ora, where Caroline rode her pony, Macaroni, and Mom took the kids on picnics, gave them baths, and read to them in bed before they fell asleep. In one journal entry, Jackie noted, these were the "things I have no chance to do in the W. House."

She wanted the children's lives to be as carefree as possible, given the limelight glare of living as the president's kids. "Jackie wanted ... to make their lives normal and fun," said her friend Eve Fout. "She applied effort and ingenuity to that." In fact, her involvement with her children was striking for a woman of her class, who usually relied on nannies to see to the daily childhood routines, tantrums and messes. The Kennedys employed a fulltime nanny, Maude Shaw. Yet Jackie personally participated in a playgroup that several Georgetown mothers organized, circulating among their homes. "She was a remarkable mother, the way she spoke and engaged the children," said Sue Wilson, a playgroup member who had also known Jackie at Vassar. One doesn't have to stretch too far to imagine that in some ways Jacqueline was making up for her own childhood filled with warring parents and maternal neglect.

A Heritage of Resiliency

Caroline and John reacted very differently to their mother's overprotection and to the revelations, which came in waves throughout their teens and 20s, about their parents' marriage.

Caroline married financier and designer Edwin Schlossberg, a man who was such a straight arrow that her brother sometimes mocked him by calling him Edwina. The couple had two daughters and a son. Caroline inherited her father's attraction to public service along with her mother's position as protector of the family name. During the Obama administration, she served as the U.S. ambassador to Japan.

She is the author of books on civil liberties, and has edited several other books, including tributes to her parents, *The Best-Loved Poems of Jacqueline Kennedy Onassis* and *Profiles in Courage for Our Time.*

She's shown a remarkable resilience, even as the revelations about JFK's affairs began to emerge in the late 1970s — with Marilyn Monroe, Judith Campbell Exner, and others. In 2011, television journalist Diane Sawyer asked Caroline whether her mother had ever discussed her husband's infidelities. Caroline looked taken aback but kept smiling. "That was really between them," she told Sawyer. "I wouldn't be her daughter if I was going to share all that."

In contrast to her mother, Caroline's attitude toward adulterous men seems unforgiving. In 2011, her cousin Maria Shriver left her 25-year marriage to Arnold Schwarzenegger, then governor of California. Shriver moved out of the family's Brentwood, California mansion when it became public that her husband had a child, then 14 years old, with Mildred Patricia "Patty" Baena, the family's live-in housekeeper.

Baena had been pregnant and working in the couple's home when Shriver was also pregnant with the youngest of the couple's four children. She left the home, but a year later she considered reuniting with her husband. Shriver had also had an affair during the marriage, which likely made her more inclined to understand and forgive. After a year, Maria and Arnold were still wearing their wedding rings. However, Caroline interceded with her cousin and also corralled a number of other Kennedys to convince Shriver to finalize the divorce.

John Jr., by contrast, grew into a rebellious teenager. He got high with his prep school pals and haunted Times Square strip joints at night. He was interested in pursuing acting, but instead enrolled in law school and earned the law degree that his mother wanted for him. He went on to found *George* magazine in 1995, which aimed to pair politics with celebrity and media in a way that would make political topics more appealing to general readers. Wildly popular when it launched, the magazine would soon struggle to attract advertising and to be taken seriously. John Jr. made the questionable choice of posing nude for *George* in 1997 to boost sales.

He clashed with his mother over his choice in women — which included leggy blond actress Daryl Hannah and pop icon Madonna. He also broke a promise he made to Jackie on her deathbed, when he vowed he would not pursue his hobby of flying airplanes. She had had a premonition he would die in a crash while piloting a plane. He did in 1999, in an accident off Martha's Vineyard that also claimed the life of his wife of three years, publicist Carolyn Bessette, and her sister Lauren.

Before they died, the couple was seeing a marriage therapist, and John and Carolyn were at odds about when they would have children. She resented that he had reverted to his old bachelor ways — pumping iron at the gym late into the night, going off on kayak trips with the boys, and, Carolyn suspected, playing around behind her back. Two days before the plane crash, he had moved out of their loft apartment in Manhattan's TriBeCa neighborhood and into the Stanhope Hotel overlooking Central Park. Their final flight together was to attend a Kennedy family wedding. The plane crash marred that event with yet more tragic young deaths for this clan. JFK Jr. was just 38.

His father's womanizing was kept out of the papers while he was still in office, per the unspoken agreement of the day between the press and public figures. Most political reporters were men; the affairs weren't viewed as affecting JFK's competence; and a journalist was expected to stay cozy with the powerful to merit news scoops and exclusive interviews. Had JFK lived, it's more than likely his affairs would have been brought to light. The early to mid-1960s witnessed a watershed for politicians when the press began to take a more skeptical view of authority, privilege, and powerful institutions.

Marion Stein & Jeremy Thorpe

Party Leader Blackmailed

On a windy October night in 1975, a twenty-something out-of-work airline pilot, Andrew Newton, invited Norman Scott for a drive in Exmoor, a hilly, open moorland in Southwest England. Scott, a male model and equestrian, was edgy and paranoid. He feared that a hitman was following him and meant to kill him in retribution for his continual blackmailing of his former lover Jeremy Thorpe, who had risen over the dozen years since their affair to become one of Britain's most prominent politicians. Newton had befriended Scott by playing on his fears and by claiming he had arrived to protect him. In reality, Newton had been paid to shoot Scott in the dark, on the deserted moor, using an ancient German pistol he had borrowed from a friend.

Scott arrived for their expedition shortly after 8 p.m., bringing along his newly adopted 5-year-old Great Dane, Rinka. Newton was horrified. He had a lifelong fear of dogs and didn't want to let Rinka ride in his borrowed yellow Mazda. But Scott insisted and said he wouldn't go anywhere without her. Newton relented. Rinka scrambled into the back seat, patiently awaiting her expected run through the hills.

Pulling over to a suitably isolated spot, Newton got out of the car, and Rinka lumbered playfully, awkwardly from the back seat. Newton didn't understand her eagerness. Thinking he was being attacked, he drew his pistol and killed her with a single bullet to the head. Scott stared in shock. Sobbing, he rushed to Rinka's side and tried to revive her with mouth-to-mouth resuscitation. Newton could have completed his murderous mission and shot Scott as well — but either the gun jammed, or he was so shaken he couldn't proceed. He got back into the car and drove off.

As Scott sat weeping beside his dead pet, four people drove past in a car, including an off-duty scout for the Automobile Association, which rescues stranded drivers. When the scout, Edward Lethaby, heard Scott's story, he called the police.

And so began the public unraveling of the life of charismatic Liberal Party leader Jeremy Thorpe, a man American journalists described as the British Jack Kennedy. He lost the trust of his chief financial backer, whose generous donations had helped make Jeremy into a legendary fundraiser for his nascent third party. He lost the leadership of the Liberals, a cause to which he had devoted two decades, building the party from near-zero to a real alternative for English voters tired of Labour or the Conservatives. He lost his Parliament seat, and he set back the fledgling gay rights movement in Britain, which had only begun gathering strength with the repeal of a law in 1967 that outlawed sexual activity between men. What Jeremy did not lose was his wife — an arts patron, concert pianist, and former English countess, Marion Stein.

Jeremy's story was replayed on British television in the mini-series *A Very British Scandal*. It aired in 2018 and starred Hugh Grant, who was nominated for an Emmy for his portrayal of Jeremy Thorpe. One reviewer called the tale "a dark moment in British LGBTQ+ history."

Marion's whereabouts on the night Rinka lay dying were not publicly recorded. As a former member of the royal family, she had been singed by the harsh media spotlight, and her life, even today, is shrouded in privacy. Her passions were music and her four boys — three from her previous marriage to George Lascelles, the 7th Earl of Harewood, and one, a stepson, Rupert, from Jeremy's first marriage. One week before Rinka's fateful day, October 23, 1975, Marion celebrated her 48th birthday. Her days were committed to tending to 6-year-old Rupert and visiting with her 2-year-old granddaughter Sophie, her first grandchild.

When Rinka was shot, Marion may have been at her cottage, Curlews, in Aldeburgh, site of annual early summer festivals for classical music lovers organized by Marion's mentor and lifelong family friend, the influential 20th century composer Benjamin Britten. Or, she may have been staying in Orme Square, the imposing London residence overlooking Hyde Park that she'd won in the divorce from her first husband.

It's possible, in October 1975, that Marion was working on one of her 30 volumes on modern piano keyboard technique. Or, she was wrapping up the aftermath of the 1975 Leeds International Competition, which she had founded 14 years earlier and which had finished the previous month. To this day, with her nurturance, the Leeds is one of the world's most prestigious piano contests. Marion launched the competition with her son's then-piano teacher Fanny Waterman, and Marion used her royal connections to give it a strong sustaining foundation. As Rinka breathed her last, Marion may also have been involved in the doings of the Royal Opera House in Covent Garden, where she served as president of the donors' friends association.

In March, 1976, Andrew Newton was tried for Rinka's murder and sentenced to two years in prison. At the trial, Newton didn't incriminate Jeremy Thorpe; however Norman Scott took the stand and repeated his assertions that Jeremy had seduced him in 1961, awakening in him "this vice [of homosexuality] that lies latent in every man," and that the affair had continued for at least three years. Scott repeated his story to many in both the press and the Liberal Party. However, because Britain's press laws require journalists to prove the truth of any disparaging or defamatory statements — a stricter standard than American journalism — corruption and incompetence are seldom exposed by the media unless the police decide to prosecute. Two legal exceptions are if the information comes out in Parliament or in court. While Jeremy survived the Rinka trial, his spurned lover's turn in the witness stand churned up public, police, and journalistic scrutiny. The talk and dirt-digging led to a trial for Jeremy, more than two years later, on charges of conspiracy and incitement to murder.

Marion's White Queen Quotient: 9

Norman Scott's sordid story, told from the dock at Exeter Crown Court, was certainly not the first time Marion had heard about her husband's sexual escapades with men. In fact, the evidence suggests she knew about his private drives from the beginning, and that when they married, their union was less based on intimacy and fidelity than on the mutual need for respectability, companionship, and a secure home life for their children; they were both single parents. Marion was arguably acting from the motives of tradition, financial security, and responsibility for her family's emotional health.

She had a rags-to-riches background. Marion was born in Vienna in 1926, and when she was 12, she fled Nazi Germany with her family to England. When war broke out between Germany and England the following year, in 1939, the British government rounded up hundreds of resident families of German origin, including Marion's father Erwin, and interned them on the Isle of Man. His wife, Sophie, and Marion survived on a weekly allowance of what is equivalent to about five U.S. dollars today.

Erwin had studied music in Vienna, which was experiencing its second great epoch of composition during his lifetime. He taught his daughter to love music as well. A decade after the family emigrated to Britain, Marion met and married fellow music lover George Lascelles, the Earl of Harewood, and a first cousin of Queen Elizabeth II. The newspapers covered the match as a fairy tale: a middle-class girl who escaped the evil empire, came to England and captured the heart of the royal couple's grandson. Within several years, Lascelles fell in love with another woman, and then spent eight years persuading Marion to divorce. It's a measure of her need for security and her desire to maintain her three sons' royal lineage that she fought so hard to stay in the marriage.

The breakdown of her marriage nearly broke her spirit. By marrying Jeremy Thorpe, she regained emotional security and reclaimed her dignity through an affiliation with a high-flying political star. She created a bountiful home life for her three sons and her stepson, and after Jeremy's scandal, she nursed him at home for the rest of their lives as he developed the debilitating Parkinson's disease.

She served as his guide and translator to the outside world, enabling him to participate in his beloved local Liberal Party club. Marion demonstrated maternal thinking not only in her choice to stay married, but also in the character she displayed as a devoted parent and friend, an untiring advocate for the arts and a mentor to her fellow musicians. With her boys, though, she exerted little control. They've had stunningly creative careers in rock music, indie filmmaking, paparazzi photography — and many serial marriages. A true White Queen would have shepherded her family's legacy, like Jackie Kennedy, with greater care and control.

A Life Blossoming Through Music

Marion Stein was born Maria Donata Nanetta Paulina Gustava Erwina Wilhelmine Stein. Her multiple middle names reflect a practice among the upper classes to embrace the names of beloved or influential relatives. She was born in Vienna, a world capital of music in which her father was deeply involved. He participated in the Second Viennese School — a wave of musical composition and performance that marked a pinnacle of achievement following the late

18th-century high-water mark set by Mozart, Haydn, and Beethoven. Marion's father Erwin was a pupil, principal assistant and friend of Arnold Schoenberg, who was intent on reviving Vienna's reputation as a great musical learning and creative center. Erwin studied with Schoenberg from 1906 to 1910 and became a respected music teacher and conductor. He married Sophie Bachmann, two years his junior, and they named their daughter Maria.

Maria was a favorite of Schoenberg and another Second School auteur, Alban Berg. They nicknamed her "Haselnüsschen," or "little hazelnut." But this intimate and productive haven of music lovers did not last long. In 1938, the Austrian people voted to annex their country to Nazi Germany, in an alliance known as the Anschluss. Although Sophie was not a Jew, Erwin was, and he feared his family would be persecuted. When Maria was 12, the Steins sold their Vienna home, packed their possessions, and moved to England.

The Steins lived quietly and modestly in London, and Maria anglicized her name to Marion. Erwin joined music publisher Boosey & Hawkes where he worked with the famed composer Benjamin Britten. They became so close that when a fire destroyed the Steins' apartment, the family lodged for 18 months in St. John's Wood with Britten and his longtime romantic partner and tenor Peter Pears. The close quarters caused them to quarrel, a living arrangement Marion later described as "not always easy."

In September 1939, when war broke out between England and Germany, the British government set up a prison camp on the Isle of Man, off the country's west coast in the Irish Sea. Worried about potential infiltration by enemy spies, the government rounded up hundreds of resident families of German origin, many of them university professors and other professionals, and interned them on the Isle. Erwin was one such "enemy alien" sent to live there in 1940.

As a teenager, Marion blossomed into a beautiful and talented young woman. She studied with pianist Kendall Taylor at the Royal College of Music and seemed destined for a career as a concert pianist. In1948, she was at Cambridge for the May Balls and met one of the most eligible men in the country, George Lascelles. He was a self-described melomaniac — a person with overwhelming enthusiasm for music. Their common interest drew Lascelles and Marion together.

After Cambridge, Lascelles wrote to Marion and took her out several times before Christmas. In March, the BBC was preparing to broadcast a concert performance of Wozzeck by Viennese Second School glitterati Alban Berg — Marion's adopted uncle from her first home. She accompanied Lascelles to the rehearsals and performance, an experience so uplifting, they decided to marry. Marion confided the almost-engagement to her father, who joked about Wozzeck having great powers over young lovers.

Back at the Harewood estate, Lascelles, 25, informed his mother that he wanted to get married. She exclaimed, "Good God," and then went silent. After a few minutes, she regained her composure and asked questions about her son's intended, whom she hadn't met. Marion came two weeks later to visit the great home in West Yorkshire. Although Countess Harewood was waited on by servants and had never had to prepare meals herself, she seemed to question the young couple's practicality — and to minimize Marion's many accomplishments by inquiring whether she could cook.

The formidable Countess Harewood was but one obstacle facing the young lovers. Under King George III's Royal

Marriages Act, all nuptials of royal family members must be approved by the King and Queen. Lascelles first approached his maternal grandfather, King George V, who responded that it seemed quite natural that he should want to marry someone with similar interests, even something as alien to the royal hunting-and-croquet crowd as music. But the King didn't tell his grandson how opposed his wife was to the match. In Queen Mary's eyes, Marion was foreign, a commoner, and worst of all, half Jewish. Lascelles walked into the interview with his grandmother unaware of her objections and that turned out to be a blessing. His guileless description of their courtship won over the Queen. The couple announced their engagement in July 1949.

Fairy Tale Marriage to a Royal Grandson

From the start, the public loved Marion and for many of the same reasons that had at first concerned Queen Mary. Marion was refreshingly unstuffy, as well as young and pretty. Marion stopped playing the piano to devote herself to motherhood and being the hostess. Their first son, David, was born in October 1950, and James exactly three years later, in October 1953. Jeremy followed 16 months after James. Marion fulfilled her official duties both at the palatial Harewood countryside estate and in London at Orme Square. It wasn't long before the press experts on the royal family had to acknowledge: Marion had won Queen Mary's affection.

The fairy tale didn't last. Lascelles continued his involvement in music, and in January 1959, he traveled to Milan to persuade opera star Maria Callas to sing in London. He came away disappointed, but while waiting for his return flight in the Air France terminal, eating a chocolate bar, his flight was called, and he offered to carry the bag of the only other person in the waiting room: Patricia Tuckwell. She was the sister of a friend, musician Barry Tuckwell, and the two struck up a conversation during the flight. The conversation led to dinner that night in Paris, and by summer, Lascelles confessed his love for Tuckwell to his wife Marion. David, James, and Jeremy were 9, 6, and 4 years old. According to Lascelles's memoir, Marion predicted he would become bored with the affair and it would pass.

Lascelles did not become bored. For nearly eight years, he tried to persuade Marion to divorce him. At one point, feeling guilty, he went to a psychoanalyst, who suggested that if there hadn't been something lacking in his marriage, his feelings for Tuckwell would never have grown into romance. Marion held on. Her marriage had secured her a safe place, in a world where she had been forced to flee her Austrian home and witness her father imprisoned as a suspected spy. Now, she had powerful friends, a standing in the arts community, money, and three boys' welfare to consider.

In July 1964, Tuckwell gave birth out of wedlock to Lascelles's son, Mark. In spite of the scandal, Marion refused to let go for another two years. At last, her divorce from Lascelles became final in July 1967. Lascelles wrote, "In the end, some eighteen months after we had finally broken — perhaps five years later than we should have — Marion agreed to a divorce." Tuckwell and Lascelles married, at a civil service in New York, and moved into Harewood.

Marion retained custody of the three sons, which was a comfort at first but which was challenging later, when they became unruly teenagers. She also kept the London house in Orme Square. But the breakdown of her marriage had wounded Marion deeply.

The Charismatic 'Jack Kennedy of Britain'

Jeremy Thorpe has been called the 'Jack Kennedy of Britain.' In some ways, the comparison was apt; Jeremy was a charismatic party-builder who could warm up an audience. Jeremy, like Kennedy, had gone to the right schools for a future leader of his country; he rose to prominence during the 1950s and 60s, had a ravenous sexual appetite, and kept his entourage of helpers always close and on guard.

Jeremy grew up in a comfortable red brick house in Kensington, the son and grandson of members of Parliament. By heritage, he should have followed their footsteps in the Conservative or Tory Party. His mother was a staunch Conservative. But Jeremy tasted liberal fruit twice in his young years: first in 1940 as a schoolboy sent to live, safely distant from the Second World War, with an aunt in Connecticut. He disliked his aunt's Republican friends but enjoyed the easygoing discipline of American classrooms. By the time he returned to England and Eton in 1943, he resented the British schoolboy toe-the-line conformity.

The second liberal influence in Jeremy's life was Lady Megan Lloyd George, daughter of David Lloyd George, a "people's champion" of social reforms in the early 1900s. Interestingly mirrored in Jeremy's future behavior, David Lloyd George's private and sexual conduct was a running scandal, and his reputation was kept intact during his lifetime by the manipulation of power. Under the tutelage of Lady Megan, who had been a girlhood friend of his mother Ursula, Jeremy learned to love the political philosophy of tolerance and freedom from prejudice that lay at the heart of liberalism.

After Eton, Jeremy entered Trinity College at Oxford to

study law. If his path was conventional, his appearance, habits, and conduct were anything but. Jeremy was renowned for wearing an assortment of Edwardian suits, silk waistcoats, opera cloaks, and trilby hats — an elegance of dress that was whispered to derive not so much from taste as from necessity. Jeremy's beloved father, and his strong champion, died when Jeremy was in his teens. Much of the romantic 19th century dress was inherited from his late father and grandfather, suggesting wealth Jeremy didn't have.

Another peculiarity was Jeremy's collection of Chinese ceramics and T'ang Dynasty paintings. He had style, but it was his verbal skill that rocketed him to the top of Oxford's student politics. A gifted impressionist, Jeremy could deliver a torrent of anecdotes and quotations in the voices of Winston Churchill, David Lloyd George, and other famous politicians. A dramatic and skilled debater, Jeremy climbed his way to the presidency of Oxford's Liberal Club and the Law Society. In 1951, he claimed a trifecta by winning the presidency of the Oxford Union, a debating society with a worldwide reputation for the cut and thrust of its disputes.[290] The Oxford Union is widely viewed as a valuable training ground for future politicians.

First drawn to journalism after college, Jeremy worked as a TV interviewer before qualifying as a barrister lawyer in 1954. British newspapers reported that he first ran for office in 1955 "with all the panache of an American congressional campaign." He kept a notebook where he made notes about the constituents he visited, reminding himself to ask next time about their gardens, a broken door, or the sick dog. His trademark was bounding over fences, reminding voters he was the energetic new breed of politician. He lost that first race, but four years later won the North Devon seat, which he held for 20 years while also resuscitating the Liberal Party. As party treasurer at 33, he created a "marginal seats" fund that gave him remarkable control over party strategy. Money from appeals and donations ballooned by 50 percent in his first year as treasurer. In 1967, he took over as party leader, and in the autumn of 1973, the Liberals won more votes than either the Conservatives or Labour, making the Liberals a force in the formation of Prime Minister Harold Wilson's administration.

Meanwhile, a liaison that Jeremy had formed in 1961 with Norman Scott continued to haunt him. Scott, 20, was working in Oxfordshire as a stable hand at Kingham Stables, which was owned by a friend of Jeremy's. On a visit, Jeremy was taken with the young man and told him, if he should ever need help, to call at the House of Commons. Soon after, Scott had a serious disagreement with the stable owner, suffered a mental breakdown, and for most of 1961 was under psychiatric care. Afterward, he approached Jeremy, who offered to put him up in a room at his mother's house. Scott said Jeremy seduced him that night, and their affair continued for three years. Jeremy continued to deny that, or any homosexual relationships for the rest of his life. In that era, homosexuals in Britain lived in constant fear of exposure.

Gay Men in Public Life

Before the passage of the Sexual Offenses Act in 1967, all sexual activity between men in the United Kingdom was illegal and subject to heavy penalties. Antony Grey, a secretary of the Homosexual Law Reform Society, wrote of "a hideous aura of criminality and degeneracy and abnormality surrounding the matter." Political figures were especially vulnerable. William Field, the Labour MP for Paddington

North, was forced to resign his seat in 1953 after a conviction for soliciting in a public lavatory. In 1954, Lord Montagu of Beaulieu, the youngest peer in the House of Lords, was imprisoned for a year after being convicted, with several others, of "gross indecency."

In November 1958, Ian Harvey, a junior Foreign Office minister in Harold Macmillan's government, was found guilty of indecent behavior and lost both his ministerial job and his parliamentary seat at Harrow East. Ostracized by the Conservative Party and by most of his former friends, he never again held such a position in public life.

However, in the 1950s and early 1960s the Liberal Party was a place where many gay men found acceptance, even while remaining closeted. Interviewed 20 years later, many of Jeremy's old friends spoke fondly of him, and several gay Liberals "revealed that they had warned senior members of the Party that Thorpe was risking everything by cruising the streets in search of young men." John Fryer, a young openly gay writer who later became Jeremy's close friend, said, "He went to places like Greece and America for sex. When he was in London he loved the danger. That was half the attraction of it all. He had an enormous thirst for getting into really tricky situations."

But Jeremy's position required him to marry and establish a conventional home life. He met Caroline Allpass, 10 years his junior, at a party at her apartment in Chelsea. She was a middle-class woman who worked as an interior designer and whose father owned a chain of furniture stores. Though one friend, Peter Bessell, claims that Jeremy went into the marriage reluctantly, it appears to have been a genuinely loving match. They married in May 1968, and had a son, Rupert, the following year. Tragically, she was killed in a car accident in June 1970; she was alone in the car when she veered into the oncoming lane and collided with a truck. Jeremy was devastated and built a monument to her memory in North Devon.

Jeremy wasn't alone for long. In January 1972, his old friend Moura Lympany invited him to a Beethoven violin concerto and dinner at Marion Harewood's. In the car on the way, Lympany told Jeremy she hoped that he and Marion would make a match. They did, and they married the following year. In his memoir, *In My Own Time,* Jeremy skips over the scandalous aspects of his life, but he clearly welcomed the culture Marion brought to his life. "One of the many joys of being married to Marion is that of attending musical events, which before I had very often turned down on the grounds of parliamentary duties," Jeremy wrote. "Marion's dowry included her close friendships with many leading musicians." His only reference to the troubles that collectively became known as Rinkagate was this: "Throughout our marriage there have been many happy moments and some less so, but there was always the background of music."

While some of Jeremy's friends found Marion cold and distant, those who got to know her realized this was a protective reserve. She'd had a difficult life and understood the pain of failure. This explained why she supported Jeremy as his life disintegrated.

A Deadly Plot

By the time of Rinka's killing, Marion had been subject to intrusions from Norman Scott for some time. Jeremy explained Scott away as a mentally ill man and a stalker. People in public life often attract strange hangers-on. Behind the scenes, Jeremy's aides in the Liberal Party gave Scott money and encouraged him to move to the United States.

In the spring of 1975, Scott drove to the Thorpes' country cottage in Higher Chuggaton to ask Jeremy for money and a favor pertaining to his national insurance card — a document he needed to qualify for unemployment pay and other benefits. Marion opened the door. They hadn't previously met, but Scott recognized her. She didn't seem surprised to see Scott, but when he asked for an interview with Jeremy, she said, "I don't think he'll see you." Scott turned to go, but was so overwrought, he couldn't back his car down the drive. He returned to ask Marion to back out the car for him, which she did.

What did she think of this alleged former lover of her husband's? Peter Bessell, Jeremy's confidant and fellow Liberal MP, who later became the chief witness against Jeremy at trial, has written that Jeremy raised the subject of homosexuality with his wife indirectly, and she was "disgusted." This is hard to believe, given Marion's close relationship to Benjamin Britten and Peter Pears, a longtime couple. After they died, she devoted herself to chairing the Britten-Pears Foundation, a labor of love that required a lot of time.

Early in 1979, Jeremy was to be tried for conspiracy to kill Scott, but the judge granted him a two-week delay so he could run for re-election. For the first time in two decades, the people of North Devon turned against Jeremy, and he lost. At the trial, both Marion and Ursula, Jeremy's stalwart mother, sat behind him. The press wrote about the devotion of Jeremy's wife, and Ursula condescended to give a reporter at the trial a rare quote: "Jeremy's been so lucky in his women."

Jeremy and his co-defendants were acquitted. On their return to Orme Square, the family drank champagne and appeared on the balcony waving triumphantly. In the annals of resuscitating events after a sex scandal, this was quite creative. Jeremy didn't have to respond to uncomfortable questions from journalists, yet he could be seen with his loyal wife by his side. However, the media mocked the balcony appearance as grandiose; such gestures are normally the prerogative of the royal family.

Many aspects of the trial and judgment sat badly with the public. The judge's summary was ridiculed as a near command to the jury to acquit Jeremy and his co-defendants. It has gone down in legal history as a model of the British ruling class chummily protecting itself against a low-class, homosexual blackmailer. England's gay community never quite forgave Jeremy for failing to take a stand and acknowledge his bisexual past.

Post-trial, Jeremy saw himself as acquitted although the public wasn't quite so forgiving. His election lost, he tried for another position in public life. A friend nominated him to run London-based Amnesty International. The subsequent outcry forced Jeremy to withdraw his name. David Astor, a newspaper publisher, urged Jeremy to confess, apologize, and devote time to charity. But Jeremy remained arrogant and aloof. In the mid-1980s, he was diagnosed with Parkinson's disease. Marion and he lived quietly together, dying within months of each other in 2014.

Scandal's Legacy for Four Sons

The four boys Jeremy and Marion raised took wild rides in life. Each in his way has visited the divide between rebellion and respectability. Perhaps that was in reaction to Jeremy hiding his nature from public view, or as a backlash to Marion holding so tightly to status by refusing to divorce her royal husband and then remaining stoically by her scandal-plagued second spouse.

George Lascelles' affinity for the big, bold stories of opera and Marion's career as a concert pianist paved the way for their three sons' love of performing arts. In contrast, however, they were ambivalent about their ties to royalty and flouted traditional values in their personal lives while delving into the 1970s rock music scene.

Eldest son David studied art at the Winchester School of Art and is a film and television producer. In 1979, he married Margaret Messenger, a lab assistant at Bristol University. The couple already had two children, Emily and Benjamin, in 1975 and 1978. Since they were born prior to their parents' marriage, the children did not automatically receive the rank of the daughter and son of an earl, and Benjamin cannot succeed to his father's earldom.

Although initially unconcerned about social convention and titles, David and Margaret had a change of heart after they married. David successfully petitioned his first cousin, once removed, Queen Elizabeth II, to allow the two elder children to bear the courtesy title of Honourable, and for Emily to assume the courtesy title of Lady.

The couple had two more children, Alexander Edgar born in 1980, who will inherit his father's title and Edward David, born in 1982. Their marriage ended in divorce in 1989. A year later, in Australia, David married a middle class painter and sculptor, Diane Howse.

David's countercultural interests are still flourishing. He raised funds to complete an animated film based on the comic book characters the Fabulous Furry Freak Brothers, whose mission is to retire to the country to grow marijuana. David and other producers are adapting the story as a stage musical.

Second-born James has lived an even more colorful and unconventional life. He took classical piano and drum lessons as a child, and later co-founded the hugely popular Global Village Trucking Company — known to its fans as The Globs. The band, the road crew, and their families lived together in a commune. They shunned bourgeois record deals and instead performed at benefit concerts and free festivals.

The Globs were the subject of a BBC documentary in 1973 about their communal living and their aim to achieve success without a record company. That year, James married Frederica Ann DuhrsSenator Soon enough, perhaps acknowledging financial pressures, the group recorded a self-titled album in 1974. James and Frederica had two children.

In 1983, James took his family on an 8-month trip in a Mercedes motor home, traveling through Europe, Egypt, Israel and Morocco. He recorded tribal music that he released on his own label. The following year, he left his family and moved to New Mexico where he started It's a Small World Band, inspired by his new interest in traditional American Indian songs. He and Frederica divorced in 1985, and he married Lori Susan Lee, known as Shadow, that same year. They also had two children, and their marriage lasted 11 years, when it ended in divorce.

Three years later, James married Nigerian actress and AIDS activist Joy Elias-Rilwan. She is the mother of four children, and is a member of the Elias family of Yoruba chieftains in Lagos. Since marrying Elias-Rilwan, James Lascelles seems to have been more settled. He has continued to record tribal music, composed music for film and theater, and runs workshops for disaffected youth throughout the U.K. encouraging the performing arts.

The youngest of George and Marion's sons is Robert Jeremy Hugh Lascelles, known as Jeremy. As a teenager, he joined brother James in the Global Village Trucking Company; Jeremy played percussion to James' keyboards. In his mid-20s, Jeremy became a tour promoter and then an executive for Virgin Records. He spent 13 years at there and rose to head the Artists & Repertoire Division under company founder Richard Branson. Jeremy searched out new talent and oversaw the artistic development of recording artists and songwriters. He left to start his own independent label, Offside Records, which was named after his favorite cricket shot. He moved onto Chrysalis Music in 1994, rising to the position of chief executive officer. He stepped down in March 2012 and was named a visiting professor at Leeds College of Music.

Jeremy married twice: to Julie Baylis in 1981 — the couple has three children — and to Catherine Isobel Bell in 1999. They had a daughter.

Jeremy Thorpe's only biological son, Rupert, was just 10 when his father went to trial. Rupert said the drama unfolded for him as the British magazine *Private Eye* hounded his dad over suggestions of homosexuality.

Rupert's career as a celebrity paparazzo is surprising given that the press doggedly pursued his family. Today, he's one of the best in the business. "Rupert has an unbelievable skill for catching celebrities on film," said a fellow paparazzo. Possessed of a trait reminiscent of his charismatic father, "He could charm his way into a convent," said another photographer.

On the picture desk of *The Sun* newspaper, Rupert became adept at crashing Hollywood premieres and exclusive parties. His photos of the Spice Girls splashing around in a

Los Angeles hotel pool were sold around the world.

In 1997, he clashed with his employer over the newspaper's plan to publish a series on his father's fall from prominence. The renewed intrusion into Rupert's family was intolerable, and he resigned. He put some distance between himself and the judgmental British public by moving to California.

"It is an irony how Rupert earns his living," said Paul Harris, a celebrity photographer who hired Thorpe when he arrived in Los Angeles. "He is a complicated character. On the surface, he is a very ebullient, outgoing, almost manic type, and yet it is hard to know what is really going on underneath."

In 2001, Rupert married Australian photographer Michelle Day, another expatriate living in Los Angeles. They each have their own successful photography businesses, with a hefty roster of celebrity clients.

For the rest of their lives, Marion took care of her husband at home. As his speech deteriorated from Parkinson's disease, she served as his interpreter for guests. The two died within months of each other in 2014. She passed away first, surprisingly, given that he had been so ill for years. After Jeremy's death in December 2014, people came forward to confirm he was likely involved in a plot to have Norman Scott murdered.

Rupert issued a generous and clear-eyed tribute to his parents after his father died, saying he had been "a devoted husband to my two mothers, Caroline, who died tragically in 1970, and Marion who passed away in March and had raised me and stood by him through everything."

Hillary & Bill Clinton

Inventing the Power Couple

President Bill Clinton's 51st birthday party in the summer of 1997 was a celebrity-filled extravaganza on Martha's Vineyard. He and his friends had reason to celebrate. He was in the midst of his fifth year in office, and his power was resurgent after the early presidential years pocked by his administration's missteps and a Republican rout taking the majority in the House of Representatives.

Bill had won a difficult re-election race in 1996 and was making headway on his second-term agenda by blending the best ideas of his opponents and supporters to craft his famous "triangulated" consensuses on the federal budget, government oversight, and more.

What the president stood to accomplish using his abundant intellect and charm was increasingly evident.

Special prosecutor Kenneth Starr in Washington seemed to be winding down his aggressive yet fruitless probe of Clinton campaign finance irregularities.

And so, the Clintons' mood was appropriately light. Bill and Hillary arrived at sunny Martha's Vineyard for their regular three-week August vacation, in historic Edgartown at the waterfront compound of hotelier Richard Friedman. For Bill's Aug. 19 birthday, actors Ted Danson and Mary Steenburgen hosted a clambake at their farm that rollicked late into the night with an eclectic mix of celebrities, high-powered lawyers, authors, and artists. They included TV mogul Barry Diller, author-humorist Fran Lebowitz and Miramax Films chief Harvey Weinstein. It was the type of crowd that had enough of its own star-power that the Clintons could relax, far from the crush of fawning fans. On the Vineyard, Bill could golf with Sylvester Stallone and Norman Lear; Hillary could take a wooded walk in solitude; the couple could stay indoors and play board games with daughter

Chelsea or pop out for a late-night drink at Carly Simon's nightclub.

However, by the following year, that 1997 sojourn began to look like the good old days. In August 1998, the Clintons' mood was silent and somber. Bill had just testified in front of a Washington grand jury where Ken Starr produced DNA evidence that the president's semen stained a dress worn by a former White House intern when she was 22. Bill lied about the intimate nature of their relationship for months after the affair first surfaced in January 1998 press reports. He allowed Hillary to go on national television and tell *Today* host Matt Lauer that a "right-wing conspiracy" was ginning up false rumors about her husband. Only when his Aug. 17 grand jury appearance became inevitable did he tell Hillary the truth: that he had invited the young intern to give him oral sex in the Oval Office among other sex play.

"I could hardly breathe," Hillary wrote of her reaction to her husband's confession in *Living History.* "Gulping for air, I started crying and yelling at him, 'What do you mean? What are you saying? Why did you lie to me?'"

After his grand jury testimony, the family left for Martha's Vineyard and attended a very different 52nd birthday party for Bill. In place of celebrity crowds and rock music, the three Clintons — Hillary, Bill and Chelsea — dined at the Martha's Vineyard home of Ann and Vernon Jordan. He was a high-powered Washington lobbyist and fixer who, like Bill, had tried for months to keep the White House intern story under wraps. Chelsea left right after dessert. Neither she nor Hillary was speaking to Bill — they brought along family dog Buddy as Bill's lone vacation companion.

Hillary slept upstairs, and Bill downstairs. Beyond the

108

marital betrayal, which would have been enough to break the spirit of any loving spouse, this prominent First Lady endured public humiliation of the most ironic kind. She had been a champion of women's rights and dignity across the globe. "I could barely speak to Bill, and when I did, it was a tirade," Hillary wrote in her memoir. "Days were easier than nights. Where do you turn when your best friend, the one who always helps you through hard times, is the one who wounded you? I felt unbearably alone, and I could tell Bill did too. He kept trying to explain and apologize. But I wasn't ready to be in the same room with him, let alone forgive him."

Yet, within three weeks, Hillary told long-time confidant, Diane Blair, she had no intention of leaving her marriage. Blair's journal entry summarized their Sept. 9 phone conversation: Hillary said Bill "has been her best friend for 25 years, her husband for 23 years, they're connected in every way imaginable, she feels strongly about him and family and Chelsea and marriage, and she's just got to try to work it through.... So — she's in it for the long haul. Partly because she's stubborn; partly her upbringing; partly her pride — but, mostly because she knows who she is and what her values and priorities are and she's straight with those — she really is okay."

Hillary Rodham Clinton survived the king of all American sex scandals and, shortly after, rose by double- digits in opinion polls. In 1998, she was named the country's "most admired" woman over Oprah Winfrey. Hillary positioned herself to become the first woman to seriously contend for the U.S. presidency. Out of tragedy, a triumph. And, yet, her twisted marital history became one reason voters gave to pull the lever for her opponent, Donald Trump.

Hillary's White Queen Quotient: 10

Although it pushed the family into a trough, the 1998 intern scandal was far from the first of Bill's philandering that afflicted Hillary. Throughout the Clintons' years in public life, there were constant rumors about his other women. Stranger still, as a young woman, Hillary was a political force in her own right. As she came of age in the late 1960s and 1970s, the anti-war and women's movements were on fire. She was elected student government president at Wellesley with the enthusiastic support of far-wealthier classmates; her gutsy 1969 graduation speech was written up in *Life* magazine as a statement that defined her generation. In law school at Yale and afterward, she was widely acknowledged among her peers as a leader. For financial security, to create a legacy, or to accomplish her patriotic goals, she didn't need to attach herself to a man's rising star. She could have had a significant career without Bill, but with him, she rightly calculated she could go much further.

By all appearances, Hillary made a deal with herself over Bill's philandering. She's a private person who hates campaigning, so her marriage to a charismatic "people person" in Bill created a dynamic partnership that propelled her, in 2016, onto the highest stage for any woman in American politics: the nominee on a major party ticket for the presidential race.

Hillary took her first step in national politics in 1994 when, as First Lady she undertook a monumental effort to reform U.S. health care. While the reform failed, this assignment from her husband gave her the opportunity to demonstrate her policy skills on a national stage. Bill's presidency in the 1990s was a time of political and personal drama in

Washington, but the rest of America experienced relative prosperity and peace, and he left office with a 65 percent approval rating. This success gave Hillary a platform to enter and win the race for a U.S. Senate seat in New York in 2000 with wide name recognition, and to go on to campaign for the presidency in 2007. While she lost the Democratic primary to Barack Obama, she leveraged her strong show of public support to become secretary of state in his administration.

When she ran again for president in 2016, Hillary's Faustian bargain tied her hands. She couldn't well attack Donald Trump for his serial philandering in a full-throated way without risking the charge that she was a hypocrite. Her biggest weakness as a candidate arose from the perception that she was untrustworthy — and her marital decisions played a role in cementing that view.

Hillary's early life choices reveal a rebellion against patriarchal domination, which she learned firsthand from her parents' marriage. Hugh Rodham was a former Navy drill instructor, unpleasant, sarcastic, profane, and stingy. He was verbally and mentally abusive to his wife Dorothy, who brushed aside his cruelty, lightly referring to him as Mr. Difficult and encouraged her three children, in their turn, to work out their marital problems. Divorce was never a realistic option in the Rodham family.

As Hillary became involved in politics, from the time she ran for student government in high school, someone as astute as she surely picked up on attitudes about the electability of independent women. She was chosen class vice president in 11th grade and ran for president the following year. When she lost, one of her male opponents told her she was stupid to think a girl could win. Many years later, after Bill lost his re-election bid for Arkansas governor in 1980, Hillary made enormous changes in her appearance to comport with how voters thought a political wife should look. She gave up her thick glasses for contact lenses, styled her hair in a flip, and lightened it to honey blond. She began wearing form-flattering skirts and blouses in pastel shades. Previously, she had kept her maiden name, but then declared she would be known as Hillary Clinton instead of Hillary Rodham. All were concessions to patriarchal politics, made in full awareness on her part. She "says she compromised by giving up her name, getting contact lenses," Diane Blair wrote in her journal after a phone talk with Hillary.

Another White Queen trait: The Clintons' partnership is infused with patriotic fervor. Early on, they referred to their life together as "the journey." They intended to inspire the expansion of their country's social consciousness, based on their own ideas and ideals, and those of their generation. Indeed, at a campaign rally in New Hampshire in 1992 when he was running for president for the first time, Bill referred to the egalitarian concept of a co-presidency. He was forced to hastily retract it after a strong public backlash. But Bill's early White House years appeared to be a full partnership — a perception that critics used to bludgeon Democrats in midterm congressional elections in 1994. Even as "co-president," a woman could cost elections in America by having too much influence.

When the Clintons met, Bill was a charismatic student leader at Yale Law School. His reputation for wooing the ladies probably made him that much more of a catch for a woman seeking to shore up an insecure ego, and Hillary may have had some doubts about her attractiveness as a woman, conceived in those formative years as a teenager. She was embarrassed by the dress she could afford for the senior prom, and her date was a fix-up who agreed to take her after she proved she was cool enough to ride a skateboard. Her high school newspaper gave her a nickname that was a humiliating commentary on her femininity: Sister Frigidaire. Bill's lifelong desire to be by Hillary's side drowns the Sister Frigidaire epithet like sunken rubbish.

Just as Hillary likely longed for the security and validation of marriage to a desirable husband, she earns high marks in another White Queen category: emotional protection of her family. When Bill ran for re-election as Arkansas governor in 1986, rumors surfaced that his opponent was going to make a campaign issue of Bill's philandering. In order to prepare 6-year-old Chelsea for the nasty things people might say about her dad, Hillary role-played press conferences with her daughter. In spite of living in the public glare for many decades, the Clintons have maintained a close-knit family; even some of Bill and Hillary's harshest political critics admire their success as parents.

When it comes to Bill, Hillary has aggressively ventured forth to defend her husband in crucial times when his philandering threatened to wreck his political career — "bimbo eruptions" in the lingo of the Clinton campaign apparatus. Hillary used her formidable legal and debate skills after the Gennifer Flowers scandal in 1992, appearing on CBS's *60 Minutes* to argue for a "zone of privacy for everyone." Six years later, she rallied a loyal entourage of men and women to report every Sunday morning to plan the week's fight as the intern scandal drew public demands for Bill's impeachment. She was the clear-eyed strategist who rallied Democratic votes against her husband's impeachment, maintaining the presence of mind to argue that Bill's enemies were bending the Constitution to suit their agenda. After years in the spotlight, defending Bill became Hillary's first reaction — seemingly even before she contemplates her own hurt and the damage infidelity inflicts on their union.

Like other modern White Queens, Hillary is conscious of her legacy and place in history, as much for her own dynastic family ambitions as for the ideal that American women be considered for election as president. Among the 32 pages of photographs in *Living History* is a Photoshop image created by a friend of Hillary's depicting former First Lady Eleanor Roosevelt styling young Hillary's hair, mother-daughter fashion. The image of Hillary is from her care-for-naught days when she wore no makeup and head-light-sized eyeglasses. Like Hillary, Eleanor had been ridiculed for her plain appearance. Emotional security figured into the decisions of both women to stay in their marriages.

Hillary mentioned her "personal heroine" when she was asked in a 2014 interview what advice she would give young women. "[Eleanor Roosevelt] famously said, back in the 1920s, that if a woman wants to be involved in the public, and in her case, she was talking politics, but it's true in professions, business, etcetera, she has to grow skin as thick as the hide of a rhinoceros. So even back then, this was an obvious point of concern and contention," Hillary recalled. "Too many young women, I think, are harder on themselves than circumstances warrant. They are too often selling themselves short. They too often take criticism personally instead of seriously. You should take criticism seriously, because you might learn something, but you can't let it crush you. And you have to be resilient enough to keep moving forward, despite whatever the personal setbacks, even insults that come your way might be. And that takes a sense of humor about yourselves and others. Believe me, this is hard-won advice that I am now putting forth here."

Eleanor stayed with Franklin after his repeated infidelities, and yet toward the end of her life, she regretted it, and advised her children to choose differently. One wonders, in admiring Eleanor Roosevelt as a role model, did Hillary only see part of the picture?

Mixed Messages from a Righteous Mother and Overbearing Father

Hillary derived her sense of social mission from her mother Dorothy, from her Methodist church and, in particular, from the church's youth minister Rev. Don Jones. Her domineering, never-approving father set the tone for Hillary's fierce ambition and her acceptance of patriarchal values.

Hillary's mother Dorothy Howell was born in Chicago in 1919 to Della Murray, a French-Scottish girl who was illiterate and just 15 years old. Dorothy's father was Edwin Howell, a 17-year-old firefighter. When she was 8, her parents divorced. She and her sister Isabelle, age 3, were put on a train bound for California by themselves — an agonizing, three-day journey that left Dorothy emotionally scarred. Their British immigrant grandparents met the train in Alhambra but were put-upon by raising the girls and were physically and emotionally abusive. Dorothy's grandmother worked her hard and confined her to her room when she was done with her chores. At 14, Dorothy took a job as a nanny in the home of a close-knit family that treated her well, sent her to high school, and encouraged her to read widely. The experience of living with a strong family taught Dorothy how to care for her own household and children, she told Hillary for her book *It Takes a Village*. Dorothy and Isabelle didn't hear from their mother Della for a decade. But when Dorothy was 18, Della wrote that she had remarried, to Max Rosenberg, and asked the girls to return to live with them. Max had a comfortable income as the owner of several Chicago apartment buildings, and he encouraged his new wife to try to make amends with her daughters. But her mother also treated Dorothy like a housemaid, and so she left. Dorothy's itinerant, insecure childhood had a strong influence on Hillary, who devoted much of her legal and political energy defending and asserting the rights of children.

For example, after law school, Hillary worked for the newly formed Children's Defense Fund in Cambridge, Massachusetts, to focus on children's legal rights. She challenged the South Carolina legal system that treated lawbreakers as adults starting at age 14 and housed them in adult state prisons. She went door-to-door in the blue-collar Massachusetts town of New Bedford to learn if children were working instead of attending school. Years later, when Bill was governor of Arkansas, Hillary spearheaded a court-ordered reform of the state's abysmal public education system, including advocating for mandatory teacher-testing. Her former Senate and State Department staff say that Hillary encouraged new mothers to take time off, keep flexible hours, and work from home so that they could be present for their children.

In 1937, after graduating from Alhambra High School and returning to her mother's home in Chicago, Dorothy met her husband-to-be, Hugh Rodham. Dorothy was 18, and Hugh was 26. She worked as his secretary, and they dated for five years during which time she suspected he was continuing a relationship with another woman. If Hugh played the field, Dorothy didn't reject him based on his embrace of this male privilege. Hillary claimed her mother was attracted to his gruff personality, perhaps taking it for strength and decisiveness.

Almost immediately after they married, Hugh enlisted in the Navy and became a chief petty officer, training young recruits in a rigorous physical education regime based on the techniques of boxer Gene Tunney. When Hugh returned home from World War II, he brought along his drill-instructor mentality, becoming impossible to satisfy — "barking orders, denigrating, minimizing achievements, ignoring accomplishments, raising the bar constantly for his frustrated children — 'character building,' he called it." When Hugh Jr. was a quarterback, for example, he completed 10 out of 11 passes in a game when his father was in the stands. Hugh told him he should have completed the 11th pass.

Hugh had a college degree and was offered his office job back when he returned from the war. But he decided instead to start a drapery business. His father had emigrated from Wales to Scranton, Pennsylvania, to take a position in a lace-making factory, so Hugh was, in a sense, returning to the family craft. He also intended to capitalize on the postwar economic boom. Hugh printed, cut, and sewed the fabric himself, making drapes, window shades and lace curtains for hotels, offices, movie theaters, airlines and homes. Like Bill Clinton, he had a big personality and was wonderful at sales. He finished at his fabric shop by 3 or 4 p.m. most days, then returned home to his easy chair, a beer in hand, and the television tuned to sports. His antisocial presence dominated the room, and he rarely rose to greet or welcome a guest.

Born in 1947, Hillary was the couple's first child. When she was 3, Hugh's business was doing well enough that he could move his family into the comfortable suburb of Park Ridge, Illinois. Within four years, Hugh Jr. and Tony were born. When Hillary became interested in politics at an early age, she mimicked her father's Republican sentiments. Dorothy was a "closet Democrat" who didn't confront her husband directly with political differences. However, she schooled her daughter in the art of speaking up for herself. When a neighborhood girl bullied Hillary, Dorothy told her the next time the girl hit her, to hit back — and she did. "There's no room in this house for cowards," she told Hillary. Dorothy set lofty ambitions for her girl and often mentioned the idea of becoming a Supreme Court justice — though at that time, no woman had yet sat on the nation's highest court.

To validate her mother's faith and to earn her father's approval, Hillary worked hard in school. She made the honor roll and competed in class debates by making sure she was well prepared. She was one of just 11 National Merit Scholars in her graduating class of 1,400. Her high school class voted her most likely to succeed.

Hillary also worked outside of school as a babysitter in the afternoons and during school vacation. She watched children of migrant Mexicans who came to Chicago for temporary work, an experience that formed her lifelong interest in immigration reform and migrant workers. In 10th grade, she met the Rev. Don Jones, 26, who hosted what he called the "University of Life" two nights a week at the First United Methodist church. His message to the youth group was faith in action, based on the teachings of Methodism founder John Wesley and theologians such as Reinhold Niebuhr and Dietrich Bonhoeffer. Rev. Jones said a Christian's role is to temper human nature with a passion for justice and social reform. He was the most important teacher in young Hillary's life, and served as her counselor over the decades and through her trials as a betrayed First Wife, advising her to cope with adversity by doing good works and being of service.

If Hillary's childhood was rich in spirituality, it was poor in other ways. At age 9, she was prescribed thick eyeglasses considered unfeminine in the 1950s. Hugh refused to allow Hillary to get a driver's license, a key rite of passage in high school, telling her to ride her bicycle instead. She went around him and got a friend to take her for the license. Hugh also objected to spending on ballroom dance lessons or on clothes for his daughter, further dousing her sense of femininity and eroding her confidence with boys.

Her first political experience outside school was canvassing the South Side of Chicago with her father. Though his Republican roots were strong, Hillary was in the habit of seeking out her own truths. After hearing a 1962 speech by Dr. Martin Luther King, Jr. in Chicago, she took a serious interest in civil rights and social justice, most likely what would become the foundation for her legal — and later political — career. She stayed in the Republican fold for a number of years and campaigned for Barry Goldwater in 1964. When she enrolled in Wellesley College in 1965, she declared a political science major and became president of the Young Republicans Club.

By 1968, Hillary developed strong opinions about the Vietnam War, and was deeply shaken by the assassination of MLK, Jr. Her fiery attitude was manifest even then, when she attempted to organize a two-day student strike, and nearly shouted down a professor who dared suggest the students strike during the weekend. That year, she supported Democrat Eugene McCarthy's presidential campaign, though she also worked as an intern for the House Republican Conference. After the protests that summer at the Democratic National Convention in Chicago, the Republican Party, as Hillary would later write in *Living History,* "left me."

In her early 20s, Hillary was thrust into the public eye when her commencement speech at Wellesley was featured in *Life* magazine. U.S. Senator Edward Brooke, a Republican representing Massachusetts, had just spoken, and Hillary put aside her prepared remarks to respond directly to Brooke's speech. The bold move led to her being one of five featured students in the *Life* feature, "The Class of 1969." Her dad had flown in for the day. After her address, he turned around and went home. Her mother wasn't there, because a doctor had advised Dorothy against traveling; she was taking blood-thinning medications due to health problems. Hillary wrote that she was disappointed, because, "In many ways, this moment was as much hers as mine." Even if she had not ambushed the Senator, Hugh would have been unlikely to embrace her and express his pride. His means of maintaining control in relationships was to withhold approval.

It's striking how much Hillary's childhood characteristics would have been spun differently if she were a boy. The British Isles temper, the pugnacious standing up for herself, the bragging about being the smartest in the class. Her high school classmates, her father, Senator Brooke — all judged her behavior as inappropriate. In a way, it was a blessing because Hillary learned to perceive the many ways women are treated as lesser. As an adult, she chose to live beyond this moment, with its backward ideas about women, and to assert her place in history.

After Wellesley, Hillary enrolled in Yale Law School. There's an oft-told tale about Robert Reich, Bill's future secretary of labor, introducing Hillary to Bill at registration that first semester. Initially, the two didn't spark. Then there's the story about Hillary walking up to Bill, as he was eyeing her from a stack in the campus library, to forthrightly introduce herself. She said to him, in effect, "Look, if we're going to spend all this time staring at each other, we should at least get to know who the other is." Every happy couple has a sweet how-we-met story, and no one is more practiced at mythmaking than couples in politics. What seems obvious is that Hillary and Bill were both campus political stars in their own right and couldn't help but revolve in one another's orbit.

An Evidently Formidable Team

Bill's upbringing was filled with even more drama than Hillary's, along with full doses of infidelity. When his mother, Virginia Cassidy Blythe, was six months pregnant, Bill's father was killed in a car accident. She named her baby William Jefferson after his likely father, William Jefferson Blythe. Virginia was rumored to be sexually involved with some of the doctors in Hope, Arkansas. And Blythe had had four or five wives by the time of his death at 28. Virginia was a free spirit by the standards of the mid-century American South, and after her husband's death was left little choice but to find work to support herself and her baby. She moved to New Orleans to study nursing, and while she was away, Bill was raised by his maternal grandparents, Eldridge and Edith Cassidy. Edith, a nurse, regularly denounced her husband, Eldridge, for affairs. Edith and Virginia were often at odds, competing for Bill's affections. Psychologically, some have speculated, Lewinsky would become the Virginia and Hillary the Edith in Bill's emotional life.

Arkansas was segregated by race when Bill was growing up. Eldridge and Edith owned a small grocery store, and despite public discouragement, they allowed people of color to purchase things on credit. This simple act likely had a deep and lasting effect on Bill's inclusive political leanings. Bill has also said that his strict grandparents instilled in him a love of learning and respect for education.

"My grandparents had a lot to do with my early commitment to learning. They taught me to count and read. I was reading little books when I was 3," he recalled.

In 1950, when Bill was four, his mother returned from New Orleans with her nursing degree. Upon her return, she married Roger Clinton, a car dealer and abusive alcoholic. Three years later, the family moved to Hot Springs, Arkansas, where Roger could work at his brother's car dealership. As a young man, Bill often intervened in Roger and Virginia's arguments. When Bill was 15, Virginia divorced Roger very briefly and then quickly remarried him; this was also the year that Bill warned Roger Sr. never to hit his mother or half-brother, Roger Jr., ever again. "That was a dramatic thing," Bill later said. Once Roger Jr. was old enough to enter school, Bill legally changed his name to Clinton from Blythe.

Soon after moving to Hot Springs, Bill decided to be baptized at the Park Place Baptist Church, nearby his new home. While Virginia usually worked on Sunday mornings, Bill walked to church to attend services alone. He came to his faith on his own: neither his mother nor his grandparents were religious.

Bill was fortunate in that his high school principal, Johnnie Mae Mackey, encouraged student leaders to consider public service as the highest form of personal success. With

Mackey as a mentor during his senior year of high school in 1962, Bill was selected to be one of two delegates from Arkansas to Boy's Nation. He traveled to the White House to meet the president. Soon after, from his TV set in Arkansas, Bill watched Martin Luther King Jr. give his speech "I Have a Dream" and was so deeply moved that he memorized it.

Bill attended Georgetown University, majored in International Affairs, and clerked for the Senate Foreign Relations Committee. He was ardently involved in protests against the Vietnam War and for civil rights. Graduating in 1968, he was awarded a Rhodes scholarship to study in England at Oxford University.

Despite his public party-boy persona (it was at Oxford that he "didn't inhale"), Bill's Oxford classmates do not remember him as a womanizer. His friend Mandy Merck said that, "Bill was plumpish, and ill-kempt, not a ladies' man, although he was flirtatious in an amiable way." If that was the impression, his image was headed for change.

By the time Bill and Hillary met at Yale in 1971, they had trod much of the same ground, and it drew them together: a strong religious faith, outrage over the Vietnam War and racial injustice, excelling in studies and student leadership to rise above their middle-class family households. They didn't share the privileged pedigree of a Roosevelt or a Bouvier, or the wealth of a Kennedy. Both Hillary and Bill ran for student government or club office, and eyed careers in public service.

As much as their common passions drew them together, their differences made them more powerful as a pair. He had the charm and the sex appeal — as Hillary put it in her memoir; he "had a vitality that seemed to shoot out of his pores." She was focused and well prepared. Bill wrote in his memoir *My Life,* "She conveyed a sense of strength and self-possession I had rarely seen in anyone, man or woman."

Even though they seemed to work as a couple on an emotional and practical level, their dreams were taking them in different directions. Bill cared deeply about going back to Arkansas to make a difference. "She sensed in him a commitment to public service that transcended mere ambition for office," wrote legendary Washington insider Carl Bernstein. "He came from a state that lagged behind the rest of the country in education, economic prosperity, and cultural sophistication, but 'he cared deeply about where he came from, which was unusual,' she noted. 'He was rooted, and most of us were disconnected'." Early on, she could see that he had the potential to do much more. A mutual law school friend, Nancy Bekavac, said people often remarked at this stage of Bill's life that he could become president. "I don't think I knew him two hours before it dawned on me," she said.

Clearly Not a One-Woman Man

At the end of Hillary's third year at Yale, she was offered a summer internship at a California law firm, and Bill asked if he could go with her — a clear sign they were becoming serious. At the end of the summer, they returned to Connecticut, and Hillary signed on for a fourth year at the university simply to be with Bill. As he charmingly wrote years later, "Hillary and I were nowhere near done with our conversation, so we decided to live together back in New Haven." After graduation, he took her on her first trip to Europe. Walking along the shores of Lake Ennerdale in England's scenic lake district, for the first time, Bill asked Hillary to marry him. She responded, "Give me time." She had serious doubts about moving to Arkansas where Bill wanted to run for office. And then, there was his womanizing.

Many times during their courtship and marriage, she was forced to face that he did not control his sexual fidelity. "She knew that Bill's history of compulsive infidelity during their courtship," Bernstein wrote, "meant the chances of a stable marriage, especially a marriage without adultery, were at best a crapshoot."

Shortly after graduation, in 1974, the two were pursuing their careers in separate locales — Hillary working on the Nixon impeachment team in Washington, and Bill jumping into his first congressional race in Arkansas. Managing his campaign by telephone, Hillary heard rumors he was spending time with an old flame, Dolly Kyle, who had just divorced her first husband. Hillary promptly dispatched her father Hugh and brother Tony to the campaign to "help out" — or, in other words, to check up on Bill. They reported back that he was involved with a half-dozen women in Fayetteville. Hillary followed up with a blistering phone call, while Bill on the other end of the line pleaded for forgiveness.

Bill lost that election, and one reason, he believed, is that he wasn't a family man. He wasn't married. With President Richard Nixon's resignation, the impeachment team closed its offices, and Hillary was free. The two married in 1975, honeymooning in Acapulco — along with her family Hugh, Dorothy, Hugh Jr. and Tony Rodham staying in the same hotel.

As close-knit a family picture as that presents, Hillary's path over the coming years would be littered with opportunities to confront Bill's philandering, and to choose each time whether to stay or to go. According to two long- time Arkansas friends, at the time Bill was running for Arkansas governor in 1978, Hillary knew about Gennifer Flowers's pregnancy and was "devastated." Bill was also rumored to be involved with leggy, blond campaign volunteer Juanita Hickey Broaddrick.

As governor, Bill's drug of choice — extramarital sex — seemed to intensify. In sworn affidavits, Arkansas state troopers Larry Patterson, Larry Douglass Brown, and Roger Perry recalled approaching several women a week for their boss. Still, Hillary resolved to stay in the marriage, in part because she may have made peace with this aspect of Bill's character years before. In 1989, at a time when Bill was involved with Arkansas divorcee Marilyn Jo Jenkins, Hillary told a confidante, "There are worse things than infidelity," according to Bernstein's largely flattering biography, *A Woman in Charge*.

During this time, the 1988 presidential race beckoned the charismatic southern governor. Bill had set himself a July 14, 1987, deadline to announce whether he would run. Two months before the deadline, the Democratic frontrunner, Gary Hart, U.S. Senator from Colorado, suspended his campaign over tabloid revelations of an extramarital affair. Bill's chief of staff, , cautioned him with a list of his rumored lovers, according to journalist Christopher Andersen, who has written more than a dozen controversial biographies of the famous, including *American Evita* about Hillary. Wright counted at least 12 rumored paramours and, especially in light of the Hart implosion, concluded that Bill couldn't run in the 1988 election. Hillary argued otherwise. Bill was ready, she said, and his accusers had credibility problems. The difficulty was manageable.

Months later, as Hillary was campaigning for Bill for president in Atlanta, the campaign had its first bimbo eruption. Bill called Hillary to break the news that the daily supermarket tabloid, *The Star,* had published an interview with Gennifer Flowers saying that she and Bill had had a 12-year affair. He denied the story to his wife. Hillary and the campaign team decided she should address it head-on prior to the New Hampshire Democratic primary. She granted an interview to Steve Kroft of CBS's *60 Minutes* to air in a prime time slot right after the Super Bowl.

Given the totality of this evidence of Bill's infidelity and Hillary's continuing responses, over many years, it's hard to reach any other conclusion than that she knew that her husband was unfaithful. What are we to make of the bargain she apparently struck with herself to look the other way — and even to go on the offensive when necessary for his political future? Perhaps she hoped the cheating would end once he was in the White House. Then again, Hillary's relatively quick decision to stay with her husband, even after Bill's testimony in the White House intern investigation, suggests she had made peace with his infidelity long before. Such "marital stoicism," some argue, is a reason that some voters distrust Hillary. They believe she sacrificed her humanity to become "co-president," to remain in power, and to fulfill her sense of her own destiny. Those arguments held their greatest force before Hillary held a seat in the U.S. Senate, ran in 2007 for the U.S. presidency in her own right, and served as Secretary of State in the Obama administration. Can one seriously argue that she still needs Bill in order to wield power? Would divorcing him wipe out her substantial record of public service and bar her from commanding the Oval Office?

Uneasiness in the Land
of Patriarchal Politics

The expected thing after each high-profile sex scandal would have been for Hillary to crumble into an emotional wreck and to head out the door. But she's a person who's most sure when listening to her own inner counsel, even to the point of defying the norm. For example, when her aide Huma Abedin was suffering her own marital sex scandal, Hillary gave her this advice: "Every woman should have the ability and the confidence and the choice to make whatever decisions she wants to make that are right for her and not be judged by it."

First Lady is one of the most tradition-bound roles remaining in America. Yet, Hillary managed to tease apart the contradictions of the institution, at one point competing in a bake-off with her predecessor Barbara Bush, and at another becoming the first sitting First Lady to run for office — and win a U.S. Senate seat from New York. It's almost as though Hillary can't help sticking a sharp elbow into the ribs of convention. As she has remarked, she's a human Rorschach test. What people observe about her and how they judge her is often most revealing about themselves.

In that sense of rebelling against tradition, Hillary is very much like Eleanor Roosevelt, a First Lady predecessor with whom Hillary has said she holds imaginary conversations. "I had been tracking her career as one of America's most controversial First Ladies, sometimes quite literally. Wherever I ventured, Mrs. Roosevelt seemed to have been there before me," Hillary wrote in her memoir. From dust bowl towns to poor urban neighborhoods, from civil rights to child labor laws, from refugee issues to human rights,

Eleanor and Hillary had common paths and interests. Like Hillary, Eleanor had suffered public criticism for daring to redefine her First Lady role. People called Eleanor a Communist agitator and a homely old meddler — reminiscent of the "vast right-wing conspiracy" Hillary says tracks the Clintons. At one point, there was a website dedicated entirely to mocking Hillary's changing hairstyles.

Protecting Her Family's Legacy — and That of Her Country

Hillary Clinton's tenacity about her legacy — and that of her family — rises to the very top among political women. In the mid-term elections of 1994, after Republicans took a majority of seats in the House of Representatives for the first time since 1952, Hillary recognized it in part as a repudiation of her high-profile role, especially her efforts to broaden health care protections. She took several steps back from domestic politics, demonstrating a willingness to take herself out of the picture for a greater cause. Instead she began speaking around the world about women's rights.

Four years later, when many were calling for Bill's impeachment, Hillary made the legal argument that it would set a bad precedent for the nation. "Even if I was undecided about my personal future, I was absolutely convinced that Bill's private behavior and his misguided effort to conceal it did not constitute a legal or historical basis for impeachment under the Constitution," she wrote. "I believed he ought to be held accountable — by me and by Chelsea — not by a misuse of the impeachment process."

Similarly, in a TV interview just days after the country learned of the allegations about Bill and the White House intern, Hillary said, "I'm here today not only because I love and believe my husband, I'm also here because I love and believe in my country." She told confidante Diane Blair, who recorded the conversation in her journal, that it's "appalling what's being done to the country and constitution. Bill has done brilliant work as president. Can't understand why Dems don't seem to have any real convictions."

If she were protecting Constitution and country, Hillary was also defending Bill's presidency, an office she had been deeply engaged in helping him win, hold, manage and guide. Had she accepted Bill's explanation that he didn't have sex with "that woman," her entire world would have collapsed. When Bill was president, Hillary had weighed in on every major appointment and had interviewed candidates. She sat in on staff meetings, ran the president's schedule, and served as his surrogate on the campaign trail for Congressional Democrats. In December 1998, the day after the impeachment vote failed, Hillary hammered home her message of a legacy of achievement that was truly important: "I think the vast majority of Americans share my approval and pride in the job that the President's been doing for our country."

After that statement, she received hundreds of letters of support, including one from Lady Bird Johnson. The former First Lady wrote that it had made her day to see Hillary standing with Bill and reminding everyone of the progress the country has made in education and health, and raising the clarion call for more. Two weeks later, in a New Year's Eve toast, distinguished former Navy chief Admiral Elmo Zumwalt Jr. addressed Chelsea as he spoke about her parents' legacy. Bill, he said, would be remembered for keeping the military strong, for ending the killings in Bosnia, Haiti, Ireland and Kosovo, and for moving peace forward in the

Middle East. Hillary, he said, would be honored "for opening the eyes of the world" to the rights of women and children, and for her support of her family in crisis.

Truly, Hillary took on responsibility for the emotional health of her family — both the one she grew up in, and the one she made. She was very close to her mother, and for years, helped her two brothers out of legal and financial troubles. She has written about the period when Bill was governor of Arkansas and she was considering divorce: "Children without fathers, or whose parents float in and out of their lives after divorce," she wrote, "are precarious little boats in the most turbulent seas." She didn't want that insecure foundation for Chelsea.

Making a Normal Family Life for Chelsea

Chelsea Victoria Clinton was born February 27, 1980 in Little Rock, Arkansas. Perhaps more than any other First Kid, Chelsea is famous for her silence — or her parents, perhaps, are famous for having kept her away from the frenzy of the media and spotlight. The silence Bill and Hillary desired permeated Chelsea's life. When she started her new school in Washington, for example, the principal asked the students and faculty not to talk about her to the media.

Chelsea never fell prey to major scandals, such as those of Jenna and Barbara Bush, two party girls who were infamously in trouble for alcohol violations in Texas and they were kicked out of Argentina. Chelsea has remained a respected public political figure.

Life in the Clinton household was as normal as possible... family breakfasts, three-handed pinochle games, parental presence at school events. Even when they were in the White House, Chelsea had a nearly direct line to Bill; staffers knew to interrupt meetings when Chelsea called. The Clintons managed to maintain a close-knit family.

Though her parents were affectionate, Chelsea's childhood was strict. She wasn't permitted to watch much TV — 30 minutes a day, tops — and wasn't allowed to gorge on sugary cereals or pizza. Pizza and cartoons, in fact, were just for the weekend. In a foreword to a book by her former professor at Stanford, Chelsea wrote that, "in our house, media had its place. Media consumption, like meals, was a shared family experience." The family spent a significant amount of time engaged in the media — together — discussing it and the effect it had on her parents.

As a very young child, she accompanied her parents as they campaigned for Bill's governor race all around Arkansas. Her parents prepared Chelsea for the difficult life in the public eye from a very early age. When she was only six, Bill would say ugly things about himself to Chelsea, to "ready her for what she might hear during his race for reelection as Governor." When the intern scandal broke, she apparently accepted the news with the steely resolve her mother displayed. Once Bill finally admitted to Hillary the extent of his relationship with the intern, Secret Service agents remember a huge fight ensuing that ended with Hillary sinking back onto the bed: "How are we going to tell Chelsea?" she reportedly asked.

Chelsea was 12 when her father was elected and 13 when she moved to the White House. Like many First Kids, Chelsea attended Sidwell Friends. Once, at a school carnival, Chelsea dressed up as a fortuneteller and read the palms of her fellow students. She told one student that she had "a long life line," that she would marry early — and that her husband would have affairs. This was in the early 1990s, before the intern scandal. If her parents had been arguing about Bill's earlier indiscretions, Chelsea would inevitably have overheard some of this. She could very well have been aware of her father's philandering.

Chelsea wasn't entirely shielded from the harsh realities of the media. Soon after her father was elected, Rush Limbaugh showed his TV viewers a picture of Socks, the White House cat. He then said, "Did you know there's a White House dog?" and put up a photo of Chelsea. She recently recalled the incident in public.

"Thankfully I had grown up in public life and knew that having thick skin was a survival skill," she said. "I do also believe if you have the right type of enemies you're doing something correct." She was bound to have some experiences that separated her from her classmates. Among these are the high-profile international trips with her mother, where she would comfortably sign autographs, joke with soldiers, and stand tall with world leaders. On one of these trips, on March 25, 1997, Chelsea spoke publicly about social issues to an informal gathering of women in Arusha, Tanzania. Asked what issues and problems face young women in the United States, she told the group she believed women in the United States probably have more opportunities than those in Tanzania but still have many of the same problems. She said women still don't feel the confidence of men in American society, and while they have equal rights under the law that does not always correspond with reality. Chelsea told the group that drugs and violence were serious problems for women in the United States, but she felt that cynicism and hopelessness were the strongest factors working against women.

Chelsea was just about to turn 18 when lurid details of the White House intern scandal broke; she was attending her second semester of freshman year at Stanford. Though she may have known about her father's past transgressions, the intern affair hit new lows of graphic detail in the media that no daughter would want to associate with her father. Kathy Lee Gifford said that "everyone feels the worst for her," and *The Washington Post* noted that even "the most acerbic pundits" stopped and stammered when commenting on the affair when Chelsea was brought up.

Perhaps most difficult for Hillary is that Bill reportedly called Chelsea the week after allegations of the intern affair were printed and told her that they were untrue. Chelsea came home in January for a Super Bowl party at the White House. One of the guests at the party was the Rev. Jesse Jackson. By one report, Jackson recognized the tension between Bill and Hillary, and realized Chelsea needed extra attention. Jackson sat next to her on the couch, and Hillary would later say that he "bonded with her immediately. He made Chelsea laugh for the first time in a long time, and I was grateful for that." Jackson recalls Chelsea as "a very strong young woman, but she was obviously in terrible pain."

After Hillary went on the *Today* show with interviewer Matt Lauer and called the intern news "a vast right wing conspiracy," she instructed Chelsea not to read the papers or tabloids — advice Hillary was following herself. She asked Chelsea to come home for a show of family unity, which she agreed to do after attending a Stanford basketball game. Bill insisted she meet her parents at Camp David... and publicity photos were taken of the reconciled family. As soon as the photos were printed, Hillary boarded a plane to Switzerland, Bill played golf, and Chelsea went back to California.

She suffered serious stress from the constant stream of news. On May 19 1998, Chelsea was rushed to the hospital with severe pains in her stomach. The White House issued a statement that Chelsea merely had the flu. When she returned to Washington at the end of the spring semester, Chelsea was stunned that her parents weren't talking. By the time allegations of the blue dress surfaced, Chelsea joined her mother in not speaking to Bill.

Professors at Stanford thought of Chelsea as extremely hard working, a student who "did an absolutely prodigious amount of work." They were especially impressed because Chelsea took a semester off to be with her parents in their last few months in the White House. She received a bachelor of arts in history *cum laude,* and her 150-page senior thesis was on the Northern Ireland peace process. After graduation, Chelsea immediately went to Oxford University to pursue a master's degree, which she achieved in 2003. Eight years later, in 2011, she re-matriculated at Oxford to pursue a doctoral degree. She completed most of this coursework from New York, and earned her PhD in international relations in 2014. Her dissertation examines international global governance structures with a focus on global health.

The poise Chelsea learned from her years as a First Kid and through her education came in handy during Hillary's 2008 presidential campaign. Only once did she appear to almost lose her cool in public, when speaking at Butler University in Indianapolis. One student asked Chelsea whether she thought the intern scandal had damaged her mother's reputation. "Wow, you're the first person actually that's ever asked me that question in the, I don't know, maybe 70 college campuses I've been to, and I do not think that is any of your business," she said.

In 2011, Chelsea was named "special correspondent" to *NBC News*. Critics called her "one of the most boring people of her generation," and commented that she didn't do much actual reporting though she was given a $600,000 annual salary. She left less than three years later to focus on philanthropic work at the Bill, Hillary & Chelsea Clinton Foundation and the Clinton Global Initiative, and because she and her husband were expecting their first child.

Chelsea married Marc Mezvinsky in a lavish, interfaith ceremony in Rhinebeck, New York, on July 31, 2010. Mezvinsky is Jewish, also a Stanford graduate, and is a financier who works on Wall Street. Chelsea remained a Methodist and has not converted to Judaism. Mezvinsky is the son of two former members of the U.S. congress, Edward Mezvinsky and Marjorie Margolies-Mezvinsky. Perhaps one common bond Chelsea and Marc share is public scrutiny and scandal. Marc's dad spent seven years in prison on 31 counts of fraud that involved nearly $10 million.

"My marriage is incredibly important to me," Chelsea has said. "It's the place from which I engage in the world every day, and the place to which I return every day." Chelsea and Marc bought a lavish 4-bedroom, 6.5-bathroom apartment on Madison Square Park in New York City in 2013. The couple announced in April 2014 that Bill and Hillary could expect their first grandchild. Chelsea and Marc welcomed baby Charlotte to the Clinton dynasty in September 2014, son Aidan in June 2016 and son Jasper in July 2019.

Arguing for a 'Zone of Privacy' for Political Families

As this chapter began, on Bill Clinton's subdued 52nd birthday, one wonders if the anger about his behavior on the part of his wife and daughter was really about his cheating. They both seem to have been aware that this was a flaw he was vulnerable to. Was their silent anger, instead, about the recklessness with which he had lied to his wife — and allowed her to play the fool by defending him in public? And by debasing their legacy so thoroughly with now-public oral sex in the Oval Office with a young, susceptible intern? His recklessness with what they had all built together seems to be the greater transgression — or at least, the one the Clinton women didn't expect to have to face.

Hillary has argued for a zone of privacy for all people in public office, and this distinction about private behavior becoming the public's business — as opposed to a private marital matter — is one she seems to have been able to follow in her personal life. However, the Clintons were unfortunate to come to power at a time when the press was deciding that private behavior was very much the country's concern. Or, if the press didn't decide that for itself, it was led in that direction by party politics. The night before the impeachment vote in the House of Representatives, Bob Livingston of Louisiana was exposed as an adulterer and forced to resign his position as House Speaker. Hillary wrote in *Living History* that he was "another unintended victim of his own party's campaign of personal destruction."

She defies this current. Speaking with Diane Blair about the resignation of Tony Coelho, a California Democrat best known for championing the Americans with Disabilities Act in Congress, Hillary said he "gave up" after getting some grief from the press about taking a loan from a savings and loan executive at a time when that industry was under investigation. He was never charged with a crime. Hillary said, "Most people in this town have no pain threshold."

After the intern scandal, Hillary gained the upper hand in her marriage and chose to run for the Senate. Just as Eleanor Roosevelt took a more public role in favor of the causes she championed after learning of her husband's betrayal, Hillary Clinton found her voice to stand on her own as a candidate for office. Her grit, and perhaps some public sympathy, won her the admiration she needed to begin her own career in politics.

Wendy & David Vitter

Anti-Sex Crusader

The outskirts of New Orleans — suburban Metairie, Louisiana — is home to Wendy and David Vitter and their four children. It's a modest neighborhood of single-family houses, green lawns, and sidewalks warping over tree roots. Metairie's majority white, largely Catholic population has swelled over the decades as New Orleans residents fled crime and racial tensions. Metairie is one of the most conservative areas of the state, while New Orleans is among the most liberal. Metairie at one time elected a former KKK grand wizard to the state legislature. It boasts 13 Catholic parishes and schools, including St. Francis Xavier Church in the town's old section.

Wendy and David serve as church lectors, reading Bible passages from the lectern on Sundays.

Metairie has been a comfortable home base for David, a roundish, preachy Harvard graduate with an astonishingly successful political career. He survived a sex scandal involving long-term relationships with prostitutes and rumors of kinky fetishes. He not only won re-election to a second term in the U.S. Senate but, in 2015, mounted a serious (but unsuccessful) run for Louisiana governor.

All this, while he presents himself on the campaign trail as a morally righteous, clean-cut family man, championing hard-right political views — such as outlawing abortion and gay marriage, and teaching abstinence as the only appropriate curriculum in school sex-education classes. In a June 2007 talk to a group of students, David said, "Saving sex until marriage and remaining faithful afterwards is the best choice for health and happiness." He spoke these words just a month before his phone number was discovered among the clients of "D.C. Madam" Deborah Jeane Palfrey. Since Palfrey had been under federal investigation for several months, David likely knew he would be caught in his philandering even as he uttered those words. The news about his phone number triggered another revelation: a yearlong relationship with a hooker from a brothel on New Orleans' Canal Street.

And yet, David Vitter carries on, almost defiantly. How is such hypocrisy possibly acceptable to David's constituents, not to mention his wife Wendy? And how does he get away with it, by winning a Senate election when other politicos tainted by insincerity — like Democrats Eliot Spitzer and Anthony Weiner — fail to accomplish a sought-after redemption at the ballot box?

One key to David's success is certainly Wendy Baldwin Vitter. A former assistant district attorney who served as New Orleans' chief of trials, she's tough, and she's comfortable in front of cameras. She was quoted once as saying she's more like Lorena Bobbitt, who cut off her husband's penis in revenge, than Hillary Clinton. "If he does something like that," Wendy said about infidelity, "I'm walking away with one thing, and it's not alimony, trust me." During the couple's I-have-sinned-and-my-wife-forgives-me press conference, Wendy stepped to the podium and addressed the media directly, pleading for reporters to stop stalking the family and to allow them to have a normal summer.

She's a craftier White Queen than some of her counterparts, such as Silda Wall Spitzer and Huma Abedin, who tried to tread the same road. Wendy Vitter has been more successful at keeping her husband's career on track. The key to their success is quite possibly silence — perhaps a tactic that, as a former trial lawyer, she understood intuitively. The Vitters have spoken publicly just once about their marital rift; they admitted to no salacious details, and then forged on. Since that 2007 press conference, David was re-elected to the U.S. Senate and sought the governor's mansion in 2015 — although he lost that race amidst resurrected publicity over his sex scandal. In conceding the governor's race, he announced that he wouldn't run for re-election to the U.S. Senate in 2016. He left at the end of his term.

Wendy's White Queen Quotient: 9

Wendy Baldwin grew up in a wealthy New Orleans suburb, Lakewood South, in a family that lost its inherited money in the Great Depression but retained its social standing. Her father was a dynamic lawyer for one of the state's most prominent firms, and he belonged to private clubs in Boston and Louisiana. With a strong family heritage, a larger-than-life father, and membership in a male-dominated faith community, it seems likely that Wendy accepts patriarchal tradition as the right way to live.

Wendy sometimes fills in for her husband at Republican events, and, at those times, friends say she is a true surrogate whose views don't deviate from her husband's. "When she speaks in public, she delivers a strong message and a consistent message," said Polly Thomas, a former Jefferson Parish School Board member active in Republican politics. "When I say consistent, I mean with David's position. She does it with great aplomb."

As for needing emotional security, Wendy had an early lesson; her mother died of breast cancer when Wendy was just 6 years old. Her father never remarried, but a large circle of cousins, five siblings, and other relatives helped raise Wendy in the absence of her mother. Two cousins took Wendy and her sisters on outings every day the summer after Beatrice Baldwin died. Wendy's grandmother, whom she called Dula, lived in an apartment at the back of their home. Wendy learned from this difficult period that when a person is vulnerable, family should surround and protect that person.

This the Vitters have done with almost superhuman willpower. David and Wendy gave a single press conference after his D.C. Madam connection was published on the Internet

— and the couple hasn't spoken about it publicly since. One benefit they've had over other political couples is that David's dalliances with prostitutes were discovered many years after they took place. This allowed the couple to claim they had dealt with it — in their marriage, and in his reformed behavior — and that it's time for everyone to move on.

At that press conference, Wendy called on reporters to respect her role as the family's emotional caretaker. Stepping up to the podium, she said, "I'm going to speak to you as a mother and hope you understand. It's been terribly hard to have the media parked on our front lawn and following us every day. ...as David returns to work in Washington, we're going to return to our life here. I would ask you very respectfully to let us continue our summer and our lives as we had planned."

Given her anti-publicity bent, Wendy hasn't talked to the press about a legacy she wants to build for her children, who, at this writing in 2021, range in age from 19 through 28. Her actions at work and at home speak of someone with a patriotic social conscience. She earned a law degree and served in the local district attorney's office, prosecuting criminals, before leaving to stay home and raise children. She ran David's first congressional campaign from their home and has helped him craft aggressive counterattacks — such as his response to enemies' questions about why he wouldn't term-limit himself when he had spearheaded such restrictions for others. By all accounts, Wendy is in step with David politically — he has called her his "most honest critic." Their unity has served his career quite well.

Early Training in 'No Nonsense'

Born in 1961, Wendy was the fifth child of Richard Clark Baldwin and Beatrice Rault Baldwin. Her lawyer father worked for Adams and Reese, a law firm representing corporate clients with offices throughout the southern United States and Washington, DC. The Baldwins had one son, Richard Jr., and five daughters: Kim, Catherine, Pam, Wendy and Kristin. Their mother was a devout Catholic, which is likely where Wendy's deeply religious roots took hold. Growing up, Wendy had a solid relationship with her father, and was also close with her grandmother, Dula. Wendy's cousin, Lise Baldwin Montgomery, said Wendy and her immediate family grew stronger after the death of Beatrice, which is why Wendy understands the importance of having extended family around.

Wendy attended the now-defunct private Catholic school, Mercy Academy, and enrolled in Sam Houston State University in Texas. Her father died before he could see her graduate, which she did in 1982 with a bachelor's degree in government, and as a member of the Golden Key National Honor Society. In 1986, she followed in the family footsteps by earning a law degree from Tulane University. After graduation, she worked as a prosecutor for the long-serving Orleans Parish District Attorney Harry Connick. A tall and slim brunette, with a long stride and a polished appearance, Wendy rose quickly through the ranks. In three years, she became Connick's chief of trials.

Connick remembers her as being a "no-nonsense, straight-ahead, competent, prepared lawyer." She met David through an office colleague, who was his best friend. They were married in 1990.

That same year, Wendy made her most celebrated court-room appearance, when she and Connick sought the death penalty for a maintenance man, Steven Quatrevingt, who was accused of raping a mildly retarded woman and strangling her with a phone cord in the bathroom of her family home. The case marked the first time DNA evidence was used in a criminal trial in New Orleans, and Wendy walked the jury through the new science of genetic fingerprinting. She also re-enacted the alleged strangling, crouching on the floor of the courtroom and pantomiming how the attacker could have committed the brutal rape.

"She took command of the courtroom," said Steven Nicholas, a former assistant superintendent at the New Orleans Police Department who became a criminal investigator for the State Police. "A lot of prosecutors and defense attorneys get emotional. Wendy never did that. She stepped up to the jury, looked right at them and delivered it." Many of her former colleagues were reminded of this intense "bulldog" approach when she stood with David after his sex scandal.

In her role as stay-home mom, she was equally passionate. Sophie, the Vitters' eldest, was born in 1993. Then came twins Lise (named for Wendy's cousin) and Airey, who were born prematurely in 1997 and needed extra care in early infancy. Jack was born in 2002. Wendy chaired school fundraisers at Mount Carmel Academy, tutors her twins in Latin, attends their volleyball games, and encourages teen-age son Jack's interest in soccer. She runs the kind of home where other parents are happy to send their children after school. "She is a fun-loving, wonderful mom," said friend Dorothy Wimberly, who was interviewed for a 2007 profile of Wendy in New Orleans' *Times-Picayune*. "She is very involved... Whenever she is home, her children always have home-cooked meals. She is a great mom to her kids and to all of her children's friends."

'The Lone Wolf of Louisiana Politics'

David also came from a large, well-to-do family; he was the youngest of six children, born in 1961 to Audrey Malvina St. Raymond and Albert Leopold Vitter. Albert was a petroleum engineer. Audrey graduated from college with a degree in social work, but stayed home to raise their children. Neither was very political, David has said, but they were "dedicated Christians and great personal examples."

In 1979, he graduated from the prestigious De La Salle High School, where he'd played first clarinet in the band. One summer, he painted floats for a Mardi Gras float-building company, which he has said was his favorite job ever. He played tennis, a sport he continued as an adult.

Unlike many successful politicians, David didn't choose that path at a young age. He said, at various times, he wanted to be a diplomat, a singer, an actor, or an astronaut. After acing his classes at De La Salle, David was accepted at Harvard University. He joined Harvard's Catholic Student Association and regularly attended Mass. He didn't run for student government — again, an unusual choice for a future politician — though he was interested in politics. His classmates speculated that he might one day run for office. He majored in economics and at the time wasn't so conservative, said his roommate of four years, Scott C. Alexander, who has described college David as left-of-center.

David graduated from Harvard in 1983 magna cum laude and Phi Beta Kappa. He won a Rhodes scholarship to study for a postgraduate year at the University of Oxford in England. It was there, his former roommate Scott

Alexander believes, that David encountered the ultra-liberal beliefs, such as supporting aid to communist East Berlin, that pushed him politically to the right. He graduated from Oxford with highest honors and returned to Louisiana in 1985. He applied to the doctoral program at Tulane University School of Law, where he was an articles editor for the Tulane Law School Law Review. He graduated with honors in 1988, became a corporate attorney, and taught law at both Tulane and Loyola universities.

Two years later, he met and married Wendy Baldwin. In 1992, he was elected to the Louisiana House of Representatives. As his academic record implies, David is intellectually accomplished. He soon set about demonstrating to his colleagues just how much he thought of himself — earning the nickname "the lone wolf of Louisiana politics." When fellow Republicans were planning to announce a new initiative, David often stepped ahead and grandstanded by holding his own press conference first. He branded himself as an outsider and a reformer by taking on notorious corruption at the statehouse. In 1993, he helped expose officials who were awarding lucrative Tulane scholarships to family members. That same year, he filed an ethics complaint against Democratic Gov. Edwin Edwards, accusing him of allowing his children to profit illegally from business with the state-regulated riverboat gambling industry. David, true to his clean-cut image, opposes gambling.

After seven years as a state legislator, David defied Louisiana's Republican old guard by running in a special election in 1999 for a seat in the U.S. House of Representatives. The Louisiana GOP had put its full establishment weight behind former Gov. David Treen. As election day neared, David Vitter's campaign distributed fliers to Black voters saying

Treen had the support of David Duke, a white supremacist and former Grand Wizard of the Ku Klux Klan. The rumor was untrue, but coming out as it did so close to the election, Treen struggled to rebut it. The smear had the effect of discouraging Black voters from showing up at the polls. David Vitter won the election.

None of his new House colleagues showed up to congratulate David at his election night victory party. Only one Republican of any consequence, U.S. Rep. Jim McCrery, placed a congratulatory phone call. Nor did David's colleagues from the Louisiana statehouse attend to celebrate his victory. "Vitter has such problems with people," said Rob Couhig, a rival Republican candidate in the 1999 House race. "Not just fringe politicians, but legitimate, honest politicians in the legislature who just can't stand him." Ironically, David won the seat vacated by Rep. Bob Livingston, who had been forced to retire over his extramarital affairs. This was the year Republicans in Washington impeached President Bill Clinton; political enemies left no cheating stone unturned. Livingston had been prepared to step into the most powerful post in the House of Representatives — succeeding Newt Gingrich as Speaker — when news of Livingston's philandering knocked him off course. David said of Livingston's resignation, "It is obviously a tremendous loss for the state. I think Livingston's stepping down makes a very powerful argument that Clinton should resign as well and move beyond this mess." Those words would turn out to haunt him.

In Washington, David became a reliable vote for the extreme right. He garnered a 100 percent rating from the American Conservative Union and continued to oppose legalized gambling — perhaps with an eye toward running for governor of Louisiana. In 2002, he perceived a chance when Gov. Mike Foster stepped down due to term limits. Yet again, the old guard GOP nominated David Treen instead of David Vitter. A Treen supporter, embittered over the 1999 House race, blurted out on a radio show that he believed Vitter had once had an extramarital affair. The muckraking *Louisiana Weekly* decided to investigate the claim by local Republican Party official Vincent Bruno. David Vitter denied the allegations, but shortly before the *Weekly* published its account, he dropped out of the governor's race, saying he needed to deal with marital problems: "Our marriage counseling sessions have… led us to the rather obvious conclusion that it's not time to run for governor."

Wendy was silent on the controversy — again. One has to admire the Vitters' smart self-restraint with the media. The prostitution story lost its sting. *The Louisiana Weekly* never closed all the holes in its account, and the alleged prostitute, Wendy Cortez, declined to speak to a New Orleans TV reporter. Two years later, when Democratic U.S. Senator John Breaux announced his retirement, David again jumped on the chance to move up. In a state with a century-old tradition of bipartisan, centrist politics, David was making headway as an extremist and an outsider. He had become an early leader of what would come to be known as the Tea Party movement. Even the Louisiana GOP old guard was finally behind him; his career had grown too big to ignore. He won Breaux's seat, and once in the U.S. Senate, David displayed the same ultraconservative pugnacity as he had earlier. At the start of one congressional session, he listed his objectives as: protecting the American flag, ending abortion, furthering public prayer, advancing home schooling, curbing illegal immigration, enforcing the death penalty, and getting rid of drugs.

D.C. Madam Publishes Clients' Phone Numbers and Fetishes

Many miles away from the Louisiana bayous, the IRS was suspicious about the source of income of D.C. Madam Deborah Jeane Palfrey. In 2006, two federal agents, a man and a woman, posed as a couple looking to buy the Victorian home in Vallejo, in Northern California, that Palfrey was attempting to sell. Under cover, they were investigating an IRS lead that Palfrey was running an upscale call girl operation from her Vallejo home near San Francisco for the lonely men of the nation's capital. Palfrey required that her employees be older than 23, have college degrees, and dress in neat pantsuits, sensible heels and discreet jewelry — she called it an Ann Taylor look. Each had to sign a contract saying she wouldn't do anything illegal while on the "dates" arranged through Palfrey's service, Pamela Martin & Associates. But the contracts were a façade. The dates paid $300, plus tips, for a 90-minute appointment, and the employees sent half to Palfrey in California.

After their undercover visit, the federal agents slapped a lien on Palfrey's home and froze her $2 million in assets. But they made one mistake. They left the Vallejo house without taking a cache in the basement: 46 pounds of phone records, including notes about the sexual preferences of her clientele. Among the notes was a detailed account of the sexual desires of one David Vitter. It said he liked to be diapered and treated like an infant.

Fourteen of Palfrey's employees testified before a grand jury, and in March 2007, she was indicted for running a prostitution enterprise. To raise money for her legal fees, she threatened to sell the phone records to the highest bidder. Instead, she gave several years' worth to ABC News. The editors at ABC didn't chase the story aggressively enough, in Palfrey's opinion, so she then posted her list of phone numbers on the Internet. An investigator hired by *Hustler* magazine publisher Larry Flynt, who has made a crusade out of exposing right-wing philanderers, connected one of the numbers to David Vitter. He had called Palfrey five times between October 1999 and February 2001 when he was in Congress, sometimes during roll call votes from the floor of the House. Because the calls were more than three years old, however, the statute of limitations had run out on any criminal charges David might have faced.

But he had other problems, namely the publicity. David at first tried to dodge media questions, but within a couple of days, he relented and issued a written statement of apology: "This was a very serious sin in my past for which I am, of course, completely responsible. Several years ago, I asked for and received forgiveness from God and my wife in confession and marriage counseling. Out of respect for my family, I will keep my discussion of the matter there with God and them. But I certainly offer my deep and sincere apologies to all I have disappointed and let down in any way."

One who was disappointed was Rudy Giuliani, the former New York City mayor who at the time was running for president. He promptly dropped David as his campaign chair for the southern region. Recognizing that the career they had built was beginning to crack, David and Wendy hunkered down for a week in their Metairie home, speaking to no one. They emerged at the end of the week and called a press conference.

David was contrite at the podium before a gaggle of TV cameras and microphones. He reiterated his apology for his "very serious sin" and expressed regret for having violated the public's trust. He didn't elaborate on the details of his "sin." Wendy stood behind him, off to the side, looking sad and horrified. But as David delivered his last lines, and a pack of reporters began barking questions, Wendy seized the podium. "To those of you who know me, are you surprised that I have something to say?" she said, restoring silence to the room. Then she began, "You know, in most any other marriage, this would have been a private issue between a husband and a wife — very private. Obviously, it is not here. Like all marriages, ours is not perfect. None of us are. But we choose to work together as a family. When David and I dealt with this privately years ago, I forgave David. I made the decision to love him and to recommit to our marriage. To forgive is not always the easy choice, but it was and is the right choice for me. David is my best friend."

Then the sadness seemed to fall from her shoulders, and she caught a defiant breath. "Last week," she said, "some people very sympathetically said to me, 'I wouldn't want to be in your shoes right now.' I stand before you to tell you very proudly, I am proud to be Wendy Vitter."

Her choice of outfit added another dimension to her statement. Instead of wearing the traditional "supportive woman" armor of power suit and tidy pearls, Wendy appeared in a chicly bobbed haircut and an animal print dress with a fitted waist. Her outfit sparked speculation that she wasn't thinking so much about how to save her husband as she was defending her reputation as a sexy woman — one who had most definitely not let herself go. She seemed to be saying, "Don't blame me for David's tomcatting. He has a beautiful wife at home."

After the press conference, David flew directly to Washington to meet with a group of Republican colleagues. At a private luncheon of his peers, he vowed not to quit his Senate job. The group reportedly jumped to its feet and broke into applause.

Within a few days, David had to face a new allegation: Jeanette Maier, a former New Orleans Canal Street madam, claimed that David had been a customer of her brothel as early as the mid-1990s. At first, David dismissed this as untrue. The following month, Hustler's Larry Flynt produced a prostitute from New Orleans who said she'd had a year-long relationship with David. Neither David nor Wendy addressed this new revelation in public. Instead, David's press officer Joel DiGrado repeated a line that would become their stock response: "Vitter and his wife addressed all of this very directly."

Meanwhile, as the criminal case against Palfrey mounted, she faced prison time. Years before, following a 1991 conviction for attempted felony pimping in San Diego, Palfrey had spent 18 months in prison. The mother of one of her "girls" had notified police, leading to Palfrey's arrest. This is why, when she started Pamela Martin & Associates, she took the precaution of hiring only women over 23 — presumably independent of their moms. Palfrey's previous time in prison had been woeful; she was terrorized physically and emotionally by other inmates. She vowed never to go back. In May 2007, after writing two suicide notes, the D.C. Madam hanged herself from a metal bar in a shed near her mother's Tampa home. Palfrey was 52.

Protecting Himself from His Own Urges

After his prostitution scandal appeared in the press, David won re-election in 2010 to the U.S. Senate, where he continued to pursue a righteous, if hypocritical agenda. Before ending his Senate career, he spoke in favor of a constitutional amendment to ban gay marriage, saying, "It's often said, but it's very, very true, and it is worth repeating — marriage is truly the most fundamental social institution in human history."

How is it possible for a man aware of his own "sins" to preach to others about marriage and fidelity? Paul Ekman, psychology professor emeritus at the Medical School at University of California, San Francisco, has observed about David Vitter, "People can believe in two opposing things. Humans are ingenious in how they can make exceptions for themselves." Another framework is offered by Judy Kuriansky, psychologist and professor at Columbia University's Teachers College. She said that men in positions of power often believe they are above the rules they impose on their followers. "Often people who speak out the loudest are trying to protect themselves from their own urges," she said in an interview with ABC *News*. "They act out one way on the public stage, but inside they have this urge. They feel it's wrong, and outwardly, they're telling themselves it's wrong. It's as if they're having a conversation with themselves."

It could also be that David is trying to walk a straighter path for Wendy and their four children. Because the family stayed out of the spotlight after the scandal, there's no coverage about what it was like for their children in the days following the revelation. David, however, did say that "like all parents, Wendy and I, our top concerns are our children."

Despite demanding privacy immediately after the sex scandal, David and Wendy have since involved the family in political events. In 2013, David organized a "Family Night with the Vitter Family at the Justin Bieber Concert" where you could join him, Wendy, Lise, Airey, and Jack — for a $1,000 donation. Wendy and young Jack appeared in wholesome campaign ads during David's 2015 gubernatorial run.

Oldest daughter Sophie Rault Vitter inherited her dad's academic talent. She graduated in 2011 from the Mount Carmel Academy high school as one of three class valedictorians. She entered Vanderbilt University to major in biological sciences, but ended up switching her major to neuroscience with a minor in business corporate strategy. She rushed and joined the Chi Omega sorority, which is known for community development projects. Sophie worked with the Vanderbilt chapter of Habitat for Humanity during college, graduated in 2015 and enrolled in medical school. In 2020, she graduated from the Louisiana State University School of Medicine in New Orleans.

Lise and Airey graduated from Mount Carmel Academy in 2015. When they turned 18, David posted a happy birthday photo on his Facebook page, and Lise responded, "thanks dad." This said something about their relationship. Not only did Lise believe that Dad, and not an aide, posted the message, she also spoke to him publicly on social media. Based on their social media pages, both girls seemed to have a very close relationship with their mother, though Lise calls her "Wendy" instead of Mom. "Wendy realizes how important that foundation is, to have parents and grandparents who really love you and show you a good path," Lise said in 2007.

The twins both excelled in school, but Airey slightly more so. She was consistently named to the county honor roll and was a National Merit semifinalist. Airey is into classic romanticism, and has created a vertical for "weddings" on her Pinterest page. Whatever affect her father's affairs have had on her, it apparently didn't ruin her belief in marriage.

The twins seem to be drawn to Washington. Lise atends the Georgetown University Law Center and worked as a staff assistant in the U.S. House of Representatives. Airey graduated from New York University with a degree in Communication and Media Studies. She interned at her dad's lobbying company and now works for a public relations firm in Washington.

David had spoken and posted on social media about taking son Jack on sports adventures: alligator hunting, fishing trips, and catching a 30-pound dolphin offshore.

We witness many scandalized couples who sought redemption in the media. Hillary Clinton defended Bill on *60 Minutes* in 1992 and on the *Today* show in 1998. Eliot Spitzer wrote a political column for *Slate* and appeared as a regular CNN commentator. Huma Abedin and Anthony Weiner spoke as a "normal family" with their new baby in *People* and tried to put the sexting behind them with one big interview in *The New York Times Magazine*. But when it comes to political resuscitation, the Vitters pursued a smarter strategy of total media silence.

After leaving the U.S. Senate, David walked away from elective politics to become a lobbyist for one of the most prominent Republican firms, Mercury Public Affairs.

He represents one client, Hikvision, which sells facial recognition and other surveillance equipment the Chinese government uses to repress its Muslim minority population, the Uyghurs. In 2016 and 2017, Hikvision installed facial recognition cameras in nearly 1,0000 mosques in Xinjiang, home to mass internment camps. When the U.S. Department of Commerce tried to ban American companies from selling components to Hikvision in 2019; David Vitter came to Hikvision's rescue.

His about-face is reminiscent of the "abstinence" speeches he gave to school children while frequenting prostitutes. In his final term in the Senate, David co-sponsored a bill that would have made a country's record on religious freedom the litmus test for whether the United States would engage in trade with that country.

Wendy Vitter has emerged as the family's political star. After her work as a prosecutor, she worked as general counsel for the Roman Catholic Archdiocese of New Orleans. In 2017, President Trump nominated her to a federal judgeship. Her nomination was nearly derailed when a judicial watchdog group found statements she had made against abortion — among them, the false claim that Planned Parenthood killed more than 150,000 women a year. During her confirmation hearing, she said she would not allow her personal views to influence her decision-making as a judge. She was confirmed in May 2019 as a U.S. District Court judge in New Orleans, a lifetime appointment.

Silda Wall &
Eliot Spitzer

Clinging to Power

The courtship between Silda Wall and Eliot Spitzer reads like an egalitarian fairy tale. They met at Harvard Law School and, after graduation in 1984, moved to Manhattan to take jobs on the legal fast track: Eliot to clerk for U.S. District Court Justice Robert W. Sweet, and Silda to practice corporate law at the high-profile firm Skadden, Arps, Slate, Meagher & Flom.

The size 2, honey blond former cheerleader from North Carolina defied all stereotypes by working 16-hour days

and billing more than 3,300 hours a year, which meant
that during her first five years at Skadden, Arps, there were
roughly two weekends when she didn't work. Dinner for the
young lovers often consisted of take-out at a law firm conference table. Sometimes after successive all-nighters, Silda
would catch an hour's sleep beneath such a table. "I felt kind
of proud that I was making more money than Eliot," she said
later. Senior members of the firm wanted her on their team
because of her sheer drive and diligence. They could always
count on Silda to come through.

Ten years into their life together, married with two
toddlers and a third baby on the way, Eliot approached Silda
with a request she didn't think she would hear for at least
another decade. He wanted to run for office, as attorney general for the State of New York. The timing was opportune;
the attorney general's seat was an open race in 1994, with
no entrenched incumbent. This was only the second time
in nearly 40 years that had been so. Silda wasn't at all sure
Eliot would be good at campaigning. The cerebral, intensely
competitive Manhattan-born-and-bred Eliot wasn't exactly
a glad-hander or someone who mixed with regular folks —
upstate dairy farmers and factory workers, suburban moms,
cops or deli employees. He would need their votes, and yet,
the Spitzer family's immense wealth placed Eliot far outside
this stratum. In 1994, his young family occupied a luxury
apartment on Fifth Avenue that his father Bernard Spitzer
had built and owned. With the building's white- glove door
attendants, servants' entrances, and Central Park views, Silda and Eliot could hardly claim a populist outlook.

What's more, Silda believed that Eliot running for office
would mean she would have to quit working. At that point
in their lives, she had left Skadden, Arps for part-time hours

practicing her passion, international law, at Chase Manhattan Bank. She had worked so hard and had come so far from her small-town roots in Concord, North Carolina, where her father was a hospital administrator and her mother a stay-at-home mom — a life choice Trilby Wall had come to regret. Silda had promised herself she would have a career, and not only that, but achieve a professional rank that would allow her to fully support a family independently. If Eliot spent months traveling the byways of New York to greet voters, Silda would be the only constant presence in their children's lives.

However, she also believed that people should follow their dreams, and this was Eliot's. More than that, she loved him. She didn't want to tell him to hold back. So, Silda said she would sleep on it. The next morning, she left Eliot a post-it note in their granite kitchen: "Go for it!" Eliot announced his candidacy on May 18, 1994. Five days later, their daughter Jenna was born. Silda completed her maternity leave from Chase and reluctantly gave up her job.

Silda's White Queen Quotient: 6

Silda's difficult decision to set aside a career she felt passionate about demonstrates how responsible she felt for her family's emotional health — including Eliot's. She's said she felt very conflicted about not working. "You don't want to give up on your dreams, but you also have to confront the reality of your life," she said. "Ultimately, it was more important for me to have my family work."

At the same time, her White Queen sense of mission soon led her down a new path. To her middle-class sensibilities, the excesses of Manhattan's tony Upper East Side were hard to bear. She took her daughters regularly to North Carolina to see the world beyond their wealthy enclave. Then in 1996, at a lavish New York party given for one of her daughter's friends, Silda came up with an idea for an organization to address her revulsion at the extravagance and inspire her social circle to awaken from its economic and moral insularity. She founded Children for Children, asked friends to downscale birthday parties, and set the savings aside for needy children. The initial budget was $2,700 but within a decade, it grew to more than $1.5 million. Well-off children volunteered at food pantries and fundraisers, and to date, more than 80,000 children have been involved as helpers or recipients; the organization has a presence in several hundred New York City public schools.

Silda's upbringing taught her to adopt the White Queen traits of submitting to tradition and internalizing a personal sense of patriotism. She was born to Robert and Trilby Wall in December 1957. She was raised in a Southern Baptist family committed to community service and giving back. When she was a child, her grandparents baked and delivered wedding cakes to poverty-stricken families. Her parents were equally civically inclined. Her mother taught children street smarts and street safety through the organization she started called Safety Town, and her father ran the Concord United Way. Silda was a Girl Scout, attended church regularly, made gifts for the less fortunate during the holidays, and visited homebound senior citizens who would have had no other visitors. "Nobody asked if we wanted to do service," she has said. "We just did it. The world I grew up in was very much about service and giving." Eliot has said Silda was raised to deflect attention from herself.

A desire for emotional security probably played a role in Silda's decision to stay with Eliot through his humiliating prostitution scandal. After her second year at Harvard, in 1982, Silda married Peter Stamos, an Oxford Rhodes Scholar and fellow Harvard Law student. They were married for only 29 days, which shocked everyone. High school friend Janet Ward-Black said that Peter and Silda were seemingly meant for each other: "Just like everything with Silda always was, she had a perfect wedding, with all her family and friends down here, to a perfect man, and then... poof!" Silda never mentions the first marriage. For a 2006 book chronicling Eliot's years as attorney general, *Spoiling for a Fight: The Rise of Eliot Spitzer* by Brooke A. Masters, Silda persuaded the author to refer to the Stamos affair as "an intense but unhappy relationship" — but not a marriage. At the time, she and Eliot hadn't even told their daughters.

When the hooker scandal hit Eliot in 2008, he was serving his second year as governor of New York State. Silda urged him to tough it out and not to resign. Was her concern at this point for his legacy, for their legacy? Perhaps. She was working as First Lady on issues that inspired her: service for young people, green energy, environmental stability and women's rights. The family put on its bravest face as the scandal unfolded. The story about Eliot frequenting prostitutes ran on a Monday morning in *The New York Times,* yet the three Spitzer girls went to school that day, as usual, and did not miss a day of school due to the furor. Months later, to celebrate their wedding anniversary, Silda and Eliot went out publicly to one of their favorite delis — a cozy, low- key place where they enjoyed a friendly celebration that was fully covered in the press. But putting on a brave show isn't the same as building a legacy. In the end, Silda decided to do that apart from her ex-husband.

Silda stood up for herself and for women's independence, which scales her down in White Queen points. Persisting as a White Queen depends on believing in one's husband, in being able to turn inward away from the world's and the media's judgment and toward one's partner toward reality you both believe in. For six years after the sex scandal that toppled Eliot's gubernatorial career, Silda seemed able to turn to Eliot for validation and reminders of their early ambitions, dreams, and love. Eliot found enough sustenance in the relationship to mount another run for public office: New York City comptroller in 2013. But the failure of that attempt also marked the failure of the Spitzers' marriage. Silda stayed with her husband, and propped him up in his electoral run, until it seemed he couldn't possibly resuscitate himself. Shortly after his loss in that New York City race in November 2013, Eliot was seen publicly with another flame, and the Spitzers announced their intent to divorce.

I think Silda lost faith in Eliot's ability to move the family toward success. His hooker obsession while governor shows a shocking lack of judgment, to the point of inviting self-destruction. Today, Silda has become "the man" she wanted to marry, in the words of Second Wave feminism. She has a successful career in investment banking, with a woman-run firm. She raises money for Democratic women and speaks publicly about having survived humiliation and defeat. Her ranking as a 6 on the White Queen scale reflects the independent life she built for herself post-Eliot.

A Southern Belle Drawn to Harvard

The name Silda comes from an old German name, Serilda, meaning "armed warrior woman" or "Teutonic war maiden." Trilby and Robert wanted to give her an unusual name, as their first child, but didn't want it to be so odd that she'd be made fun of. This is why they shortened Serilda to Silda. Silda jokes that the "experiment must have failed, because her parents named their next babies [her younger siblings] Susan and Jim."

Regardless of her reputation today as a poised Southern belle, "a lady," as close family friend Jan Constantine has said, when Silda was a child she was a tomboy who had dreams of becoming a football player. She wanted to be North Carolina's first woman football player because she thought she could run through everyone's legs and not ever be tackled.

Though she admittedly grew into less of a tomboy, Silda still wanted to play sports in high school. Basketball and tennis were the only sports available to girls. As a sophomore, she lobbied for permission for girls to run with the track team, but by the time permission had been granted, she was a junior and had other interests. These extracurriculars included cheerleading, marching band (she played the French horn), class secretary, lifeguard at the local pool, swimmer on a local team, and drama group. It was with the drama club that Silda first visited New York City. The club saw *Grease* and *A Raisin in the Sun* and ate at Sardi's, an iconic restaurant in Manhattan's theater district. She never in a million years thought she would live in the big city. Janet Ward Black, a high school friend, said Silda "was perfect," and ran with a popular crowd, not the nerdy, brainy one.

She was also a very good student. One of the most prominent influences in her youth was her high school English teacher, Frances Ward Black Holland. Though other students thought Holland was too tough, Silda "thought she was just wonderful." Silda gravitated toward teachers who were the most challenging, the ones who demanded much of their students. Holland encouraged Silda to study harder — and so she did.

After high school, Silda attended Meredith College, a small Baptist women's school in Raleigh. Applying for college was an awakening of sorts for Silda. When she was filling out college applications, Trilby asked her not to write "homemaker" under mother's profession, but "home administrator" instead. "Growing up, I felt it was very important to have a career," Silda has said. "I watched the frustration of my mother, who had gone to college and was extremely capable but didn't have the opportunities she might have had in another time."

During two summers while at Meredith, Silda worked at Cannon textile mills in a neighboring town. As an undergrad, she first studied art because she had a burgeoning interest in restoring old paintings. But her work was not received well at the college, and she began to feel she was wasting her parent's tuition payments. She also didn't feel the she was using her brain the way she needed to. She wanted to return to her family's philanthropic and socially minded roots. Knowing she was interested in research and international issues, she mentioned to her father she might like to study law. He suggested that she speak with a church friend, who was a lawyer, and the paralegal who worked for him. Silda discovered the paralegal worked as much as the lawyer, but was paid about 20 percent of his salary. This is when she committed to becoming a lawyer and achieving financial independence.

She finished Meredith *summa cum laude* with a degree in history and English. Though Silda had not expected to leave North Carolina, she couldn't turn down the opportunity to attend Harvard Law School. She was, as she had always been, a driven and disciplined student, though she wasn't especially ambitious. A classmate of theirs at Harvard, Jim Cramer, said Silda "didn't set out to change the world like Eliot did. She worked at Chase, for God's sake. If she weren't so pretty, you'd have called her a geek."

Harvard Law was just 25 percent women at the time, and Silda stood out in part for her feminine charms: self-possessed, slender, with soft blond hair, perfect white teeth and preppy clothes. But her sense of justice was as notable as her beauty. She was active in a student human-rights group rallying against apartheid in South Africa. She joined a campus women's group but argued against excluding men. She felt "there are men out there who care about women having equal access to things as well."

In their third year at Harvard Law, Eliot and Silda met on a skiing trip in Vermont. The year was 1984. Tall and athletic with intense blue eyes, Eliot exudes charisma, but when he initially asked Silda on a date, she turned him down. Eliot's friend Cliff Sloan told Eliot he didn't have a chance with the hard-working southern beauty. On Valentine's Day, Eliot ran into Silda, who was carrying a large bouquet of flowers. Always fascinated by a challenge, he decided to ask her out again. This time she said yes. Seeing them together, Sloan soon changed his tune, noting that Silda was the only one who could keep up one-liner for one-liner with Eliot. "It was like a champion Ping-Pong player finding another one," he said.

Moving to Manhattan after graduation, the couple often met for dinner and a movie — they preferred a diner called Silver Star within walking distance of Silda's office. They couple bonded over their mutual lack of interest in showy, see-and-be-seen Manhattan behavior. "Eliot's a lot of fun to be with," Silda said in 2005, "but he's very unpretentious and he doesn't need to have a whole lot of fanciness around him."

Silda has said she fell in love with Eliot because they had a deep connection she will never understand or be able to explain. "Where we were [in our lives] and the values of our families — it all just kind of made sense," she said. They married in 1987, in a Central Park boathouse with Judge Sweet officiating.

Pressure to Perform in a Rising Dynasty

In contrast to Silda's church-going, middle-class world in North Carolina, Eliot came from a wealthy, non-religious home in the metropolis of Manhattan. However, his parents made their own fortunes and taught him a work ethic as strong as that of his wife. His parents, Anne and Bernard Spitzer, lived "an accelerated version of the classic Eastern European Jewish success story."

Bernard's parents, Morris and Molly, emigrated from Poland to New York after World War I; Morris had served as a communications officer in the Austrian army. They lived above their printing shop on Manhattan's Lower East Side and then in a series of walk-up railroad flats without hot water on East Fifth Street. Eliot's mother, Anne, was a neighbor but lived in slightly better circumstances: in a co-op building with a guard and an elevator. Her father, Joseph Goldhaber, was a teacher who had emigrated from Palestine.

Anne and Bernard met at a modest resort in the Catskills, when she was 14 and he was 18. Bernard earned a degree in civil engineering from City College. He was planning to enlist in the Navy as an intelligence officer serving in Europe. The two married before he left, when Anne was still a teenager. She stayed home and finished her bachelor's degree at Brooklyn College and then went on to earn two master's degrees. Eventually she became an adjunct professor of English literature at Marymount Manhattan College where she was still teaching at age 77.

When Bernard returned from the war, he attended Columbia University on the GI Bill and earned a master's degree in engineering. After working in the field, he found it deadly dull. He chose next to go into construction. He formed his own company and began building luxury high rises. When Eliot was born in 1959, the family moved to a modest town house in the Riverdale section of the Bronx. There was no lawn, but their town house was across from a city playground. Three years later, the family moved into a 1928 Tudor in the wealthy Fieldston community. With a backyard and front field, there was room enough for the kids to play basketball and soccer. The three Spitzer children — Emily, Daniel and Eliot — attended private school. Soon, the family bought a second home in Rye, and each of the children enrolled in an Ivy League university: Emily at Harvard and the two brothers at Princeton.

By some accounts, Eliot was Bernard's favorite. When Bernard died, he allegedly left Eliot $6 million more than he'd left to Emily or Daniel. Anne remembered Eliot's older siblings competing for his attention. When Eliot was present,

Daniel said, the family's energy level was higher. As the family's intellectual leader, he "had ideas that galvanized other people."

As progressives, both parents wanted their children to have a serious impact on society. Young Eliot thought he might hold high political office when he grew up. But when family friends referred to Bernard as "a Jewish Joseph Kennedy," Eliot called it nonsense. At the family dinner table, Bernard engaged the children in discussions of the thickness of the Earth's crust, the Vietnam War, how a steam engine works, and the economic implications of double-digit inflation. At 10, Eliot was reading *The New York Times* each morning. By 14, he'd subscribed to *Foreign Affairs*.

Never parents to cut their children slack, the Spitzers set high standards: "even using games of Monopoly as opportunities to school them in the hard realities of business." Bernard once reduced a 7- or 8-year-old Eliot to tears by ordering Eliot to sell him a piece of property, and then refusing to pay. "Never defer to authority," Bernard counseled him.

Eliot served as co-captain of both the soccer and tennis teams at Horace Mann high school, and he played enforcer on the soccer field. In 2005, he told interviewer Stephen Colbert that, though he wasn't a great athlete, "you play hard, you play rough, and hopefully you don't get caught."

Though he scored a 1590 out of 1600 on his SATs, Eliot was rejected from Harvard. A fellow student, Bob Faggen, remembers Eliot slamming a locker door and kicking a backpack when he got the news. One history teacher wrote a letter of protest to Harvard, but it did not reverse the university's decision.

The experience made Eliot even more determined to succeed at Princeton. He woke up daily at 6 a.m. to read the

Times and hardly ever missed class. He found time to go home on weekends to tend to his duties as treasurer of the Ben Franklin Democratic Club in the Bronx. He was active in Princeton student government and ran for office almost immediately. As a sophomore, he plastered the campus with leaflets stating: "Vote Performance," and won a seat as student council chair. While fellow student government members were active in sit-ins and demonstrations, Eliot "promoted resolutions and negotiated with Princeton's president over lunch." As chair, he played hardball, firing critics — and their girlfriends.

He showed a wacky, rebellious side too. A friend from Harvard Law and former *Slate* publisher Cliff Sloan remembers attending a Boston Celtics game with Eliot, in which Eliot cheered loudly for the opposing team: the New York Knicks. "For Eliot, it was a true act of principle — or maybe insanity. He just laughed it off."

Eliot declared a major in public and international affairs at Princeton's Woodrow Wilson School — the university's most selective undergraduate major. During the summers, Eliot worked in D.C. for a Congress member from the Bronx and Ralph Nader. One summer, he took a sabbatical to travel the country alone, taking odd jobs "in a sort of self-study course on living life without privilege," i.e., mopping floors in Atlanta, stacking fiberglass insulation in New Orleans, and picking tomatoes in upstate New York. This trip, he said later, "opened my eyes into a part of life I hadn't seen."

After Princeton, Eliot attended Harvard Law School. Susan Estrich, a professor in Eliot's first year, remembers him as "smart and ambitious, which certainly didn't set him apart from the rest of his classmates... what did, and what brought him to my door, was that he was interested in a career in politics." Estrich advised Eliot to be a prosecutor because Democrats needed to be able to prove what "side they're on when it comes to crime," and by being a prosecutor, he'd earn a reputation as being tough.

Eliot was named editor of the *Harvard Law Review*. He and Cliff Sloan assisted Prof. Alan Dershowitz in the appeal by Claus von Bulow, who was convicted of the attempted murder of his wife. As a result, Eliot was ringside for one of the most highly publicized cases of the century — an early predictor of his good timing. Dershowitz remembers that Eliot "was just off-the-charts brilliant. The last thing anyone in my office thought that he was going to become was a politician."

Given Eliot's impression on his friends and professors at Harvard, it's hard to believe Silda was surprised by his 1994 declaration that he wanted to run for office. She thought he might wait until their kids were older; when he first ran for attorney general, they had three daughters under age 5. But jumping on an opportunity was perfectly in character for Eliot, who had polished his ego by outshining his older siblings. As worried as Silda was about escaping her mother's role as homemaker, Eliot wanted to avoid ending up in his father's business.

Silda knew, at least, that if he got the job, he would be good at it. And he was. He lost the first race but was elected New York's attorney general in 1998 when he began turning Wall Street on its ear. Spitzer prosecuted the phony, pumped-up investments and gold-plated Master of the Universe bonuses that proved to be harbingers of the hubris leading to the worldwide financial meltdown in 2008. In the process, he earned the nickname "The Sheriff of Wall Street."

Eliot spent the years between his loss in 1994 and his

next race for attorney general visiting and building his credibility with voters around New York State, the nation's third largest. By 1998, as the Democratic frontrunner for the job of attorney general, he was in demand as a news commentator. When Bill Clinton's Oval Office sex scandal broke in Washington, Eliot spoke on 10 separate programs in a week. He lamented how a criminal investigation had turned into a political issue. Silda had her opinions, too. She couldn't understand why or how Hillary Clinton stood by Bill under the klieg light of such personal humiliation. If she were in Hillary's position, Silda remarked to a friend, she would be walking out the door. Silda, like most of us, couldn't imagine herself staying until she was forced into confronting a similar situation in her own life.

By his second term as attorney general, Eliot's star was soaring. His aggressive pursuit of Wall Street fat cats transformed him into a national celebrity. A profile in *The Atlantic Monthly* pronounced him "the Democratic Party's future." His environmental cases had been equally innovative. For example, he successfully prosecuted an Ohio power plant for exporting its pollution to New York. He loved his life in elected office. "You're fighting fights that are interesting and important — nothing can hold a candle to this," he said in an interview. Eliot was the odds-on favorite to become the next governor.

Silda sought advice from Hillary, then representing New York in the U.S. Senate, about being a political spouse — "about how to maintain a private sphere for our family and how to be helpful in my husband's campaign," she said. In 2006, with Children for Children running strong, Silda stepped down as board chair to help with Eliot's campaign. She and the girls were proud of his work. And they softened

Eliot's rough edges. For the holidays, the family sent out hundreds of jars of homemade jam, along with an annual holiday card, often featuring a charming family photo. Silda moderated her husband's headstrong and combative impulses and helped shape his public image by advising on his television campaign. The TV ads presented him as a caring father speaking quietly about the needs of his children, rather than the fast-talking Ivy League son of a millionaire, spouting legalese.

Silda was warming to her role. She shook hands, hosted fundraisers and made speeches on Eliot's behalf. In deference to convention, she even started using Spitzer as her last name. Her transformation from ambivalent political spouse to a White Queen concerned for her family's legacy ascended apace with Eliot's soaring political fortunes.

In the 2006 vote for New York governor, Eliot won in a landslide; nearly 70 percent of New York voters chose him to lead. After his victory, the Spitzers decided the family would stay in Manhattan, with Eliot spending some nights in the governor's mansion. They would rendezvous on weekends in between the city and the state capitol at Pine Plains, their 160-acre farm in Dutchess County. Eliot consulted Silda fully on every decision, from appointments to major policy initiatives, and her White Queen patriotism began to show in a new way. She chose to have offices in both places, Albany and Manhattan, and treated her new position as First Lady as a real job. After years of sacrifice for Eliot's career, this was her chance to matter in public life, too.

When campaigning, Eliot had promised to bring his "Sheriff of Wall Street" attitude to challenge the entrenched interests in New York state government. In 2006, such a shakeup was badly needed. Powerful union and business lobbies drove the state's stratospheric budget deficits; and, elected officials were regularly indicted for corruption. Eliot came on like "a f---ing steamroller" — a self-description he uttered as a private threat to a political opponent. But he made a mistake importing his take-no-prisoners attitude to his new role as governor. He was no longer living in the good-versus-evil world of the prosecutor. Instead, a governor needs allies to pass bills and budgets. Picking fights with one and all is a grave miscalculation. Within months of taking office, he had alienated nearly everyone in Albany. Marlene Turner, Eliot's chief of staff, said, "How did we get here? It's only February, and we have no friends left to defend us." After high-profile battles with Albany denizens, Eliot's poll numbers had roughly reversed by the anniversary of his election: Where 70 percent "hired" him to run the state, less than one year later, just 30 percent of New Yorkers thought he was doing a good job.

Silda Wonders, 'Who is This Guy?'

A close family friend, Lloyd Constantine, began referring to the 2007 Eliot as "The Imposter." At lunch that first year, Silda asked Lloyd, "Who is this guy?" Eliot's constant battling with other political leaders made him seem more concerned with being right than being successful. He was no longer recognizable as the brilliant and decisive leader they had known. Constantine believes that Eliot's off-camera behavior — his secret liaisons with hookers — was "steadily dripping venom into his mind" causing him to act erratically.

But if those two close partners were in the dark about Eliot, others were beginning to suspect his terrible secret. In July 2007, North Fork Bank raised a red flag about one of Eliot's transactions. The Bank Secrecy Act requires all financial institutions to file currency transaction reports with the

Treasury Department for any deposit or withdrawal of more than $10,000. Eliot was moving around thousands of dollars to pay for prostitutes employed by a service called Emperors Club VIP. His compulsive arrangement of "dates" with Emperors Club call girls had all the hallmarks of an addiction. On one day, he contacted the service three times to arrange to meet a prostitute. He didn't care which one it was; he asked the escort service to send whoever was available.

There was still another mark of addiction: Eliot's behavior was dangerously self-destructive. From his days prosecuting high-priced hooker services, he knew the bank transactions would eventually put investigators on his trail. Indeed, the first time he wired $10,000, he asked the bank to make the sender anonymous. Eliot was risking Silda discovering him, too. On a long weekend visit to Puerto Rico in the autumn of 2007, Eliot had an Emperors Club escort named Angelina meet him at the Ritz-Carlton in San Juan. Angelina flew back to New York on the same day that Silda was arriving to spend the rest of the weekend with her husband.

At about the same time, investigators from the Financial Crimes Enforcement Network, a branch of the U.S. Treasury Department, showed up at the office of Manhattan's District Attorney Robert Morgenthau asking for advice about tracking prostitution rings, including payment methods. Prostitution rings are hardly usual territory for federal agents, and Morgenthau probed for their real target. The feds acknowledged they were looking into "a well-known politician." Several years earlier, Eliot had worked for the Manhattan DA. Now, Morgenthau figured out within a few hours of talking to the federal agents that they were after Eliot.

Prosecutors also sought assistance from a confidential informant, a woman who had previously worked as an escort for Emperors Club VIP. With her evidence of illicit activity, prosecutors obtained a judge's approval to tap the cell phones of some of the people thought to be involved.

Meanwhile, Silda was concerned about the growing strain in her marriage. Eliot was short with her, sometimes in public. She responded by throwing herself deeper into her work. She was hoping she could help him by pushing forward with her initiatives promoting green buildings, encouraging community service, and trying to stem the population exodus from upstate New York. She got testy with *The New York Times,* which she said was ignoring Eliot's many achievements in its coverage. Silda went so far as to conduct a background check of one *Times* reporter who she suspected had undisclosed ties to Republican Senate Majority Leader Joe Bruno, one of Eliot's political foes. Silda was in full White Queen protective mode.

By March, just 15 months into Eliot's term as governor, federal agents had enough evidence to file charges against the Emperors Club. The agents' affidavit listed details about a dozen Club clients, but one especially stood out for its lengthy, precise description of dates, locations, sexual behaviors, and recorded phone conversations: Client number 9. One reporter writing about the case called the affidavit "a humiliation bomb," intended to lead the press to Eliot and discredit him. As attorney general, Eliot had frequently used similar methods against his Wall Street and polluter targets.

The affidavit had its intended effect. On March 9, 2008, Eliot told his wife and daughters that the next day's *New York Times* would carry a story about him frequenting prostitutes. Over the next several days, as senior staff, friends, and family gathered at the family's Upper East Side apartment to debate Eliot's future, Silda, their daughters and a few close friends tried to convince him not to resign. They argued that other politicians had survived scandals and remained in office — most notably, former President Bill Clinton. And Silda was fully involved in her role as New York's First Lady, passionately working for the causes that inspired her. She had given up so much to achieve this platform.

One aide described Silda's initial reaction: She "probably thinks, 'I could have just been a rich Park Avenue wife, or a big lawyer. Instead, I gave ten years of my life to this political bullshit, so you're not going to just walk away.' It was likely a combination of that and being completely delusional: 'I'm married to the governor of New York, and he's the greatest thing that ever happened to this state.' She really wanted him to fight it out."

On the other side of the resignation question, prominent state Republicans were calling for Eliot's impeachment. An affair was one thing, but prostitution is illegal and shone a hypocritical light on the "Sheriff of Albany." He had strengthened the laws against sex trafficking shortly before becoming a client of the Emperors Club. Eliot reached out to the leader of the Democrat-dominated state Assembly, Speaker Sheldon Silver. Eliot asked if there was an impeachment drive, could the speaker hold it off? Silver was not encouraging. As Eliot announced his resignation at a press conference on March 12, Silda stood off to his side. The situation, and her stricken image, made her the subject of national pity. If Eliot was the errant party, why drag Silda onto the stage to share in his humiliation? Was she a prop, meant to convey that there was some element of solidarity, forgiveness, or a normal family life?

'The Wife is Responsible for the Sex'

Some explained Silda's show of support as a way to prevent even more hounding by the news media. "Quite frankly, if she's not standing there, the first question everyone will have is: 'Why isn't she standing there?' " said one seasoned New York political consultant. "It punts the question of a divorce to a different day." Many had theories about why Ms. Wall Spitzer faced reporters with her husband. Was it a show of strength for the sake of their three teenage daughters, or a calculated political strategy? Was it her decision or his?

Anna Harvey, professor of politics at New York University, said politicians often try to paint allegations of sexual misconduct as a family matter. "What you're trying to do when you have your spouse accompany you in a public forum like that is you're trying to frame the issue as a private one," she said. Silda's public show of support brought on savage criticism. A *New York Post* headline called her a "doormat," and the *Dallas Morning News* referred to her as Eliot's "Silda shield."

On the *Today* show, conservative commentator Dr. Laura Schlessinger opined to Meredith Viera, "When the wife does not focus in on the needs and the feelings sexually, personally, to make him feel like a man, to make him feel like a success, to make him feel like her hero, he's very susceptible to the charm of some other woman making him feel what he needs. And these days, women don't spend a lot of time thinking about how they can give their men what they need."

Privately, Silda did blame herself to some extent. She spent time looking for reasons and reading about testosterone and power, according to Lloyd Constantine. She considered Eliot's emotionally straight-jacketed upbringing, and how little outlet he had for expressions of weakness or pain. She asked whether she should have done something differently? She told Constantine, "the wife is supposed to take care of the sex. This is my failing. I wasn't adequate."

Publicly, Silda resolved to move beyond the image of victimhood. In May, she made her first post-scandal appearance at the annual Children for Children gala, held at Christie's auction house. She arrived alone and dressed in a magnificent burnt orange gown. Emcee Cynthia McFadden said, "She looks pretty hot, doesn't she?" and the crowd gave her a standing ovation. Silda responded to the audience, "I hope that your spring has been less eventful."

In October, she attended *Fortune's* "Most Powerful Women" conference in California, and introduced herself as a "media storm survivor" — again to great applause. Five months later, she spoke at the "Women in Power" series in Palm Beach, where she displayed before-and-after photos of herself: "before" at Eliot's resignation press conference and "after" in her orange gown at the auction house gala. By then, she had taken a job as managing director at a women-run hedge fund, Metropolitan Capital Advisors.

Everyone wondered if Silda would divorce Eliot. There was so much at stake — 20 years of marriage and three wonderful girls. Eliot seemed committed to making it work. They went to counseling. Eliot "told anyone who would listen how lucky he was that she'd forgiven him." In *Client 9: The Rise and Fall of Eliot Spitzer,* Peter Elkind wrote that Silda began to take a larger perspective on Eliot falling prey to temptation. "No man is without flaws," she reasoned, in Elkind's view. "And although Eliot's sins had massive ramifications, they were ultimately personal failures. In Silda's eyes, he remained true to his public promise, battling tirelessly on behalf of the citizenry against powerful forces bent on doing him in."

Trying to Mend the Family

The three Spitzer girls were the first in the family to face the cameras on Fifth Avenue when they left for school Monday morning, March 10. Eliot said of it later: "I just hoped beyond hope that they would be able to walk out the front door without the media being too obtrusive... I wanted to create a sense that, yeah, their dad had done something unforgiveable, but we were still a family and we were going to make it through this."

In the early years after the scandal broke, Eliot was reported to be spending a significant amount of time with his family, attempting to smooth the future of their lives together. In June 2008, the family — all five together — took a vacation in Southeast Asia where they visited Laos. Back in Manhattan, Eliot moved more fully into his role as a hands-on dad, making breakfast and walking the girls to the corner to catch the bus for school.

Eliot's daughters were at particularly tender ages when news of their father's scandal broke: Elyssa was 18, Sarabeth 15, and Jenna 13. Psychologists said they were likely shocked, angry, and in disbelief. While sons tend to be disappointed in a father's infidelity, daughters often ally with their mother. What's more, Silda was losing some of the respect she had earned in Upper East Side social circles. Psychotherapist Jenn Berman, author of *The A to Z Guide to Raising Happy, Confident Kids,* said the Spitzer girls likely felt as if "a warm security blanket had been ripped off their backs" because of the betrayal.

Elyssa, then a senior and editor of her school paper, worried about her college prospects — needlessly, as it turned out. She was admitted to both Princeton and Harvard and chose the latter. At college, Elyssa was a staff writer for the *Harvard Crimson,* the college's daily newspaper, and chair of its weekly magazine section. She concentrated on social studies at Currier House, one of 12 undergraduate residential houses at Harvard College. Like her father, she spent five months working on a Massachusetts farm harvesting crops after graduation, and then returned to Harvard to work as a research and policy analyst at the Harvard Union of Clerical and Technical Workers. She graduated from Harvard Law School and is the Senior Fellow in Law and Neuroscience at the Harvard Law School and the Center for Law, Brain & Behavior.

When Eliot's scandal broke, psychologist Joy Brown said it was possible Sarabeth could become the "peacemaker, a daddy's girl, the apologist who believes he has feet of clay and that 'everyone is out to get him.'" She also attended Harvard, focusing on psychology. She helped Eliot canvas for petitions during his 2013 bid for New York City comptroller. Silda, by contrast, did not campaign for him.

In 2012 Jenna graduated from Horace Mann, a college prep in the Bronx, and chose to take a gap year — most likely inspired by her family's travel. She spent a month on a Buddhist retreat in Ladakh, India, and then, for two months more, took Hindi classes in Varanasi — a challenging locale for a sheltered young woman. After briefly returning home, she left for Jordan to work for a nonprofit that organizes sports programs for refugee girls, and for intense study of Arabic. After returning to New York, and in an effort to help her hometown become more sustainable, Jenna took an internship helping to write regulations for energy-efficient buildings.

The Spitzer daughters are well on their way to leading independent, meaningful lives, post-scandal. No matter how anti-wife and anti-woman Eliot's hooker episodes appear, the daughters' strength derives from their parents' belief in a woman's independence. Silda and Eliot spent six years trying to rebuild their life together, an effort that merits notice. However, by the time Eliot announced a run for New York City comptroller in 2013, Silda had given up on this version of public life — and the intense public scrutiny it brings.

On the campaign trail, Eliot told the press he had Silda's approval to run. But she was all but invisible, issuing no statement of support and not once appearing at his side. It was a stark contrast to her trekking to Niagara Falls and Buffalo during the 2006 gubernatorial race. Friends said she was conflicted, offering assent but privately preferring he had chosen not to run. Karen Finerman, who runs the hedge fund where Silda works, said, "It's not in her nature to say to him, 'No, you can't'." But clearly Silda was unwilling to reprise her 2008 role as a public doormat or enabler. Eliot eventually had to concede that his wife probably wouldn't be joining him on the campaign trail.

Shortly after Eliot lost the primary, the two announced their divorce. Silda received a $7.5 million divorce payout, including the Fifth Avenue apartment and an annual stipend of $240,000.

Silda has continued to work in finance and to champion children's, environmental, and women's causes. She raises money for female Democratic candidates, including Hillary Clinton. Eliot experimented with punditry for a while, commenting on the 2008 financial crisis for various news outlets.

In 2014, after his father passed away, he took the lead in his family's real estate business. He sold two apartment buildings in Manhattan and used the money to build in the South Williamsburg section of Brooklyn. In 2019, Eliot announced his engagement to Roxana Girand, founder and president of the real estate agency Sebastian Capital. The couple took out a marriage license and had planned to marry in April 2020, but postponed the wedding because of Covid-19.

Huma Abedin &
Anthony Weiner

A Woman of Confidence

Huma and Anthony had been married for 10 months when the sexual messaging scandal hit. She was to attend a state dinner at Buckingham Palace with then-Secretary of State Hillary Clinton and President Barack Obama. That afternoon, Huma had been writing Anthony a letter from a "spectacular" room in the palace, saying how grateful she was for their life together: "I cannot believe what an amazingly blessed life that we live, these incredible experiences we've both had."

Back at their apartment in Queens, it was Memorial Day weekend 2011, and Anthony was amusing his 43,000 Twitter followers with his in-your-face humor: "My TiVo ate the hockey game! #WhoCanISue?" Moments later, he attempted to send a very different tweet to a 21-year-old female follower in Washington State: a photo of his genitals in gray briefs. But Anthony messed up, and tweeted the photo to his thousands of fans. Conservative blogger Andrew Breitbart grabbed and posted the photo, claiming that it came from Weiner's Twitter account. Anthony responded by telling a Politico.com reporter that his account had been hacked. As the accusations and denials flew, Breitbart responded that he had much more material on Anthony. In the heat of this scandalous stew, Anthony reached out to his wife in London: "When are you going to be here?"

Within days, new photos and new women began to come forward. Yet Anthony continued to deny everything — and Huma believed him. Like her boss, Secretary Clinton, she knew there were political rivals and enemies who would like to see their husbands crushed. Anthony's Twitter account being hacked, women lying to embarrass him — all of this was perfectly plausible. A week later, on June 6, ABC News released a cache of sexting images, emails, Facebook posts, and cell phone-call logs proving that Anthony had an illicit virtual affair with Megan Broussard, a 26-year-old single mother from Texas. Nine days after that, porn star Ginger Lee held a press conference and read aloud some of the explicit Twitter messages Anthony had sent to her.

During these terrible days, Anthony finally sat down with Huma privately and confessed. He said he'd had six women sext partners over three years — their entire engaged and married life. "I felt like I couldn't breathe," Huma recalled.

Two days later, she boarded Hillary's plane for a week-long trip to Africa, with a stop in the United Arab Emirates. Work was her normal and her refuge. At a stop in Abu Dhabi, Hillary arranged to have Huma's mother Sahela and her brother Hassan flown in to the Emirates Palace hotel. As the family spoke to Huma about her marriage and Anthony's sexting, there were many painful silences. Was she going to have a husband who would be good to her — and to their child? Only the family knew: Huma was pregnant.

Learning to Defend Herself and Her Culture

Huma was born in 1976 in Kalamazoo, Michigan to parents who were academics. Her father, Syed Zainul Abedin, was born in New Delhi, India. Syed had earned his master's degree in 1947 from Aligarh Muslim University in India. Afterward, he stayed on as a faculty member and lecturer in English literature. Huma's mother, Saleha Mahmood Abedin, is Pakistani. Huma's full name combines her parents' names: Huma Mahmood Abedin. Her parents met while studying for their doctorates at the University of Pennsylvania. He was working at Western Michigan University when Huma was born. When Huma was two, the family moved to Jeddah, Saudi Arabia. There, Syed founded the Institute for Muslim Minority Affairs, which was devoted to Western-Eastern and interfaith understanding and reconciliation. The institute's academic magazine, the *Journal of Muslim Minority Affairs,* published extensively about

Christian-Muslim relations, Islamic fundamentalism, and the difficulties of Muslim minorities living in the West, including the Islamophobia he encountered in America.

Saleha worked as an editor for the journal, as did Huma as a teenager, her older brother Hassan, and her younger sister Hiba. Syed died unexpectedly in 1993, following complications from surgery, and Saleha took over as the director of IMMA and editor of the journal. In September 1999, she went to help establish one of the first private women's colleges in Saudi Arabia, Dar Al-Hekma University, where she has taught sociology and served as vice president. Following in his parents' footsteps, Hassan also became a professor. In a family of academics, Huma dreamed of working in journalism. At 15, she conceived of a life plan to become the next Christiane Amanpour.

Despite this adventurous vision for her future, Huma has said that her upbringing was very traditional. She's fluent in Arabic and is a practicing Muslim. Her father had an ideal of the perfect British education and created a system for the order in which Huma was supposed to read great literature. *Silas Marner* was among the books Syed categorized at level one. Later, Huma moved to *Anna Karenina* at level six, *The Count of Monte Cristo* at level 15, *The Adventures of Huckleberry Finn* at level 19, and so on.

Her upbringing in a country with the strictest gender apartheid in the Middle East arguably bred in Huma an assumption that men should be in charge. Today, Saudi culture is undergoing some changes. However, for years, Saudi women were prohibited from leaving their homes without male guardians, were not allowed to associate publicly with men other than their direct blood relatives, were barred from many jobs, and were forbidden to drive cars. These restrictions have resulted in unions where Saudi women exert power behind the scenes — they manipulate within their marriages and extended families to achieve their goals. Speaking generally, women in Saudi Arabia are indirect; they don't leave, and they don't confront.

The country's founding in 1932 is the origin of its strict fundamentalist gender roles. That year, a powerful family, the House of Saud, forcibly united autonomous tribes and provinces on the Saudi peninsula into a monarchic state that the family would rule. To solidify power, the House of Saud struck a bargain with ultra-conservative Arab clerics, giving them free reign over social matters. Because of Saudi Arabia's vast oil wealth, its citizens are exempt from paying taxes and they receive free education and health care. No citizen is allowed to belong to or to form any political group; free speech is curtailed, as are individual liberties.

To the chagrin of many Muslims, Saudi Arabia is seen as the custodian of Islam because it follows Wahhabism, a particularly rigid and reactionary school of Sunni jurisprudence that aims to purify Islamic theology by enforcing the most literal interpretation of Islamic law. Huma grew up in this society that walls off free thinking, infantilizes its citizens, and all but physically attaches every woman to a male guardian. To believe this background hasn't affected Huma's choices in her marriage to Anthony would be naïve.

After her father's death when she was 17, Huma returned to the United States to attend George Washington University. She graduated in 1996 and began working as an intern in the office of First Lady Hillary Clinton. Huma didn't meet Hillary until November after Bill's re-election as president. The two women first met in Arkansas. Huma immediately became a Hillary devotee — an effect she says her boss has on many others. "Once people see her and meet her," Huma has said, "they change their minds" about her.

After interning, Huma was hired as an assistant to Hillary's chief of staff, Maggie Williams. The job gave Huma a front-row seat in 1998 to President Bill Clinton's Oval Office sex scandal. Huma was next promoted as Hillary's aide and advisor, and given the title traveling chief of staff — sometimes referred to as a "body woman." Huma was in charge of making sure Hillary got to and from her appointments, interrupting interviewers or curious fans, when necessary, to move the day along. Many of the people around Huma have described her as indispensable. "She's always thinking three steps ahead of Hillary," said Mandy Grunwald, a Clinton family adviser. Mike Feldman, a personal friend and former traveling chief of staff to Al Gore, said Hillary and Huma "have a unique relationship. Watch them together, and there's this nonverbal communication between them. Sometimes it's as little as a glance, but the senator knows she can hand off a head of state, a senator, or an important donor to Huma and that the conversation is going to end well."

Huma is known for being particularly stylish and remarkably unflappable, but few know much about her inner life. She's said to have an uncanny ability to allow people to get close to her without really letting them in. For example, in her first major profile, published in *The New York Observer* in 2007, her closest friends described her as Jordanian, Iranian, 26 years old, 36 years old, having two kids and living with the Clintons — none of which was entirely true. The late Oscar de la Renta, a close friend and ardent supporter of the Clintons, knew Huma for nearly a decade. He noted that she had spent time as a guest at his Dominican Republic compound. "I don't really know much about her history," de la Renta said, "because Huma is not such a talkative girl." He did, however, observe that Huma is as much of a workaholic as her boss. When the two women visited him, he joked with them that just because they were sitting in the sun as they pored over emails didn't mean that they were relaxing in full vacationing spirit.

A Middle-Class Son from Brooklyn and Queens

Unlike many successful New York City politicians, Anthony didn't come from a powerful or politically entrenched family. Born in Brooklyn Sept. 4, 1964, he lived his toddler years in a Mitchell-Lama Housing Cooperative, named for a city program developed to provide affordable housing for middle class New Yorkers. His mother, Fran, taught math at Midwood High School, and his father, Mort, was a lawyer who worked out of a ramshackle neighborhood building. Fran and Mort had three boys: Seth, the oldest, was killed in a hit-and-run accident in 2000. Anthony was their second son, and then Jason, who grew up to become a restaurateur and chef in tony East Hampton. Their parents divorced in 1990 shortly after Jason graduated from high school.

Like many of his hardworking, middle class constituents, Anthony attended New York City public schools. Though busy, the family had dinner together often, and Jason recalled that it was "a lot like Talmudic scholars dissecting." The family discussed politics and ideas, and dinner was "a bit like debate club practice." Fran was the open intellectual; Mort required his sons to defend their views. Anthony was clearly the child with the most brainpower, and when he skipped seventh grade, his parents were determined that he should go to Stuyvesant High, a top public school in the city system. Anthony took the entrance exam but fell one point short. Afterward, he went to summer school to make a second attempt at Stuyvesant, but he was not accepted.

Instead, he went to Brooklyn Technical High School where he played ice hockey and ultimate Frisbee. He wasn't quite a jock — he grew his hair long and remembers taking the subway to West 4th Street to see the avant-garde Rocky Horror Picture Show — but he also didn't party much. Jason recalls drinking at parties but said Anthony never socialized quite like that. A friend remembers him fighting bullies and otherwise standing up for "people who could not fend for themselves." Anthony graduated in 1981 and enrolled in the State University of New York in Plattsburgh. He declared a political science major and won a seat on the student government with corny slogans like, "Vote for Weiner, he's on a roll."

It was during his senior year in college that Anthony began thinking about pursuing national politics. Harvey Schantz, Anthony's faculty adviser, recalls that the younger man wasn't sure at the time whose congressional district he lived in. Though Anthony spelled his congressional representative's name wrong in his letter asking for an internship, Charles "Shumer" hired him anyway. Anthony worked six years for Schumer, first in Washington D.C., and then in Brooklyn. Schumer became a mentor to the extent that when Anthony decided to resign after his sexting scandal, one of the first calls he made was to the senator. During that phone call, both men cried.

Working at Schumer's side, Anthony decided he wanted to run for office. He was hyper-verbal, clever and engaging; he had a knack for listening patiently to older constituents. It's "what [Anthony] lives for," said Jon Stewart, host of *The*

Daily Show, who shared a summer rental with Anthony in 1985. "He's just one of those guys who likes to be in it." In 1990, when the New York City Council expanded from 33 to 51 seats, Anthony saw his chance and ran for one of the new posts. He was 26 when he began campaigning on "no promises, just hard work," and became the youngest person to serve on the city council. He was so brash that Mayor Rudy Giuliani, who hated to be upstaged, ordered city officials not to speak to Anthony, thereby denying him more material for his exuberant public persona.

Seven years later, when Chuck Schumer ran for the U.S. Senate, Anthony stepped up to succeed him in the House of Representatives, from a district that straddled Brooklyn and Queens. Anthony emerged victorious by just 489 votes — in a squeaker over Melinda Katz, the favored candidate of Queens Democrats. Ungraciously, Anthony boasted that "hard work beats a big county organization, it beats big money and hard work wins elections."

Anthony threw himself into Capitol Hill social life, playing in the softball league and on an amateur ice hockey team. Anthony's cockiness made him a bad fit, however, as one of 435 House members. He didn't work on forming alliances and instead got a reputation as a lone wolf in the Democratic caucus. In the days after his Twitter fiasco, he appeared on the House floor and did something he had never done before. He sat down in the far left side of the chamber, with the Congressional Black Caucus, and engaged in prolonged, lighthearted chatter. Because it was so out of character, one caucus member said, "We knew then he was guilty of what was being reported."

His brother Jason said Anthony's pugilistic political persona bled into his personal life and made him "hard to take." Anthony would explain to his subordinates, in high volume, why they were idiots. One day Huma showed up at the office and while standing in the reception area, heard him viciously chew out a staffer. She stepped into his office with a horrified look and asked, "What is going on here?" There were things about Anthony, it was apparent, Huma didn't know.

After less than a decade in Washington, Anthony began to think about returning to his hometown. He perceived himself in the mold of former Mayor Ed Koch, who led New York City from 1978 to 1989: an outer-borough fighter, off color, whip smart, fast-talking and "unafraid (actually, proud of being) a royal pain in the tuchis." Toward that goal, Anthony was driven, insanely, to the point of making life miserable for everyone who worked for him. He wanted a breaking-news statement issued daily. He wanted his legislative staff to focus on creating events and messages rather than on bills coming out of committees. He lunged at every legislative opportunity to ingratiate himself with the Big Apple's law enforcement community.

He ran for mayor the first time in 2005, shooting a commercial from his Brooklyn stoop.

Anthony ultimately lost the race to billionaire media mogul Michael Bloomberg, the incumbent mayor. But Weiner had put up a surprisingly good showing that took many fellow Democrats off guard. He seemed at ease promoting himself among New Yorkers. Here, he could be the Park Slope middle-class son of Mort and Fran; he could be the guy who once sold bagels at an outer-borough shopping strip; he could sit on stoops and also shoot the bull at diners. He sat out the 2009 race, which the incumbent Bloomberg again dominated. Anthony set his sights on 2013.

Throughout his rising political career, Anthony was no

stranger to relationships or to women, and many have called him a playboy. At the office, however, he was overly cautious when it came to women. If he and a female staffer were the last two remaining in his office at night, Anthony would invariably leave, leaving the staffer to lock up.

In the spring of 2008, when Anthony was 43 and Huma 31, they were rumored to be dating. It was one of the first times Anthony remained tight-lipped to the press about his love life. When asked if he was aware of the risk he was taking by dating a Muslim who grew up in Saudi Arabia, he responded that the relationship was "not the product of a political calculation." He denied having spoken to Hillary about the relationship, and he refused to say what his Jewish mother thought about the pair.

The 'Most Competent, Graceful Person' in Politics

Anthony began to notice Huma in Washington in 2001 after Hillary was elected to the U.S. Senate. "It's not like she's this lightweight beautiful person in fancy outfits," he recalled. "She's like this intriguing, fascinating creature… She is the most competent, graceful person I've met in all my years in politics."

Nearly a decade passed between Huma and Anthony's first date and their wedding.

At a Democratic National Committee retreat on Martha's Vineyard in August 2001, Anthony asked Huma if she wanted to go out for a drink. She said no; she had to work. Anthony went to Hillary and asked her to give Huma the night off. Others in the room say that Huma was behind Anthony waving, "No, no!" — but Hillary agreed.

At the restaurant, Huma ordered tea and that was the first clue Anthony had that Huma doesn't drink alcohol. When she excused herself to go to the ladies' room, several of her friends were at his table within minutes telling him to stay away from her. "She wants no part of you," they said. Huma took a long time coming back to the table — she said she kept running into people she knew — but Anthony says she ditched him. Eventually he left without her.

Over the next six years, they continued to run into each other in Washington. The ice between them thawed in 2007 when Anthony sat between Hillary and her new rival, Barack Obama, at President George W. Bush's State of the Union address. Huma texted Anthony, "I appreciate you looking out for my boss." Afterward, they went out for coffee and realized they were very much the same. They were "two hyper-drive young brains that just clicked," one friend said. "She liked his Borscht Belt humor." Both had very intense professional lives and were all but married to their jobs. Huma was relieved that he got that about her. They were married in July 2010 in Huntington, New York at the ostentatious Oheka Castle with Bill Clinton officiating. Huma's old friend, Oscar de la Renta, designed her wedding dress, which was heavily influenced by Indian and Pakistani style. He has said it was like dressing Scheherazade, the stunning Persian queen and legendary storyteller from *One Thousand and One Nights*.

The following May 27, Huma sat at a writing desk in a gilt-edged room at Buckingham Palace reserved for visiting heads of state. She was traveling with her bosses for a formal dinner with the Queen. White tie, tiaras and silver serving plates had been arranged. From her spectacular quarters, Huma could survey London's largest private garden as she began her hand-written note to her husband. Her life had a Camelot feel. As the newlywed cherished her full heart, this was the moment Anthony texted her from across the ocean, claiming that his Twitter account had been hacked: "When are you going to be here?"

At first, Anthony told Huma the photo wasn't him. Conservative blogger Andrew Breitbart was disreputable. But four days later, on June 1, Anthony said publicly that he could no longer say "with certitude" whether the picture was of him. Then, with ABC *News* closing in on the story, Anthony finally told Huma the truth as they were packing to return home from a weekend trip to the Hamptons. "I don't understand," she recalled responding. "What is going on? What's happening to our lives?"

Huma didn't want him to resign, and Anthony returned to Washington to confer with congressional Democratic leaders. He offered to take a leave of absence to seek counseling for his sex addiction. Never popular with his peers, however, Anthony drew the wrath of House Democratic Leader Nancy Pelosi. She was courting press attention for her initiatives on job creation and righting the economy but instead, "Weinergate" was absconding with media attention. Pelosi and Democratic National Committee Chairwoman Debbie Wasserman-Schultz called publicly for Anthony to step down, saying that his sordid behavior had become a distraction. President Obama weighed in, telling reporters if he were in Anthony's position, he would quit because the Congress member had done a disservice to the public that elected him. Finally, on June 16, Anthony held a four-minute press conference and announced he would leave his job of 12 years.

He stood at a podium on Capitol Hill alone, without

the standard wife-in-humiliation at his side. Feminists and pundits praised Huma for declining to act as a prop: the wounded wife standing by her man. The implication of her presence would have been, if she can forgive him, the public should too.

For a year after the sexting scandal forced him to resign from Congress, Anthony lived quietly outside the public spotlight. But private life post-Congress proved stultifying, so he and Huma plotted his return to power. In June 2012, the couple posed for People magazine with their 6-month-old son, Jordan. Huma told the *People* interviewer that Anthony was doing the laundry and other house-husbandly tasks. He claimed to have become a "very different person" since the birth of their child, and said he was "trying to be the best dad and husband [he] can be."

The interview was published the following month. At the same time, Huma was cajoling Anthony to sit for another interview — this one bigger and more serious, which was to be the final word on the sexting mess that had ended his congressional career. She wanted to clear the air, put that behind them, and get back on track toward their dreamed-of life in politics.

That next spring, on April 14, 2013, *The New York Times* Magazine published a rambling, confessional profile. "Weiner and Abedin have realized, it seems, that the only way out is through," wrote Jonathan Van Meter. Anthony summed up the troubles that had ended his seven terms in Congress as "one fateful Tweet."

The magazine profile ended with Anthony saying that Huma wanted him to run for New York City mayor, a position he had long coveted — and shortly afterward, he announced his candidacy. He immediately shot to the top of the field over four solid Democrats. He had the name recognition and the money — more than $4 million, much of it from Orthodox Jews in his Brooklyn-Queens district who backed his Zionist stance on Israel. As the basis of his platform, he developed a 64-point booklet of policy initiatives, Keys to the City. Paid pollsters had assured him that New Yorkers were willing to give him a second chance in public office. By June, he was leading in the polls among voters.

The 2013 mayoral race made Anthony and Huma feel comfortably like their former political selves. Huma made fundraising calls as she held a laminated sheet and inquired about the engagement of the man on the other end of the line. When she hung up, she turned to Anthony and said, "He's going to max out, and his wife's going to max out" — give the maximum financial donation allowable to the Anthony Weiner for Mayor campaign.

"Cha-ching!" Anthony responded jubilantly. As he was topping the polls, he recalls saying to Huma, "You know, we're back."

But so was a pseudonymous alter ego, Carlos Danger. Between sitting for the *People* photographer in June 2012 and the publication of the cozy family photos the following month, Anthony had reached out to a new sext partner. The relationship escalated quickly. Soon, the two were having phone sex as many as five times a day, and Anthony — Carlos — had proposed buying a condo in Chicago's tony South Loop neighborhood where they could meet. His sexting partner, Sydney Leathers, exposed him as Carlos Danger to TheDirty.com. Anthony went from leading the pack of Democratic contenders to running dead last.

Leathers said she thought all along that Huma knew about Anthony's sext habit — and tolerated it for the sake of their ambition as a couple. Leathers told the *New York Post* that Anthony's attitude was that he could do whatever he wanted. His wife would "forgive [him] no matter what," Leathers recalls of Anthony's mindset. "I just always kind of assumed she knew how he was from the first time around. I think they both are very ambitious and they are better off together than separately."

There is some evidence that Huma knew that her husband continued his sexting compulsion, even after quitting Congress in disgrace. According to friends and family who spoke to the *New York Post,* Anthony confessed to her in September 2012 that he was at it again.

That knowledge might have convinced another couple to hold back from the 2013 mayoral race, but Huma and Anthony pursued it with enthusiasm. "She was eager to get her life back in politics, to clean up the mess I had made," Anthony told the documentary filmmakers who followed his 2013 campaign in *Weiner.* "Running for mayor was the straightest line to do it."

A sense of public mission is how Huma rationalized encouraging her husband's pyrrhic mayoral attempt. In an essay for the September 2013 issue of *Harper's Bazaar,* timed to publish just as Democrats would be going to the polls, she wrote that her husband is a smart, caring, and dedicated public servant. "I love my husband, I love my city, and I believe in what he wants to do for the people of New York," she wrote. Since bringing a child into the world, and beginning to raise him in their Manhattan neighborhood, Huma said the couple had begun to see the world differently. They worried about their son's education, his health, and his safety. New Yorkers needed "a fighter in City Hall," someone who is fearless and relentless. "This campaign isn't about

Anthony," she wrote. "It's about the people of this city and how to make their lives better."

For twenty years, Huma had participated on the national stage as one of Hillary Rodham Clinton's key aides. She could calculate the risk the couple was running by entering the mayoral race. Yet she not only stayed by Anthony's side, she encouraged his hurtle into this fresh humiliation. They were counting on their two lifetimes in politics to allow them to navigate the scandal and present a narrative of redemption: Anthony had become a family man, had faced up to his compulsion, had suffered the loss of his congressional seat and was putting that behind him to fight for middle-class New York as the city's mayor. It was a calculated gamble to get their political life back, and it failed spectacularly.

Within weeks of Anthony's entry into the mayoral race, TheDirty.com published Carlos's lurid sexts for all to see. Now everyone knew: Even a resignation, even a new baby and a magnanimous wife, hadn't quelled Weiner's sexting obsession.

As her essay in *Harper's Bazaar* magazine was hitting the streets, Anthony plummeted in the polls. He grew more combative with the press and belligerent with people on the street. Heatedly, he got into a shouting match with an Orthodox Jew in Brooklyn, after the man heckled Anthony about being "married to an Arab" and setting a bad example with his sexting behavior. "What rabbi taught you that you're my judge?" Weiner responded sharply. It was a toxic and ultimately fatal posture. On primary day, of five Democrats, Weiner came in fifth.

A Sex Scandal Adapted
to 21st Century Media

Anthony has theorized that worldwide press attention to his scandal resulted in part from his relationship with Huma; they were an ultimate power couple. He also blames his last name, which became a headline writer's dream. But it was the compulsive nature of his sex-talk and photo-sharing that did him in. He took it to an extreme, ending by engaging with an underage girl and a conviction as a sex offender.

Politically, Anthony's offense was to ask people repeatedly to keep forgiving the same sin, behavior he might have survived in pre-Internet days. "To me, [the sexting] was just another way to feed this notion that I want to be liked and admired," he said. "And if it wasn't 2011 and it didn't exist, it's not like I would have gone out cruising bars or something like that." In the documentary Weiner, he said he viewed sexting almost like playing a video game and that he didn't have the capacity to judge it as inappropriate. "I had a huge blind spot about it, and that blind spot was a pretty big one."

Huma's White Queen Quotient: 10

If Anthony had had even a somewhat successful mayoral campaign — not necessarily a win, but a decent showing — their gamble might have worked. For the rest of eternity, they could argue that he had put the past behind him, the sexting issue was addressed, fully asked and answered, and was no longer a relevant subject for the media, in the same way the Vitters have dismissed his history with women he'd paid for sex. A successful primary would have preserved the life Anthony and Huma had fashioned for themselves in politics and would have paved a path for their son to follow — building the legacy modern White Queens covet.

Indeed, Huma addressed the legacy issue directly. She has said she would not be able to face the couple's young son, Jordan, if she had left his father when he most needed her. Anthony has said that Jordan's impression of him drives his thinking. "I am quite confident that my son will have the ability to look at the totality of the experiences he has with his father, and the record that I've got, to judge me appropriately," Anthony said in a 2014 interview. "Maybe, you know, it teaches him a little something about adversity and everything doesn't go great all the time."

This couple's boldness doesn't quite add up to a desire to protect their son in the conventional sense. Will Jordan really benefit from "looking back on his mother's excruciating display of lack of self-respect?" asked one columnist after the Carlos Danger revelations. "Does she believe that the fact that she is essentially condoning Weiner's behavior sets a good example for her son?"

In August 2016, however, Huma could no longer hide behind maternal protectiveness. The *New York Post* printed two front-page covers of Anthony sexting with son Jordan beside him on the bed or in his arms. Anthony boasted to a sext partner that he used the boy as a "chick magnet." At the end of August, Huma announced that the couple would separate, and the following year, she filed for divorce.

Huma's childhood in patriarchal Saudi Arabia inclined her to shoulder her husband's behavior. She blamed herself for dropping out of couples counseling, instead of holding accountable the perpetrator of the illicit activities. This is a classic dodge for a woman who can't bring herself to confront her husband.

Financial security played a strong role in the couple's decision making. When Anthony resisted resigning his congressional seat, he was still years away from a congressional pension. That may have been one reason he resisted the calls to step down — to continue building credit toward a federal pension. On the other hand, if he hung on in Congress, he might have faced legal expenses to defend himself in an ethics inquiry.

As a member of congress, Anthony was drawing $174,000 annually, and Huma was earning between $123,758 and $155,500, given her GS-15 rank in the federal government. Running for mayor in 2013 allowed him to tap his $4 million campaign account, which by law cannot be used for personal expenses. His running also made him eligible for some $1.5 million in public matching funds through New York City's campaign finance system. His race allowed Huma to use her connection with Clinton to solicit money from a vast network of financial donors.

Clinton helped the couple financially in more direct ways as well. In June 2012, Huma was reclassified as a "special government employee," advising Clinton part-time from her home in New York. Huma and Anthony's 2012 tax returns — a year when Anthony was unemployed — showed joint income of $490,000.

That year, the couple sold their 2-bedroom condo in Forest Hills, Queens, and moved to Manhattan into a 4-bedroom, 3.5-bath apartment that listed for $3.3 million. The owner, Rosen Partners' chief executive Jack Rosen, has made political contributions to the Clintons as well as to Anthony.

Social Media Obsession Helps to Sink Hillary Clinton Campaign

Huma and Anthony spent their entire adult lives in high-profile lives in the public eye. It's ironic, then, that Anthony's downfall was his infatuation with the new clandestine flirting, sexting, and remote sexual flirtations that social media enables. A guy like Anthony can be texting about a hockey game one minute and sexting the next.

Huma and Anthony were conditioned to second-guess media reports, to fend off attacks leaked by political enemies, and to rely on their own version of reality. They were each other's trusted confidantes inside the armor they created to wall off embarrassment and criticism — so much so they very likely didn't realize how odd these choices appear to people who bump up against the regular reality checks of life lived outside the most powerful circles on the planet. In that sense of an extreme loss of privacy, Huma and Anthony are the evolution of the other couples profiled here.

They separated not because Anthony was virtually unfaithful — that seems to have become routine for this couple — but because the publicity had grown too glaring to ignore and the political stakes too high. Huma had to choose: Anthony Weiner or Hillary Clinton. In the end, it may not have been Huma's injured wifely feelings that ended her marriage so much as her professional pride and ambition.

In late August 2016, Huma was the most senior aide to presidential candidate Clinton, who was making a historic run as the first American woman topping a major party ticket — and her victory seemed virtually assured. No one — not the polls nor the press, not even her opponent Donald Trump — thought Clinton would lose the election. Within

204

weeks, the Clinton campaign would have a transition team in place and would be interviewing candidates for the 4,000 positions they expected to fill in Washington in their new administration. The Trump team, not nearly as confident of winning, wasn't thinking that far ahead.

Not only did Clinton lose the election, but in a bizarre twist, Anthony's sexting was instrumental in her loss. In September 2016, the FBI learned that Weiner had been texting a 15-year-old. Given her age, this was a crime, and the FBI opened an investigation. Within days of the upcoming election, FBI Director James Comey announced that the investigation had revealed a new cache of emails, forwarded by Huma on Anthony's laptop, during Clinton's tenure at the state department. That reinforced public concern that Hillary Clinton was reckless. Then, just two days before the election, Comey told Congress the new emails contained nothing of interest in regard to Clinton — but if he intended to clear the air, Comey's announcement had the opposite effect of energizing Trump supporters to show up at the polls and vote.

Weiner's lawyer said the former lawmaker likely exchanged thousands of messages with hundreds of women over the years and was communicating with as many as 19 women when he encountered the 15-year-old online. He was convicted in federal court and served 18 months in prison. Although Huma filed for divorce in 2017, the two later discontinued the case and negotiated their separation privately. Anthony is living a private life, once again, as chief executive officer of IceStone, a manufacturer in the Brooklyn Navy Yard that makes countertops out of broken glass. He issued a press release in September 2020 to let the world know.

Huma continues to work within Clinton circles, including work for Teneo Holdings, a New York-based strategic planning and financial services firm. The firm was co-founded by Doug Band, a former chief adviser to President Clinton. Huma and Anthony are sometimes seen together on the streets of Manhattan, with Jordan.

Melania & Donald

American Czarina,
Immigrant First Lady

Two girls grew up with few frills in communist countries. They dwelled in monotonous concrete apartment buildings and had next to no access to news or images from the West. Their parents worked at low-level jobs where advancement was available only through personal, Communist Party connections.

The girls' prospects were limited, and their parents wanted better for them. Each girl used every avenue, talent, and connection to leave her homeland for the United States.

And one day at different times, both girls would grow up to marry Donald Trump.

This traces the early lives of two of Trump's three wives: Ivana and Melania. Their similarities suggest that they were ambitious, clever, opportunist, and comfortable with the strong-man style of Eastern European men in their former countries of Czechoslovakia and Yugoslavia.

Each in her turn was drawn to the win-at-all-costs Donald Trump. Each has accepted, to one extent or another, his philandering, compulsive lying, absentee parenting and narcissism. Ivana left that behind, but Melania has stayed in her marriage.

It is curious that Donald Trump was attracted to two very similar women. Yes, it may be true that people have a "type" of partner that sparks chemistry. But one has to circle in the same orbit to meet that partner.

Most people think of Donald Trump as a builder, former casino owner, and a guy who excelled at firing underlings on *The Apprentice*. But he is likely most familiar with the social circles where he accumulated the majority of his wealth — in connection with some of the most powerful underworld figures in Russia and its former satellites. Over the past three decades, at least 13 people with known or alleged links to Russian mobsters or oligarchs have owned, lived in, and even run criminal activities out of Trump Tower and other Trump properties.

Investigative journalists who have followed Trump's career report that he owes his wealth to post-Soviet Eastern European kleptocrats. In the early 2000s, "the influx of

Russian money did more than save Trump's business from ruin — it set the stage for the next phase of his career," Craig Unger wrote in *The New Republic* in 2017.

The very nature of Trump's businesses — all of which are privately held, with few reporting requirements — makes it difficult to root out the truth about his financial deals. But his personal love life speaks of someone who travels in these circles. Ivana and Melania grew up in dictatorial societies in which coming out on top required ruthlessness and contempt for the rules that govern ordinary folk.

Trump has expressed open admiration for totalitarian strongmen: Vladimir Putin, Kim Jong-un, Recep Tayyip Erdogan. And he sought to undermine and invalidate the democratic U.S. election that ejected him from office in November 2020. This may all have seemed normal to Melania — so normal that she provided no check on his authoritarian actions. Her influence at key junctures in his political life reveal an imperiousness. She doubled down on birtherism conspiracies about Barack Obama and has baited "liberals" and the media, most famously with the haughty "I don't care" message she wore painted on her coat when visiting the southern U.S. border where refugee parents were detained and separated from their children.

In Melania Trump, the United States may have imported its first First Lady who believes in and supports authoritarianism in her man — and then, in her president. She doesn't share the values of a democracy. She is less the kind of First Lady Americans had come to know, and more the compliant wife of a mob boss.

No Compromise, No Apologies

By the time Melania Knauss met Donald Trump in 1998, her modeling career had begun hitting speed bumps. She had spent her childhood in a small town in Slovenia, which was then part of communist Yugoslavia. Her mother developed patterns in a factory that made children's clothing, and her father worked as a chauffeur and he also sold cars. Melania modeled clothes made by her mother beginning at age 7. In 1986, when she was 16, she accepted an invitation from a Slovenian photographer to pose in a series of black-and-white shots that were subsequently published in catalogs.

Melania continued to model through high school and into university, when, in 1992 she won second place in *Jana Magazine*'s Slovenian "Face of the Year" modeling contest. The honor inspired her to make her way to bigger modeling circuits in Milan and Paris. She polished her image by changing her first name from Melanija to Melania and Germanizing her surname from Knavs to Knauss.

Playing on this bigger stage paid off for Melania. Paolo Zampolli, an Italian businessman with broad business interests, scouted the European catwalks each year for his New York modeling agency. Zampolli searched for models who not only had the looks but also the survival skills to take on New York City's arduous modeling scene. He brought Melania to New York in 1996 on a modeling contract and work visa, and she proved herself, in his words, "stable and focused." She saved her money, avoided the party scene, and took assiduous care of her body. One payoff for her self-care included a sexually explicit photo shoot, showing her bare breasts for the French men's magazine *Max*. When Melania dated, she would be home by 1 a.m., a former roommate told *GQ* magazine. There were no all-night dance clubs on the roster for this ambitious 25-year-old.

Yet her efforts weren't making her as sought-after as she had hoped. There were days she had no work. She would go to casting calls only to have someone chosen over her—increasingly, someone younger.

In 1998, she made an exception to her careful homebody routine. Her benefactor Zampolli was throwing a party during New York's Fashion Week at a Manhattan nightspot called the Kit Kat Klub. Zampolli liked to populate his parties with models, and he invited the statuesque young Slovenian to lend the event a touch of beauty. The story that Melania and Donald tell about the evening is that he arrived with a date—a more famous model—and was instead drawn to Melania. As the story goes, he asked for her number, and she said no. Instead, she asked for his number. In a later interview with *GQ* magazine, Melania explained that she wanted to understand Donald's intentions. "It tells you a lot from the man what kind of number he gives you," Melania said. "He gave me all of his numbers." Presumably, a man looking for a quick affair would give just a mobile number, or in some other way confine her to a small space in his life.

Melania said she waited a week before calling Donald. She has commented that this delay might have communicated her reserve, and impressed upon the well-to-do Trump that she was a woman to be taken seriously. "I'm not starstruck," she explained in an interview with *GQ*. "We had a great connection, we had chemistry, but I was not starstruck. And maybe he noticed that."

Days later, Donald could be found escorting Melania in a black stretch limousine, along with dinner guests Zampolli and the magician David Copperfield. They dined at a Trump favorite locale, the Cipriani balcony restaurant inside the majestic Grand Central Station. The evening was a celebrity Manhattanite version of sweeping a woman off her feet.

In short order, New York City society columnists began writing about Donald and his new girlfriend. She "maintains her own apartment," *The New York Times* noted. Appearing on the Howard Stern radio show, Trump bragged about their sex life. Afterward, the *New York Post* ran a cartoon depicting Melania in bed with Trump. Above her head was a thought bubble in the form of a dollar sign. Indeed, the relationship had begun to help Melania's career. She graced a 50-foot billboard outside the Trump casino in Atlantic City; her chiseled cheekbones and icy-green eyes became increasingly recognizable.

Within a year, as Donald began publicly musing about running for president on a third-party Reform ticket, the couple was sufficiently established that the press asked Melania about her ideas for becoming First Lady. At the time, few people thought Donald Trump would run, much less be elected. However, Melania responded to interview questions as though she was seriously considering the role. "I will be very traditional like Jackie Kennedy," Melania told *ABC News* in December 1999. "I would support him. I will do a lot of social obligations."

However, by the following month, the high-profile couple had broken up. Twenty-six-year-old Melania had reportedly dumped Trump, 53, after she caught him cheating with another model and former flame, Kara Young. Melania told a friend that Trump was "back to his old ways," and she wouldn't have it. This is why she had kept her own place, she emphasized, because of Donald's terrible reputation for womanizing. Another friend told the press that Melania was heartbroken and is "a one-man woman."

What happened next between Melania and Donald we can only conjecture. The couple got back together, of course. Did Melania extract a promise of fidelity they both had ample reason to doubt Trump would ever keep? Given his lifelong mania to not only seduce beautiful women but to ensure the world knew all the enviable details, this seems un-likely. The only explanation that makes sense is that Melania got over her aversion to his "old ways" and made a deal with herself to somehow accept Donald Trump as he is. After their son, Barron, was born, Melania granted *Parenting* magazine an interview in which she said, "I think the mis-take some people make is they try to change the man they love after they get married. You cannot change a person."

At the same time, it seems likely that the couple agreed that Donald's philandering would be conducted in a way that would not embarrass his wife. He would be discreet enough to allow her to wear the mantle of deniability. This probable accord came to light later, in 2016, in Melania's reaction to the publication of the *Access Hollywood* interview. Melania flat-out refused to go on TV with her husband for an apolo-gy.

The infamous tape was recorded in September 2005, eight months into the marriage, as Donald bragged to TV host Billy Bush that he could just start kissing beautiful women. "It's like a magnet. Just kiss. I don't even wait," Trump told Bush. "And when you're a star, they let you do it. You can do anything. Grab 'em by the pussy. You can do anything."

The tape was made public in October 2016, one month before Americans went to the ballot box to cast their votes for either Donald Trump or Hillary Clinton. The timing was a classic "October surprise" by Trump's political opponents, calculated to remain uppermost in voters' minds in the early November election. Here was the Republican presidential candidate declaring himself a sexual assailant in his own words — an admission that made Democrats salivate as Trump competed for votes against the historic feminist candidacy of Hillary Rodham Clinton. In response to the airing of the tape, Trump dismissed his earlier words as braggadocio. In an interview with *The Washington Post*, he called it "locker-room banter" between alpha males. However, a second wave of bad publicity awaited the candidate. After the tape's release, a deluge of women came forward to accuse Trump of varying degrees of sexual misconduct. To date, his accusers number at least 23.

The *Access Hollywood* talk and the affair with *Playboy* Playmate Karen McDougal were a revelation to Melania, according to *Washington Post* reporter Mary Jordan. Trump's campaign was more focused on his chances at the ballot box.

Advisers initially suggested that Trump and his family take the route paved by Hillary Clinton. Just before the New Hampshire presidential primary in 1992, when Bill was running for president, a supermarket tabloid, *The Star*, published an interview with Gennifer Flowers, who said she'd had a longtime affair with Bill. The Clintons initially denied the affair. But within days of the accusation, they decided to take on the many rumors of Bill's infidelities more directly. They booked an interview on *60 Minutes,* scheduled to air directly after the Super Bowl for maximum viewership. Still denying the Flowers affair, Bill admitted to having caused "pain" in the marriage. Hillary, sitting by his side, said she had forgiven him and they had moved past the difficult times. Both argued that his infidelity was a personal matter and should not be a factor in voters' choice for president.

"You know, I'm not sitting here, some little woman standing by my man like Tammy Wynette," Hillary said, waving her clenched right hand. "I'm sitting here because I love him, and I respect him, and I honor what he's been through and what we've been through together. And you know, if that's not enough for people, then heck — don't vote for him."

Following the release of the *Access Hollywood* tape and the sexual misconduct allegations, the Trump campaign was in freefall. Would any woman vote for him now? In his book about the 2016 election, journalist Bob Woodward describes Republican National Committee Chairman Reince Priebus ticking off a list of big donors who were closing their wallets and pulling their endorsements. Adviser Rudy Giuliani began estimating Trump's chances of winning at about 40 percent. Another strategist, Kellyanne Conway, proposed they halt the damage by having Trump appear on *60 Minutes* to say he was sorry and to repent his behavior. In Conway's vision, Ivanka and Melania would be seated on either side of him, reminiscent of the *mea culpa* interview the Clintons had conducted 24 years earlier.

As Conway proposed this aloud in a room with the Trumps and other campaign advisers, Melania seethed. She wandered behind the couch where Conway was seated. "Not doing that," Melania said in her Slovenian accent, dismissively waving her hand. "No way. No, no, no."

Instead, Melania released a face-saving statement: "The words my husband used are unacceptable and offensive to me. This does not represent the man I know. He has the heart and mind of a leader. I hope people will accept his apology, as I have, and focus on the important issues facing our nation and the world."

While some of the seamy details may have been a revelation to Melania, hers was an incredibly bold-faced defense. Whatever may have been happening inside the marriage, for public consumption, Melania's stance was denial: This is my story, and I'm sticking to it.

For his part, to blunt the criticism, Trump invited four women who had accused Bill Clinton of sexual assault to the next debate against his rival, Hillary.

Melania's adamant objection to public penance brings into sharp relief an arrangement that she and Donald had been living for more than a decade: highly independent lives within a marriage that benefited both. Theirs was a transactional marriage, in the words of one of Melania's close friends, Stephanie Winston Wolkoff. Others say the couple demonstrates a sincere affection for each other, but they operate independently. They never really merged their lives.

Trump adviser Roger Stone, in an interview for this book, said Melania has expressed indifference about politics. "She's said it to me," Stone said. "I think what she would say, and she said it to me, is 'It's not my thing. It's Donald's thing.'" On the other hand, Melania hasn't discouraged her husband's ambition. Stone continued, "I don't think she wanted him to be 90 years old and saying I should've, I could've."

Donald seeks Melania's advice on how to position himself and how to win. But her greater passions lie elsewhere. She's a hands-on parent to her son, with the close involvement of her parents, who moved from Slovenia and became U.S. citizens. She has a Manhattan-Hamptons-Aspen-Palm

Springs lifestyle, and has dabbled in luxury skin care and jewelry businesses. She and Donald are infrequently in the same residence together, and when they are, they keep separate bedrooms.

"Was she dying to be a political wife? No, not at all," said Michael Caputo, a Trump administration official and longtime adviser. "I thought that it didn't interest her at all. They had a perfect life, and she was probably quite happy the way she was with her boy and her home in the Tower and the life they led. It was a perfect life."

There's a second aspect to avoiding a *60 Minutes*-type confession when it comes to the persona Melania has crafted for herself. Bart Rossi, a political psychologist, said that Melania has created an icy, stony exterior that serves her well as she copes in public with her husband's infidelities and other controversial behavior.

She's got a steely look, aloof, almost indifferent, Dr. Rossi said. "She can protect herself from him by being that way. Everything bounces off when you're like that." One might say the same of Jackie Kennedy's persona. "She knows he's going to run around, he's already done that," Dr. Rossi continued. "That is the way to handle that and still be a person with her [own high] profile. She gets a persona that is a certain type: I'm more reserved, I'm more demure, I'm classy, I'm sexy, I'm beautiful. The more reserved I am, the more attention I may get to that kind of a profile."

"She may look classy in some regards, but on the other side of it, there's a lot of shallowness and question marks about her being with him," Dr. Rossi said. "Her understanding and dealing — because I know she does — with the Stormy Daniels and McDougals, and god knows how many other women."

Trump has denied claims of infidelity but confirmed payments to porn star Stormy Daniels and Playboy model Karen McDougal.

Humbling themselves in public for a television camera is not the Trump way. In that, they proved a departure from so many of the couples, with cheating husbands, that preceded them, such as the apologetic Weiners, Spitzers and Clintons. A U.S. Congressman from New York, Anthony Weiner resigned his seat after a sexting scandal. He was married to one of Hillary Clinton's top aides, Huma Abedin. Eliot Spitzer was a crusading Wall Street prosecutor and then governor of New York, when he was caught hiring hookers and stepped down. The Trumps turned the political playbook back to defend, deny and ignore. This was a strategy pursued by the Kennedys, Roosevelts and Vitters; in 2007, former U.S. Senator David Vitter was revealed to be a client of the infamous "D.C. Madam" who ran a prostitution ring in the nation's capital. He and wife, Wendy, gave a single press conference to address the scandal and have refused to speak publicly about it again.

America elected Donald Trump, and with a certain portion of the electorate, he enjoys support for his decision to weather the womanizing criticism — and, indeed, any criticism — with brashness and bravado. His wife, in a fashion reminiscent of European political wives, has chosen to look the other way, not in a manner that's humiliated or meek, but flavored with a type of bravado of her own.

Melania's White Queen Quotient: 10

As a woman who, by her own admission is indifferent to politics, how strongly does Melania measure up to the five traits of the White Queen shared by contemporary political wives whose husbands have cheated?

Melania's rating on the scale of White Queen traits is not a science but more a matter of judgment, comparison, and intuition. Melania rates highly on the first four measures, and not as much on the last. It's not that she's unpatriotic. Rather, other forces appear to be stronger motivators in her life.

There is little doubt Melania is devoted to family, trait No. 1. She famously refused to move to Washington, DC, for months after her husband's election, preferring to keep their son Barron in his New York City classroom until the end of the school year. Melania also recognized her moment of leverage over her husband, who needed a First Lady for public appearances if for nothing else. She began to renegotiate her pre-nuptial agreement, as reported in the book *The Art of Her Deal: The Untold Story of Melania Trump*. The renegotiated prenup offers "proof in writing that when it comes to financial opportunities and inheritance, Barron will be treated as an equal with Trump's oldest three children."

Melania sponsored her parents, Viktor and Amalija Knavs, in their move to the United States. Most days, Barron's grandparents escort him to school and pick him up afterward. Like other presidential parents, Melania shielded her young son from publicity and prying eyes. Her official entry onto the campaign trail with her husband, on a snowy April night in Wisconsin, began with Trump introducing her as "an incredible mother."

Melania also serves as an emotional caretaker, a sounding board and refuge for her husband, say people close to them. For all the speculation about her desire to escape the marriage — from the #FreeMelania meme on Twitter to Omarosa Manigualt Newman's contention that Melania is sending political messages via her sartorial choices — there is a straight line of determined intensity that runs through the woman's history. She gives advice privately but doesn't upstage her husband. Michael Caputo, the former senior adviser to Trump who spent time with the couple, said Melania provides something like the fortress of solitude — the arctic cave to which comic book Superman retreated when he needed to restore his strength. "I'm saying that to be kind of funny, but I think when the president goes to the residence, he has an incredible support apparatus there," Caputo said. "He draws a lot of strength." At the same time, in public, Melania only echoes her husband's political views — speculating about the authenticity of Barack Obama's Hawaiian birth certificate, for example — and keeping mum about any opinions she may hold. She told an interviewer about the advice she gives her husband, "Nobody knows and nobody will ever know."

With a husband like Donald Trump, a wife's emotional caretaking will be closely tied to living carefully within patriarchal traditions — trait No. 2. He's competitive to the point of needing to dominate every encounter and openly admires other strongmen leaders like Russia's Vladimir Putin and China's Xi Jinping. Trump has swept aside civility when it comes to the press, political opponents or others who stand in judgment of him. Instead, he returns to crowds of faithful followers, campaign-style, in a manner that seems to buoy his spirits and confidence. He loves pomp and mused on several occasions about mounting a military parade, complete with tanks and flyovers, to cruise the streets of Washington, D.C. His children are deferential, and the women in his life are invariably stunning. In a Republican primary campaign dispute, Ted Cruz questioned Melania's fitness to become

First Lady by publicizing a magazine photo of her lying nude on a bearskin rug. Trump's people responded by juxtaposing an unflattering photo of Heidi Cruz, Ted's wife, with a glamour shot of Melania. The message from Trump: My wife is hotter. It was a schoolyard-level putdown inserted into a dispute that had nothing to do with physical beauty.

Looking more closely at Melania's upbringing, her parents emphasized male brutishness — to the extent of indifference to an out-of-wedlock child — as well as outward feminine perfection.

Melania's well-begotten marriage, along with the manner in which she raises their son Barron, speaks to a woman who sought not only financial security but a position for herself and a legacy — traits No. 3 and No. 4 in the White Queen scale. She calls Barron "little Donald" and wants him to become a businessman and a golfer. He almost always dresses in suits. She has said, "He's not a sweatpants child." With her statuesque beauty and international social connections, Melania could have married any of dozens of wealthy men. Instead, she chose one who brought with the wedding ring instant recognition and fame, if not infamy. "This whole thing is a case where this is not a marriage just for money," said Bart Rossi, the political psychologist. "My view is more that she wanted a legacy. It was about enhancing her profile and her situation in life much more than money."

Finally, as we turn to patriotism, Melania's respect for U.S. laws extends about as far as they benefit herself and her kin. She moved here to work as a model, and did so, some claim, before she had the right to work here legally. Her husband helped her obtain a green card under the elite EB-1 program — nicknamed the Einstein visa. This citizenship entrée is normally reserved for renowned academic researchers, multinational business executives and those in other fields — Olympic athletes, Oscar-winning actors — who have demonstrated "sustained national and international acclaim."

Melania sponsored her parents to also become U.S. citizens. Yet as First Lady, when she visited an immigrant detention center holding children who had been separated from their parents at the U.S. border, she wore the infamous green jacket with "I really don't care, do u?" painted across the back. Former friend and aide Stephanie Winston Wolkoff has written that Melania wore the jacket to drive "liberals crazy. You know what? They deserve it."

In the context of the motivations of political wives, patriotism expresses the idea that a person has greater ideals for the direction of the nation. By this measure, and compared with other prominent political wives, Melania seems somewhat indifferent. She encouraged her husband to run for president, reportedly so that he would not live to regret missing his opportunity. But when the vote was tallied on Election Night 2016, Melania is said to have wept at the result. Then, she made a mental calculation of her new leverage in the marriage and renegotiated her prenup.

Melania lived up to the task of being First Lady, but not enthusiastically. She adopted a broad but nebulous campaign, "Be Best," focusing on well-being for youth and advocating against cyberbullying and drug use, particularly opioids. This position was a winner within her marriage, where her husband would never stand for someone who outshone him in any way. Indeed, the author of *The Art of Her Deal* argues that this is the quality Donald most prizes about Melania. He knows that she is the only one in his inner circle who doesn't have an agenda other than to see him succeed. For these reasons, the canny Melania merits a White Queen-style ambition rating of 10.

Trump Childhood:
Lessons in Social Climbing

So much has been published about Donald Trump: his business ventures and bankruptcies, his litigations and how he stiffed his creditors, his combats and conquests and publicity-seeking. He's an enormous personality whose perfect apotheosis was playing a clamorous, dictatorial business executive on NBC TV's *The Apprentice* ... until he ascended, unpredictably, to an even more powerful role, as U.S. president, where his many personal oddities were on display on the largest stage on earth. Rifling through this man's past, we can see that two facets of his character are crucial to understanding his relationship with his third wife. One is his drive for commercial success, a drive so excessive that it suggests a person trying to prove himself to himself and to ward off a deep insecurity. The other is the way he reacts to women. It's as if their value is tied up entirely in their physical beauty. Again belying a fragile ego, Trump surrounds himself with beautiful women as one way to prove to the world — and to himself — that he is a success.

Commercial ambition and desirable women were intertwined early in the Trump family history in America. Donald's grandfather, Friedrich Trump, emigrated to the United States in 1885 at the age of 16, to avoid facing mandatory military service in Germany. He settled in Seattle and opened The Dairy Restaurant, which included a curtained-off area that "likely served as a low-rent whorehouse," according to Gwenda Blair, an official Trump family historian. Friedrich would try two more bordello-style ventures, one about 30 miles north within Washington State, and the next in Canada's Yukon Territory. He followed the gold-seeking miners who paid well for liquor and prostitutes.

Sixteen years after he left Germany, at age 32, Friedrich returned as a successful entrepreneur and began fielding his mother's attempts to find him a wife. He spurned her matchmaking and instead took up with a 20-year-old busty blonde named Elizabeth Christ. His mother disapproved, and she wasn't the only one to find fault with Friedrich. In 1904, angered by his years-ago draft-dodging, the German government ordered Friedrich, his wife Elizabeth, and their infant daughter to leave the country. He returned to America to work as a barber in New York, a relatively non-lucrative profession that some speculate served as a front to give him access to the city's organized crime circuit. He anglicized the family name from Drumpf to Trump.

In 1918, a deadly flu that killed 20 million people around the globe also spelled the end for Friedrich. His son, Fred, the middle child, was just 12 years old. Two years later, at age 14, Fred joined his mother in a residential building company, Elizabeth Trump & Son. They were a formidable team. Elizabeth had contractors build houses on empty lots Friedrich had owned, sold the houses and supported herself and her three children with the mortgage payments. Fred began building his first home at age 23, partially financed by his mother. They constructed hundreds of homes in Queens over the next several years. This resilient matriarch stayed involved in the family business and lived near her son Fred as he raised his own family in Jamaica, Queens, during Donald's formative years.

Fred was a blond, mustachioed, serious man whose passion was business. In 1935, as he was turning 30, he attended a party and met a woman a half-dozen years his junior, Mary Anne MacLeod. Mary Anne, the youngest of

10 children, was at the party with her married sister, with whom she lived in Queens. She had emigrated from Stornoway, Scotland, arriving in America on her 18th birthday. Mary Anne had brown hair and bright blue eyes and spoke English with a heavy Scottish Gaelic accent. The couple married in January 1936 and went to Atlantic City for their honeymoon.

Before the year was out, Fred Trump received approval from the federal housing administrator in New York State to build a 450-home project in East Flatbush — a permit the official Trump family biographer called "the most important event of Fred Trump's life." To squeeze the most out of the land, he built attached row houses with common walls. Soon, "Trump homes" lined the streets of central Brooklyn. Between August 1936 and July 1938, Fred sold 500 homes. A local newspaper dubbed him "the Henry Ford of the home-building industry" for his application of mass-production techniques. Fred continued to use Federal Housing Administration financing to build many thousands of apartments in Brooklyn and Queens.

At the time, the FHA was subsidizing Fred and other mass-producing builders, with the stipulation that none of the homes be sold to Blacks. The federal government's justification was that if Blacks bought these homes in the suburbs, the property values of FHA-insured homes would decline, and the loans would be at risk. One result was to push Black families and other families of color into urban housing. So, while Fred Trump didn't invent the racial discrimination for which his row house developments were known, he appears to have been comfortable going along with it. His reputation for racial animosity was fueled by his arrest at a KKK rally in Queens.

In 1950, folk songwriter Woody Guthrie moved into a Fred Trump apartment in the Beach Haven section of Brooklyn. Guthrie noted that all the residents were white and wrote lyrics about the rental policies: *I suppose that Old Man Trump knows just how much racial hate; He stirred up in that bloodpot of human hearts; When he drawed that color line; Here at his Beach Haven family project.*

Mary Anne MacLeod Trump is remembered as a kind and patient mother who raised five children on Wareham Street in Jamaica Estates. The family lived in a two-story mock Tudor that Fred had built. By contrast, Fred was a demanding parent, opinionated and stern. He kept regular hours, was tight with money, and, after returning home each night for dinner, resumed doing business on the telephone. Years later, Donald said his father freely dispensed criticism but rarely praised.

Fred didn't involve his two daughters in the family business, but he expected his sons—Fred Jr., Donald, and Robert — to learn the business from the ground up. He drove them regularly to his properties in his blue Cadillac. The boys swept out storage rooms, emptied coins from basement washers and dryers, and made minor repairs as the maintenance crew supervised. As they got older, they collected rents. Fred paid them, but they also had trust funds from the time they were in diapers. Donald's share was about $12,000 a year. In the late 1940s, that was roughly four times what a full-time worker made in a year.

As the business grew, the family moved out of the too-small Wareham Street house into another Fred Trump home: a brick colonial-style edifice with 23 rooms, 9 bathrooms, and room enough for a maid, a Black chauffeur and two Cadillac limousines with license plates FT1 and FT2. Fred engaged in social climbing: taking a Dale Carnegie course to work on his shyness, telling people he was of Swedish ancestry instead of German, and, mindful of the growing prominence of Jews in the real estate industry and in politics, he became active in Jewish philanthropies. His son, Fred Trump Jr., continued this affinity as a college student at Lehigh University where he said he was Jewish in order to pledge to the Jewish fraternity.

Donald was pugnacious as a child. In his book *The Art of the Deal,* he bragged about slugging his music teacher in second grade because he didn't think the teacher knew the subject. There's some doubt as to whether this story is true, but it fits the general narrative. As a child, Donald threw rocks at other children in playpens and provoked disputes with his peers. He admits he got into a lot of trouble — and as a result, his father shipped him off to the New York Military Academy when he was a teen.

Donald was competitive with his siblings, most especially his sister Maryanne, who would grow up to become a federal district court judge, and later an appellate judge. They would try to top each other to make points about politics and business — anything, really, according to Donald's first wife Ivana. Speaking up and shouting down was how the Trumps related to each other.

Mary L. Trump, Fred Jr.'s daughter and a clinical psychologist, has described the family dynamic in darker terms. "Donald ... (needed) to prove to his father that he's the tough guy, the killer, the best, you know, that he's winning all the time, and above all, that he's not weak. And the ways to be weak in my family were to be kind, to admit mistakes, and to apologize."

Donald turned 18 in 1964 when the Vietnam War was

fully inflamed. He received four student deferments from the military draft and one medical deferment because of a bone spur in his foot. Donald attended Fordham University in the Bronx, close to home, and then in junior year, he transferred to the University of Pennsylvania in Philadelphia. His niece Mary has written that Donald paid a friend to take the SAT so he could be admitted to Penn. He received a Bachelor of Science degree in economics, but he didn't study at the exclusive Wharton School at Penn, as he often claims.

Donald was self-conscious about his image. On a date with another Penn student, the actress-to-be Candice Bergen, he wore a three-piece burgundy suit with matching leather boots. He was the heir apparent to the Trump construction business. Fred Jr. was not interested in succeeding his father, Fred Sr. recognized a kindred spirit in his second son. Donald began modeling himself after his father, first by driving a Cadillac with the license plate DJT.

Two years after obtaining his degree from Penn, Donald was still living in Queens. He was effectively an "outer borough guy" — a somewhat derogatory term among New York City denizens — and he wanted to join the tribe of fashionable Manhattanites. He has boasted that during this period, he was on the hunt "almost every night" for "beautiful young women."

Donald moved to Manhattan and rented what he called a crummy little apartment on Third Avenue and 75th Street, with a dismaying view of a water tank. He set out to join Le Club, which he regarded as "the hottest club in the city" — like the more famous Studio 54 at the apex of its renown. Le Club membership included some of the most successful, attractive men and women. It was the sort of place, according to *The Daily Beast,* where you were likely to see a wealthy

75-year-old guy walk in with three blondes from Sweden. The sort of place, in other words, where women are valued above all as beautiful ornaments, and being in their company is an outward sign of a man's success.

One of Donald's favorite ways to meet women was to attend runway fashion shows populated by glamorous models. In 1976, he encountered a blonde Czechoslovakian model, Ivana Zelníčková, who was in New York City to promote the Montreal Summer Olympics. While she and several other models were waiting for a table at Maxwell's Plum, Donald introduced himself, saying he knew the manager. He got them a table, paid the bill, and showed up after their meal in a limo to drive them back to their hotel. The next day, he sent Ivana 100 red roses: "To Ivana, with affection. Donald." He invited her to lunch and showed up in a 3-piece business suit. "He looked like a smart businessman," Ivana wrote in *Raising Trump,* "which, I was coming to realize, was his look."

Not only did Donald meet his first and third wives at fashion events, but he took his son, Don Jr., shopping for women at such a gathering years later, in 2003. Donald went up to a stunning blond, Vanessa Haydon, who was a model in the show, as well as an actress and outstanding tennis player. "Have you met my son?" he asked her. At the show's intermission, the elder Trump introduced the two again. "Have you met my son?" he asked, and she responded, "Yes, a few minutes ago." Don Jr. and Vanessa began dating after meeting for a third time at a friend's dinner party.

In Ivana, Donald found a person who could not only compete with his dad's flashy Cadillac style but also one-up the old man. Her first meeting with the Trump family was for brunch at Tavern on the Green in New York's Central

Park. The entire clan arrived on time, which by Fred's watch meant five minutes early. Present were parents Fred and Mary, sisters Maryanne and Elizabeth, brothers Fred Jr. and Robert, along with their spouses and children. Everyone ordered the steak; Ivana unsettled them by choosing a filet of sole. At subsequent black-tie events, Ivana has said, she scandalized Fred Sr. by wearing cleavage-baring gowns, while his daughters Maryanne and Elizabeth dressed modestly.

Ivana encouraged Donald's drive for commercial success. Not only did she approve of his "look" as a smart businessman, she reflected in her memoir, *Raising Trump*, that their initial attraction contained an element of ambition. "We had the same kind of drive and energy," Ivana wrote. "Not a lot of people are like us, and we recognized those qualities in each other."

At the time, Donald was working 7 a.m. to 7 p.m., anxious to prove himself as a developer in the merciless New York City real estate market; he would come home at night and take Ivana out to dinner. Six months after they met, in April 1977, the couple married at the imposing Marble Collegiate Church on Fifth Avenue, where the Trumps had been going for decades. Six hundred people attended the ceremony, performed by Pastor Norman Vincent Peale, who besides his work as a Methodist minister wrote prolifically about the power of positive thinking. Ivana's mother wasn't feeling well and stayed in Czechoslovakia. Ivana's father, Dedo, made the trip to America and met Donald for the first time. Donald would display a similar disinterest in the family origins of his third wife, Melania. He visited Slovenia just one time, and then stayed only for dinner with her parents.

Ivana and Donald took a two-day honeymoon in Acapulco before going back to work: he, to finalize the deal to turn the Commodore Hotel into the Grand Hyatt, where

Ivana would take control of interior design and rebranding. Meanwhile, he started financing another project, Trump Tower. The work kept him constantly busy, and Ivana shared his zeal. After their first child, Don Jr., was born, she took just two days of maternity leave before returning to the Grand Hyatt.

Ivana's account of raising her three children has an arm's-length quality, especially when compared with how she recounts her career helping to build Donald's empire. For the design and branding of Trump Tower, Ivana writes in *Raising Trump*, "I picked out every piece of marble and every golden fixture in the place. The famous fountain in the lobby? My idea. The steel-and-glass façade? I pushed for that."

Ivana would not allow playdates at Trump Tower. She employed nannies to do all the dropping off and picking up. "I avoided playdates like the plague," Ivana has written. For school performances, she would take a car to the school, watch the performance, kiss her child afterward, and head out the door to be "back at my desk within an hour."

Time with Dad was similarly curtailed. The children would rise at 6:30 a.m., and then their mom or a nanny would take them down to the 28th floor of Trump Tower, where Donald had his offices. They said a morning hello to him before walking to school. According to Ivana, Donald had no idea how to engage the kids at their respective ages and converse on their level. The children didn't know how to talk to him, either. When Ivanka was old enough to talk business, it was a "breakthrough."

Bedtime was 7 p.m. sharp with no discussion. Ivanka remembers her parents going out nearly every night. She would have dinner and a bath, and then spend 45 minutes with her mom as she got ready for her evening.

"Mom incorporated us into every aspect of her life," Ivanka wrote in a contribution to *Raising Trump*. "Not many kids sat on the floor of their mother's office while she was on the phone, tagged along onsite inspections, got to go with her to lunch with her friends, or greeted guests when she entertained."

Ivana believes that, as a career woman, she was a role model for her children. But that emphasis on work, she has said, also probably doomed her marriage. "My huge professional wins came at a personal cost," she wrote. "My husband and I became more like business partners than spouses. We'd talk about work all the time, about the bottom line, the high rollers coming in that weekend, what was going on at the Plaza."

She's gone so far as to say that Donald loved what she did for his company, and he felt as though she was outshining him. "In our marriage," Ivana wrote, "there couldn't be two stars. So one of us had to go."

Echoing Donald's early competition with his siblings, as well as his father's social climbing, Donald and Ivana encouraged competition in their children. During the annual Trump Christmas ski trip to Aspen, Ivana recalls the Trump kids racing the Kennedy children on skis. The Kennedys, an Irish immigrant family, whose scion rose to become president, racing against the newer immigrant family from Germany and Czechoslovakia. "It was Trump vs. Kennedy," Ivana wrote, "and Trump always won."

The family bought the 126-room estate Mar-a-Lago in Palm Beach, Florida, in 1985, when the children were ages 1, 3 and 7. They learned tennis at the next door bath and tennis club, Ivana wrote, and the kids were "savagely competitive, especially when playing against each other."

Ivana and Donald had been married for more than 12 years when Ivana could no longer ignore his infidelity, and particularly the presence of one woman in Donald's life: Marla Maples. In December 1989, at the family's annual Aspen retreat, a young blond woman approached Ivana in the food line at Bonnie's restaurant and said, "I'm Marla and I love your husband. Do you?" Ivana told her to get lost; the children witnessed the exchange. Later, Donald and Ivana raged at each other in a fight the kids also overheard.

Returning to New York in January, Ivana couldn't turn on the TV without hearing about her troubled marriage. The Trumps appeared on the front page of the *New York Post* eight days in a row. Ivana's exotic Czech name became synonymous in the American mind with a "cheated-upon wife." She filed for divorce in March 1990, when the children were ages 6, 8 and 12.

Ivana and Donald's divorce was finalized in March 1992. Seven months later, Marla gave birth to a daughter, Tiffany. The baby was a little more than two months old when her parents, Donald and Marla, married at Christmas 1993. None of Ivana's children attended the ceremony.

Ivana is proud of having stood up for herself by leaving Donald — although it's unclear whether she really had much of a choice. Donald's flagrant parading of Marla Maples appears to have been calculated to back Ivana into a corner, to strip her of the ability to look the other way. Still, she embraces her choice to divorce as a blow for womankind. In 1992, as news coverage about the affairs of presidential candidate Bill Clinton raged on, Ivana attended a speech by Hillary Clinton. Afterward, Ivana wrote, she went up to Hillary and asked: "How do you deal with it?"

"She knew I was talking about the cheating," Ivana wrote. "She just looked at me and walked away. I've often wondered what course her life would have taken if she'd left Bill after the Monica Lewinsky scandal. Nowadays, I look at political wives who stand by their cheating, lying husbands at press conferences with a glazed look in their eyes, and I can't believe they put up with it. How do they explain it to their children?"

Ivana can say that now. But her public statements also ring of regret for having given up what turned out to be the starring wifely role of U.S. First Lady. In an interview in October 2017, a year after the election and as her book *Raising Trump* was being published, Ivana told Amy Robach of ABC *News* that she had believed Donald could run for president in 1992. However, she felt — wrongly, as it turned out — that the affair with Marla Maples ruined his chances. "Every American woman hated him," Ivana said she had thought at the time, "and every American hated him. There was no way he could run."

Ivana went on in this interview to tout her own abilities as a businesswoman and public figure, in a fashion that deliberately reminded viewers of Melania's many missteps: the early disarray in the East Wing staff, the speech plagiarized from Michelle Obama. "Would I straighten up the White House in 14 days? Absolutely," Ivana said. "Can I give the speech for 45 minutes without teleprompter? Absolutely."

She said she has the direct number to the White House and speaks with the president every two weeks or so, at his request. "Because I'm basically first Trump wife," Ivana told the interviewer, with a laugh. "I'm First Lady, okay?"

Melania's response, through a spokesman, was harsh: "Mrs. Trump ... is honored by her role as First Lady of the United States. She plans to use her title and role to help children, not sell books. There is clearly no substance to this statement from an ex... unfortunately only attention-seeking and self-serving noise."

Even though Donald was the U.S. president when Ivana published her memoir, she did not ask his permission. She wrote that the divorce was brutal, and it took about two years to reach the settlement. Donald approached it as a business deal, she said, and "he cannot lose. He has to win."

An Improbable Rise: Melanija Knavs

The Knavs family were in many ways similar to the Trumps, if you had transported the Trumps from the opportunity-rich postwar outer boroughs of Manhattan to a little village in a communist country. The chance of upward mobility was not great in the hilly town of Sevnica, in what was then communist Yugoslavia. But it was not for lack of effort on the part of the Knavses.

"He was pretty successful over there," Trump has said of his father-in-law. "It's a different kind of success than you have here. But he was successful."

Viktor and Amalija met in 1966 and raised their daughters, Ines and Melanija, in an ordinary concrete apartment building in the hilly town of 4,500 people. Humble Sevnica was known for its medieval castle and annual salami festival.

Even in those days, when Yugoslavia was a communist country and times were lean, Amalija—nicknamed Malci — was always impeccably dressed and coiffed. She worked in a government-owned textile factory, walking across a bridge to work every day in heels. She drew patterns for children's clothes and later designed them. In the evenings after work, she found time to make fashionable clothes for her daughters.

The family lived a little above their neighbors, striking a "worldly image" by vacationing in France, Germany, and Italy. Malci traveled to France and Germany for work and brought home western fashion magazines, which interested and inspired her daughters.

Viktor spent a lot of time on the road as a traveling salesman of cars and motorcycles. He doted on his Mercedes sedans and a Maserati, which were rarities in his small town. One neighbor, Joze Vuk, said of Viktor, "He always wore a tie, smart clothes and carried a briefcase. You could not avoid noticing him." He joined the Slovenian Communist Party, an exclusive club whose members sometimes pledged because of career ambitions as much as ideology.

Viktor was a jocular, larger-than-life personality who carried himself in a self-assured way — an obvious parallel to Melania's future husband. Both are tall, portly men with blond hair and sharp suits; brash men who like the finer things in life. They are only five years apart in age. Friend and neighbor Tomaz Jeraj said, "Trump reminds me of Viktor. He's a salesman. He has business in his veins."

Melania concurs in the view that they're a lot alike. "They're both hard working. They're both very smart and very capable. They grew up in totally different environments, but they have the same values, they have the same tradition. I, myself, am similar to my husband. Do you understand what I mean? So is my dad; he is a family man, he has tradition, he was hard working. So is my husband."

Viktor, like Trump, was also viciously litigious when it came to his personal life. Before meeting Malci, he allegedly impregnated a woman who bore him a son, Denis Cigelnjak. Viktor fought the order to pay child support all the way to Slovenia's highest appellate court, and lost. Under court order, he paid child support until Denis was 18, but Viktor never reached out to meet the young man. "I missed being able to say, 'Hey, Dad, let's go for a coffee'," Denis has said.

For high school, Melania left Sevnica for Ljubljana, the capital city of Slovenia. Viktor had rented an apartment in the capital so that the girls could study at city schools, which were superior to those in their village. Melania joined Ines in Ljubljana and attended the Secondary School of Design and Photography. After her high school graduation, Melania began college at the University of Ljubljana, studying architecture and design. She dropped out after a year, and she and Ines decamped to Milan in northern Italy. Ines wanted to break into fashion design in this capital of couture, while Melania had decided to pursue modeling. They changed their last name to Knauss, from Knavs. Her first name changed from Melanija to Melania.

This intense pursuit of professional opportunity reflects the new freedoms of the times, according to Mitja Velikonja, a professor of cultural studies at the University of Ljubljana. Slovenia began moving toward democracy, from communism, in 1989. Dr. Velikonja is a contemporary of the Knauss sisters.

"We were/are still living in a patriarchal society, in which it is 'normal' that women get married and have kids. So there was a sort of 'soft' social pressure," she said in an email interview for this book. "However, formally and informally, girls were encouraged to study, to engage in public, to step out of the shadow... So, in a way, they were suggested to be both: caring mothers/wives and good, ambitious workers — which is also a sign of 'silent patriarchalism' that doubles the demands/expectations to women. In short: not very different from our times."

After leaving Sevnica, Melania rarely returned to visit her old friends. This presaged what was to become a signature Melania character trait: moving on to grab the next opportunity without looking back.

In Milan, at age 18, Melania signed with a modeling agency. In 1992, she was named runner-up in the *Jana Magazine* "Look of the Year" contest, held in Ljubljana, which promised its top three contestants an international modeling contract. This work brought her to the attention of Italian-born businessman Paolo Zampolli, who invited her to model for his agency in New York.

In 1996, now taking her chances in the uber-competitive city of New York, Melania pursued her career with vigor. Fashion photographer Antoine Verglas said Melania stayed away from "the scene," hung out in her modest apartment and had "no history of boyfriends" in New York. "That was very unusual in our business," he said.

She was now 26, and she began playing up her advantages by going on casting calls for alcohol and tobacco ads, which her underage competitors couldn't be hired for. She landed a Camel ad, on a billboard in Times Square. Around this time, she went for breast implant surgery, according to photographers who have seen her surgical scars. However, Melania denies having had implants.

After she met Donald Trump in 1998, her career prospects improved measurably. Trump began introducing her around town as a "supermodel," although Melania could hardly make a claim to such a title. One of her big breaks was posing for a multi-page spread in British *GQ* magazine, inside Trump's custom-built jet, under the spicy headline, "Sex at 30,000 feet. Melania Knauss earns her air miles." The sexy photo essay about jet-setters claimed Melania was "wearing a sparkly necklace and not a stitch of clothing." In fact, according to photographer Verglas, though she appears to be nude, she discreetly covered some parts and "there were certain sittings she would not do."

The photo essay was published during Trump's Reform Party presidential bid. *GQ* quoted Melania as saying, of the possibility of being first lady, "I will put all my effort into it, and I will support my man." Talk show legend Larry King invited Melania onto his show for an interview. She described how she met Donald, telling the story about Fashion Week and the Kit Kat Klub, which some say was an invention, a convenient "meet cute" for the couple to tell. In fact, friends say, the couple had been seeing each other for some time before the Klub. Larry King asked Melania what drew her to Donald. She said she fell in love with "his mind. His amazing mind."

The pair make for a dynamic team, say people who know them. Trump trusts Melania's political instincts, and she is a force that keeps him grounded. Michael Caputo met Melania in 2013. He was advising Trump at the time about whether to run for governor of New York. He recalls being wowed, not only by her beauty but by her deliberative presence.

"She came with a jacket on her shoulders but not her arms," he said. "I knew that she was a beautiful person, a beautiful woman, from her pictures. But I was astonished at how much better looking she was in person. She's a remarkable woman. Everything she says, she has thought about. I've never, ever seen her make a mistake… She's very deliberate in everything she does. It's a real big contrast to the president."

Another Trump adviser, Roger Stone, emphasizes that Donald trusts Melania because she never tries to upstage him. Her advice is only given with Trump's best interest and success in mind, Stone said. "She's discreet," he said. "We don't know what she says to her husband." For that reason, he said, "she is probably one of the few advisers he listens to."

Her perceived calming effect on him was so great that Trump's pals and at least one of his adult children exhorted her to come to the White House as soon as possible after he was elected. Melania delayed her move from Trump Tower in Manhattan, she said, to allow their son Barron to finish out the school year with his classmates and friends. The pair didn't arrive in Washington until June 11, 2017 — more than seven months after he won the presidency.

The Next Generation: Raising Trump

Donald Trump's three oldest children echo the values of their parents. Ivanka, like her mother Ivana, is a work-comes-first mother to her three kids. She has weekly lunch dates with the oldest, daughter Arabella, at her office. The marriage of Don Jr. — father of five — broke up over rumors that he was unfaithful, and he has adopted an aggressively conservative, divisive political persona — just like Dad. Eric, like his father, has been called to task for directing charitable contributions to Trump family businesses, in defiance of federal tax rules as well as state laws that ban self-dealing and misleading donors.

Headlines refer to Tiffany, Donald's fourth child, with Marla Maples, as the quietest Trump. She graduated from Georgetown University Law Center in Washington, D.C. and is engaged to Nigerian-American Michael Boulos, whose family owns a multibillion-dollar conglomerate based in Nigeria and is active in more than 10 West African countries.

The couple has spent Thanksgiving and Easter holidays with Donald and the clan. Ivanka has given Tiffany advice about living life in the spotlight, such as what colors look best on camera.

Indeed, being famous is something this younger generation has handled well. During the 2016 presidential campaign, at a town hall debate between candidates Hillary Clinton and Donald Trump, the moderator asked each one to say something nice about the other. Hillary's response was, "I respect his children."

Donald Jr., Ivanka, and Eric never graced the tabloid headlines, the way other wealthy Manhattan teenagers did in the 1990s and 2000s, when they were growing up. No doubt, the Trump children lived in opulent luxury. To give just one example, after birthday parties, the family sorted the gifts of toys, sports equipment, clothes and games into piles. One pile was for keepers, the things they loved and were genuinely excited to have. Another pile was for the doubles or triples of that year's hot toy, which went for donation.

The children attended separate private schools and vacationed in Saint-Tropez and St. Moritz. However, while other rich kids in their circle were flying to Ibiza and Las Vegas for nightclub benders, or to Rodeo Drive for shopping sprees, the Trump children received a modest allowance, a curfew, and no personal credit cards.

Eric has said he was raised to avoid tarnishing the family name. "We knew our family had a reputation to uphold. We're one of (the) last families you'd ever see going to a club and dancing on tables," he told AOL.com in a 2011 interview.

No doubt Donald and Melania's son, Barron, will follow a similar path.

Will the Trump Marriage Last?

What does the future hold for Donald and Melania? Their marriage is more a negotiated deal than a traditional union. "Transactional" is the phrase used by Stephanie Winston Wolkoff. Longtime Trump aide-now-estranged Omarosa Manigault Newman called it "the ultimate merger." She wrote in her 2018 tell-all *Unhinged* that Trump behaved "like a dog off the leash" at events Melania did not attend, and "Only Melania knows the bargain she made in her own mind to tolerate her husband's behavior."

Melania knew he would be a question mark in terms of his fidelity as a husband, but as his wife, she could build her own profile. She got to be a somebody by marrying him. The marriage has enhanced her image in a way that was a step beyond what she could have created on her own, even as a successful model. Becoming Mrs. Trump improved her status and position in life. "She looks to me like she's a person who wants to be well known and viewed by everybody," said psychologist Dr. Rossi. "Even if she's rather quiet at times and not in the public eye… she likes her position, put it that way."

Even so, people who've spent time around the couple say they love each other. Michael Caputo has known Trump for many years — from Caputo's days as a high-stakes blackjack player at a Trump casino in Atlantic City, to his position in the Trump administration as an assistant secretary for the U.S. Department of Health and Human Services. "If you've ever been in their presence when they're relaxing, you know that there's real love between them," Caputo said, "the way he looks at her and no one else."

Caputo has experience in the Slavic world professionally as a consultant, as well as personally; he is married to a Slavic woman. He says that background gives Melania a built-in determination that an American woman might not have.

"She comes from nothing, and she has a good memory," Caputo said. "She remembers what it was like growing up in the village. I think Melania takes all the qualities of being a Slavic woman — which is you're focused on your family, your beauty, your education, your power — and tries to put all four of those things into making a good home life for your entire family and yourself."

No doubt her past helps her deal, emotionally, with Trump's "side action," Caputo said. "It's still far better than being married to a Slavic man. On bad days, she probably says to herself, 'Well, at least I'm not married to Constantine.' I mean, I met many good men in Russia, Ukraine and elsewhere. But it's a much lower percentage. Their challenges are different. It's just a really unfulfilling life as a male in the former Soviet Union."

Perhaps looking at it that way, Melania's deal makes a good bit of sense. Yet, the speculation about whether this couple would stay together began the day the presidential election results were in. Touching down at the Palm Beach, Florida airport to start their post-White House life, Donald paused to wave to the photographers, while Melania walked on leaving him alone. She doesn't have to play the role anymore. With Trump impeached a second time and vulnerable to prosecution, staying by his side can't be an attractive proposition.

One lawyer who specializes in high net worth matrimonial cases, Jacqueline Newman, managing partner of Berkman Bottger Newman & Rodd, was quoted saying, "I think the next year or so will be very telling as to how things will play out with their marriage."

Melania has established herself as a worldwide figure probably well beyond her wildest dreams when she left Ljubljana for Milan and then New York. She has a son she adores and whose future she solidified by leveraging her First Lady status to renegotiate her prenup. She has fulfilled her side of the marital transaction, adorning her husband's grandiose ambitions with her striking good looks, style, and affectionate family life. Time will tell if this deal continues to suit Melania.

Conclusion

I decided to write about these couples after noticing that our public conversation about them had remained frozen in place. When the Oval Office intern scandal broke in 1998, we asked, "Why does Hillary stay with Bill?" More than two decades later, we're still wondering.

I've been married for 25 years, and it's a strong, nurturing union that has been essential to my happiness and my growth as a person. It would take a lot for me to leave. The repeated public humiliation the wives profiled here have suffered would have been enough to break me.

As I studied their stories, I found some commonalities. Often, they have a stultifying view of marriage, which I've called patriarchal. Sometimes, like Jack and Jackie Kennedy, they've been raised to believe that men cheat and women stay with them, and that's just the way it is.

Infidelity is a male privilege. Lady Bird Johnson reportedly looked the other way regarding her husband's affairs, wielding power inside the White House as compensation.

In other cases, such as Hillary Clinton's, the many good things that came from marrying Bill seem to have persuaded her that their union was worth the price of enduring infidelity. Her acceptance of the institution of marriage formed as she witnessed her parents' difficult relationship and through her conservative Midwestern Methodist faith. Later, I believe, she saw that politically in America, a woman is limited — and a divorced woman, especially one who leaves a popular Democrat, cannot aspire, with any success, to the nation's top office. I think those attitudes about women in politics have their roots in patriarchal culture as well.

The Trump marriage veered furthest away from my concept of the union — and surprised me most as a student of American politics. Donald and Melania seem to inhabit separate realms and to come together when necessary, when one could not move forward without the other. The presidency was one instance in which they were forced into a joint undertaking. If my choice of language sounds businesslike, that's because that's how I've come to view the Trumps. Having learned more about each partner's history, I believe they are two highly ambitious individuals who benefit from their partnership. It's a transaction: he gains a beautiful woman on his arm, a solid-seeming marriage, a son, and a savvy adviser. She gains wealth and international cachet. If we're honest, many if not most marriages are transactional; they're deals forged in emotional currency, if not always a prenup.

U.S. voters surprised me. I didn't expect them to dismiss Donald Trump's transgressions with women sufficiently to elect him. Stepping out on three wives, bragging about his sexual conquests to gossip columnists and radio hosts, dismissing assault allegations from nearly two dozen women — it still confounds me that this behavior didn't matter more to voters. For journalists like me who believe it's fair and important to report on the private lives of politicians, the Trump presidency was a reckoning. I believed — and still do — that a political leader must have good character.

Press coverage of politicians' personal lives is important because how a person has conducted himself or herself is our measure of what to expect from that person in the future. There will be situations that arise that no one can predict, and character is what steadies a leader in precarious times. Voters can't be in the room; we need to have a certain amount of trust in the person in charge.

When a politician lies about an affair, people ask themselves, what else have they lied about? Each new discovery of a politician cheating erodes public trust. The result is cynicism and apathy among voters.

Researching the women profiled in *Why They Stay*, I observed a stubbornness not to depart the marriage that reminded me of the days when women had nearly no means to survive outside of a union with a man. I employed the White Queen analogy to sum up this determination to stay, to seek security, to care for the family's emotional health, and to build a family legacy. Including women who were raised outside of Western culture helped bring into relief, for me, the strength that conservative, patriarchal views about marriage can exert. Saudi Arabia's fundamentalist version of Islam restricts women's lives in ways that are easy to observe. The contrast helped me see more clearly the more subtle sexism in the United States and in England. Within Western culture, the realm of politics is especially filled with rituals, hierarchies, decorum, and unwritten maxims that benefit men and people who live by male-established rules. Staying married was long thought to be crucial for male politicians, and it may still be for women.

A commonality among the modern White Queens was the passion for a patriotic mission, whether it took the form of Eleanor Roosevelt reassuring a nation shaken by war and the Great Depression, or Hillary Clinton defending children's legal rights, or Silda Wall Spitzer starting her Children for Children foundation. At first, I thought the motives behind this patriotism were selfless and noble. I still believe that, but I also think that when one acts for the good of the country, or the good of one's political husband, there are personal benefits, too. As Elizabeth Edwards said about discovering that her husband John had been unfaithful, it was easier to bury herself in their shared anti-poverty crusading than to wallow in self-pity. The patriotic work may be a way to salvage some view of the marriage as not a waste, to resuscitate good feeling and self-respect.

Lastly, I observed that the public nature of these marriages, betrayals, and patriotic causes intensifies the emotions of all of it for the people involved. Political consultants say that when an elected official seems to have lost touch with what ordinary people are thinking and seeing, that person is living in a bubble or echo chamber. Perhaps he or she is avoiding reading the papers or listening to the news altogether — as Hillary Clinton did and advised her daughter Chelsea to do while her father's White House Oval office scandal was playing out. Not only are the spot-on reports too painful, but no media account can realistically seem 100 percent accurate to the people living through the events. So, they come to distrust what's said in public and to turn inward and toward their spouse and family for a reality check.

Enough time in the political trenches reinforces this reaction. As we've seen with the women profiled in this book, their inclination is to defend the husband when he's under attack — whether it's by building a legal and journalistic war room to fight an impeachment, declaring love for him before a bank of New York City press microphones, pleading with Louisiana reporters to let the family continue their summer plans, or simply standing off to the erring husband's side as he confesses his infidelity.

The many eyes on every move must be frightening and intoxicating, as well. The publicity allows the women who stay to view themselves as loyal, and perhaps to bask in other ego-assuaging activities. I think of Jackie Kennedy setting tastes for women around the world, or Silda Wall Spitzer urging Eliot not to resign the governor's mansion, just as she had begun to position herself as an advocate for environmental causes and public service for young people. Or, Eleanor Roosevelt joining the first United States delegation to the United Nations and chairing the committee that would write the landmark Universal Declaration of Human Rights. Without their marriages to famous political men, would these women have had these opportunities? To leave the marriage would be to go from being extraordinary to ordinary. They would no longer be rubbing shoulders with the influential and the history-making. They might themselves no longer make history.

Endnotes

Prologue

Anderson, Christopher. *American Evita: Hillary Clinton's Path to Power* (New York: William Morrow, 2004).

Andrews, Helena. "Wendy Vitter 'stands by her man'," Politico.com, July 19, 2007.

Bernstein, Carl. *A Woman in Charge* (New York: Alfred A. Knopf, 2007).

Bernstein, Elizabeth. "Back to Happily Ever After," *The Wall Street Journal,* May 1, 2012.

Brands, H.W. *Traitor to His Class: The Privileged Life and Radical Presidency of Franklin Delano Roosevelt,* (New York: Doubleday, 2008).

Bynum, Chris. "Overcoming infidelity," *Times-Picayune* (New Orleans) July 27, 2007.

Chester, Lewis, Magnus Linklater and David May. *Jeremy Thorpe: A Secret Life,* (London: Fontana Paperbacks, 1979).

Collier, Peter with David Horowitz. *The Roosevelts: An American Saga* (New York: Simon & Schuster, 1995).

Davis, John H. *The Kennedys: Dynasty and Disaster, 1848–1983* (New York: McGraw-Hill, 1984).

Dubin, Murray. "Chelsea's quandary: Living with infidelity," *The Philadelphia Inquirer,* Aug. 19, 1998.

Edwards, Elizabeth. *Resilience: Reflections on the Bur- dens and Gifts of Facing Life's Adversities* (New York: Broadway Books, 2009).

Elkind, Peter. *Client 9: The Rise and Fall of Eliot Spitzer* (New York: Portfolio, 2010).

Freeman, Simon and Barrie Penrose. Rinkagate: *The Rise and Fall of Jeremy Thorpe*, (London: Bloomsbury, 1996).

Garcia, Justin R. Garcia, J. MacKillop, E.L. Aller, E.M. Merriwether, D.S. Wilson and J.K. Lum. "Associations between Dopamine D4 Receptor Gene Variation with Both Infidelity and Sexual Promiscuity," *PLoS One*, 2010 Nov 30; 5(11): e14162. doi: 10.1371/journal.pone.0014162.

Gersen, Jeannie Suk. "The Sexual-Assault Election," *The New Yorker*, Nov. 6, 2016.

Gilligan, Carol. *In a Different Voice: Psychological Theory and Women's Development* (Cambridge, MA: Harvard University Press, 1998).

Goldenberg, Sally and Leonard Greene. "It's Huma's Nature: I Blame Myself," *New York Post*, Aug. 1, 2013.

Gordon, Claire. "Anne Sinclair Named France's 'Woman of the Year,' Reveals Different Perception Of Political Wives," *HuffPost Women*, Dec. 20, 2011.

Jacobs, Ben and Amber Jamieson. "Donald Trump goes low by parading women accusing Bill Clinton," *The Guardian*, Oct. 9, 2016.

Johnson, Rebecca Johnson. "The Survivor," *Vogue*, March 2009.

Kennedy, Helen. "Hil and Rupert dine on sly," *Daily News* (New York) July 18, 2006.

Klein, Edward Klein. *All Too Human: The Love Story of Jack and Jackie Kennedy* (New York: Pocket Books, 1996).

Lachkar, Joan. *The Many Faces of Abuse: Treating the Emotional Abuse of High-Functioning Women* (Lanham, Mary- land: A Jason Aronson Book, Rowman & Littlefield Publishers, 1998).

Lake, Celinda and Stan Greenberg. "Re: Research on Hillary Clinton" (Clinton campaign memo, Washington, DC, May 12, 1992.

MacPherson, Myra. "Into the Fray; Testing the Waters; Joan Kennedy Campaigns Down on the Farm," *Washington Post,* Dec. 12, 1979.

"Marion Thorpe," obituary, *Yorkshire Post* (England) March 15, 2014.

May, Vanessa. "Divorce in Finish women's life stories: Defining 'moral' behavior," *Women's Studies International Forum,* 28.6 (Nov.–Dec. 2005).

McGreevey, Dina Matos. *Silent Partner: A Memoir of My Marriage* (New York: Hyperion, 2007).

Mitchell, Andrea and Alastair Jamieson. "Trump Planned Debate 'Stunt', Invited Bill Clinton Accusers to Rattle Hillary," NBCNews.com, Oct. 10, 2016.

Nogales, Ana. "Happily Ever After? On overcoming cheating," *Orlando Sentinel* (Florida) Aug. 14, 2009.

Nogales, Ana with Laura Golden Bellotti. *Parents Who Cheat: How Children and Adults Are Affected When Their Parents Are Unfaithful,* (Deerfield Beach, FL: Health Communications, Inc., 2009).

Okimoto, Tyler G. and Victoria L. Brescoll. "The price of power: Power seeking and backlash against female politicians," *Personality and Social Psychology Bulletin* 36:7, July 2010: 923–36.

Pengelly, Martin. "Melania Trump's photo snub prompts speculation over post-White House path," *The Guardian,* Jan. 22, 2021.

Ridley, Jane and Eloise Parker. "The sins of the father. A powerful dad's transgressions can be powerful problem for his kids," *Daily News* (New York) March 12, 2008.

Roosevelt, James with Bill Libby. *My Parents: A Differing View* (Chicago: Playboy Press, 1976).

Rosenblum, Emma. "Scenes from a Marriage: Julianna Margulies enters Silda Spitzer territory with *The Good Wife, New York Magazine,* Sept. 21, 2009.

Ruddick, Sara. "Remarks on the Sexual Politics of Reason," *Women and Moral Theory,* ed. Eva Feder Kittay and Diana T. Meyers (Totowa, NJ: Rowman & Littlefield, 1987).

Salario, Alizah. "How Infidelity Affects Kids," *Daily Beast,* May 28, 2011.

Sanford, Jenny. *Staying True,* (New York: Ballantine Books, 2010).

"Silda steps up for Dems," *New York Post,* Jan. 24, 2014.

Smith, Glenn, Robert Behre and Schuyler Kropf. "Sanford gets second chance: On political scrapheap 4 years ago, ex-governor wins 1st District seat," *Post & Courier* (Charleston, SC), May 8, 2013.

Smith, Sally Bedell. *Grace and Power: The Private World of the Kennedy White House* (New York: Random House, 2004).

Today show, interview with Hillary Clinton and host Matt Lauer, NBC, Jan. 27, 1998.

Wilcox, W. Bradford, Elizabeth Marquardt and David Popenoe. *The State of Our Unions 2010: When Marriage Disappears: The New Middle America* (report, The National Marriage Project, University of Virginia, VA, 2010).

Eleanor and Franklin Roosevelt

Burns, James MacGregor and Susan Dunn. *The Three Roosevelts: Patrician Leaders who Transformed America,* (New York: Grove Press, 2001).

Collier, Peter and David Horowitz, *The Roosevelts: An American Saga* (London: Andre Deutsch Ltd., 1995).

Cook, Blanche WieSenator *Eleanor Roosevelt: Volume One 1884–1933* (New York: Viking Penguin, 1992).

Lash, Joseph P. *A World of Love: Eleanor Roosevelt and Her Friends,* 1943–1962 (New York: Doubleday, 1987).

Lash, Joseph P. *Eleanor and Franklin: The Story of Their Relationship, based on Eleanor Roosevelt's Private Papers* (W. W. Norton & Company, 1971).

Longworth, Alice Roosevelt Longworth and Michael Teague. *Mrs. L: Conversations with Alice Roosevelt Longworth* (New York: Doubleday, 1981).

Murphy, Lawrence R. *Perverts by Official Order: The Campaign Against Homosexuals by the United States Navy* (Philadelphia, PA: Haworth Press, 1988).

Persico, Joseph E. *Franklin & Lucy: President Roosevelt, Mrs. Rutherfurd, and the Other Remarkable Women in His Life* (New York: Random House, 2008).

Roosevelt, Eleanor. "Diary," (Franklin D. Roosevelt Presidential Library & Museum, February 1919) Box 4.

Roosevelt, Eleanor. *This I Remember, vol. II* (New York: Harper & Bros., 1949).

Roosevelt, Eleanor. *This is My Story, vol. I* (New York: Harper & Brothers, 1937).

Roosevelt, Elliott and James Brough, *Mother R.: Eleanor Roosevelt's Untold Story* (New York: Putnam, 1977).

Roosevelt, Franklin D. to Sara D. Roosevelt. "Roosevelt

family papers" (letter, Franklin D. Roosevelt Presidential Library & Museum, March 28, 1918).

Roosevelt, James with Bill Libby, *My Parents: A Differing View* (Chicago: Playboy Press, 1976).

Roosevelt, Theodore. *An Autobiography* (Oakland, CA: University of California Libraries, 1913).

Ward, Geoffrey C. *A First-Class Temperament: The Emergence of Franklin Roosevelt* (New York: Harper & Row, 1989).

Willis, Resa. *FDR and Lucy: Lovers and Friends* (London: Routledge, 2004).

Jackie and Jack Kennedy

Adams, Cindy and Susan Crimp. *Iron Rose: The Story of Rose Fitzgerald Kennedy and Her Dynasty* (Beverly Hills, CA: Dove Books, 1995).

Andersen, Christopher. *The Good Son: JFK Jr. and the Mother He Loved* (New York: Simon and Schuster, 2014).

Cassini, Igor writing as Cholly Knickerbocker. *New York Journal-American,* 1947.

Coontz, Stephanie. *Marriage, A History: From Obedience to Intimacy, or How Love Conquered Marriage,* (New York: Viking Penguin, 2005).

Davis, John H. *The Kennedys: Dynasty and Disaster, 1848–1983* (New York: McGraw-Hill, 1984).

" 'Don't do it, don't be a fool!': Caroline Kennedy 'against her cousin Maria Shriver's reunion with Arnold Schwarzenegger'," *Daily Mail* (London) Jan. 4, 2012.

Heymann, C. David. *American Legacy: The Story of John and Caroline Kennedy* (New York: Simon and Schuster, 2008).

Heymann, C. David. *Joe and Marilyn: Legends in Love* (New York: Simon and Schuster, 2014).

Howe, Caroline. "Jackie Kennedy wanted to divorce her philandering husband and was given $1m to stay," *Daily Mail* (London) June 3, 2014.

"Jacqueline Kennedy: In Her Own Words," two-hour special hosted by Diane Sawyer, ABC *News,* Sept. 13, 2011.

Klein, Edward. *Just Jackie: Her Private Years* (New York: Random House Publishing Group, 2009).

Shriver, Maria. "Jacqueline Kennedy: Historic Conversations on Life with John F. Kennedy," Q&A with Caroline Kennedy," Sept. 14, 2011, http://mariashriver.com/blog/2011/09/qa-caroline-kennedy-jacqueline-kennedy-historic- conversations-life-john-f-kennedy/

Smith, Sally Bedell. *Grace and Power: The Private World of the Kennedy White House* (New York: Random House, 2004).

Swanson, Gloria. *Swanson on Swanson: An Autobiography* (New York: Random House Inc., 1980).

Marion Stein and Jeremy Thorpe

Bessell, Peter. *Cover-Up: The Jeremy Thorpe Affair* (Oceanside, CA: Simon Best, 1980).

Chappell, Connery. *Island of Barbed Wire: The Remarkable Story of World War Two Internment on the Isle of Man* (London: Robert Hale, 1984).

Chester, Lewis, Magnus Linklater and David May. *Jeremy Thorpe: A Secret Life,* (London: Fontana Paperbacks, 1979).

Fox, Margalit Fox. "George Lascelles, 88, Earl and Opera Writer," obituary, *The New York Times,* Aug. 5, 2011.

Freeman, Simon and Barrie Penrose. *Rinkagate: The Rise and Fall of Jeremy Thorpe,* (London: Bloomsbury, 1996).

Grant, Kitty. "How Russell T. Davies Changed LGBTQ+ Representation on British TV, Redbrick.com, accessed April 17, 2021.

Hickling, Alfred. "Film & Music: Classical: 'Unlike many, we have never been tainted with a whiff of scandal'," *Guardian* (London) Aug. 7, 2009.

Lascelles, George, 7th Earl of Harewood. *The Tongs and the Bones: The Memoirs of Lord Harewood* (London: Weidenfeld & Nicolson, 1981).

"Lord Montagu on the court case which ended the legal persecution of homosexuals," *London Evening Standard,* July 14, 2007.

"Marion Thorpe," obituary, *Yorkshire Post,* March 15, 2014.

Notes for David, James and Robert Lascelles drawn from jameslascelles.com, omnilexica.com, britishpathe.com, and "The Royal Rich Report," *Daily Mail* on Sunday, Oct. 21, 2001.

Parris, Matthew. *Great Parliamentary Scandals: Four Centuries of Calumny, Smear and Innuendo* (London: Robson Books, 1996).

Rosenbaum, Martin. "Jeremy Thorpe: Was there an establishment cover-up?" *BBC News,* UK Politics, Dec. 8, 2014.

Service, Tom. "Britten centenary: Marion Thorpe on her friendship with the composer," *Guardian* (London) Nov. 21, 2013.

"Star Snooper," *Sun-Herald* (Sydney) March 6, 2003.

Tapsfield, James. Ex-Liberal leader Thorpe dies at 85; 'Fighter for underprivileged' acquitted of murder plot," *Daily Post* (North Wales) Dec. 5, 2014.

Thorpe, Jeremy. *In My Own Time: Reminiscences of a Liberal Leader* (London: Politicos Publishing, 1999).

Hillary and Bill Clinton

Anderson, Christopher. *American Evita: Hillary Clinton's Path to Power* (New York: William Morrow, 2004).

Andersen, Christopher. *Bill and Hillary: The Marriage* (New York: William Morrow, 1999).

Andersen, Christopher. "Sex, Lies ... and Chelsea," *Orlando Sentinel*, Aug. 25, 1999.

Bennet, James. "For the Clintons, Stanford Parents' Day Won't Come Soon Enough," *The New York Times*, Sept. 18, 1997.

Bernstein, Carl. *A Woman in Charge* (New York: Alfred A. Knopf, 2007).

"Bill Clinton Biography," Biography.com, accessed Jan. 22, 2015.

Bingham, Amy. "Chelsea Clinton's Childhood: No Pizza, Cartoons on Weekdays," ABC *News*, May 7, 2012.

"Biography: Hillary Rodham Clinton," The American Experience, *PBS*, accessed Jan. 21, 2015.

Blair, Diane. Journal entry, Sept. 9, 1998; Thanksgiving Day, 1996; late December 1998

Brock, David. *The Seduction of Hillary Rodham* (New York: Simon and Schuster, 1998).

Chafe, William H. *Bill and Hillary: The Politics of the Personal* (New York: Farrar, Straus and Giroux, 2012).

"Chelsea Clinton Goes Public," AllPolitics, CNN/Time, March 25, 1997.

Clinton, Bill. *My Life* (New York: Vintage Books, 2005).

Clinton, Hillary Rodham. *Living History*, (New York: Simon & Schuster, 2003).

Dart, Bob. "Chelsea's just one of the gang at Sidwell Friends," *Baltimore Sun*, May 10, 1993.

Gallup poll, Dec. 31, 1998.

Gartner, John. *In Search of Bill Clinton: A Psychological Biography,* (New York: St. Martin's Press, 2008).

Goldberg, Michelle. "QAnon Believers Are Obsessed With Hillary Clinton. She Has Thoughts." *The New York Times,* Feb. 5, 2021. https://www.nytimes.com/2021/02/05/opinion/qanon-hillary-clinton.html

Hoffman, Matthew. "The Bill Clinton We Knew At Oxford," *Independent* (London) Oct. 11, 1992.

"It All Began in a Place Called Hope: President Bill Clinton," The White House, accessed Jan. 22, 2015.

Lee, Esther. "Chelsea Clinton Talks Growing Up in the White House Under 'Very Firm' Parents, Says Marriage Is 'Incredibly Important'," *US Magazine,* March 17, 2014.

McClelland, Edward. "How 1968 changed Hillary," *Salon,* April 8, 2008.

Mooney, Alexander. "Watch Chelsea Clinton field a question about Monica Lewinsky," *CNN News,* March 26, 2008.

Purdum, Todd S. "Chelsea Clinton, Still a Closed Book," *The New York Times,* June 17, 2001.

Roberts, Roxanne. "Life With Father," *The Washington Post,* Jan. 27, 1998.

"Rush Limbaugh said I looked like a dog," *Daily Mail* (London) April 2, 2012.

"The Class of 1969," *Life,* June 20, 1969.

Thomas, Ken. "Chelsea Clinton gets PhD from Oxford: For what?" *Associated Press, Christian Science Monitor,* May 10, 2014.

Today show, interview with Hillary Clinton and host Matt Lauer, NBC, Jan. 27, 1998.

Van Meter, Jonathan. "Anthony Weiner and Huma Abedin's Post-Scandal Playbook," *The New York Times Magazine,* April 10, 2013.

Willey, Kathleen. *Target: Caught in the Crosshairs of Bill and Hillary Clinton* (Washington: WND Books, 2007).

"William Jefferson Clinton Biography," Clinton House Museum, accessed Jan. 22, 2015.

Women in the World Foundation summit, April 3, 2014.

Wendy and David Vitter

Alford, Jeremy. "Sinator Vitter," *Gambit Weekly,* Jan. 20, 2009.

Alford, Jeremy. "The Men Behind the Ads," *Gambit: Best of New Orleans,* Nov. 2, 2010.

Allen-Ebrahimian, Bethany. "Opinion: What a lobbyist's remarks behind closed doors tell you about Chinese money in Washington," *The Washington Post,* Oct. 29, 2019.

Alpert, Bruce. "Wives both play roles for Senate campaigns," *Times-Picayune* (New Orleans) Oct. 29, 2010.

Campbell, Susan. "A Wife's Forgiveness of Infidelity is Not for Us to Question," *Hartford Courant,* July 22, 2007.

Goldman, Russell. "Your Cheating Heart: Why Pols Don't Practice What They Preach," ABC *News,* July 11, 2007.

Itkowitz, Colby. "Senate confirms Wendy Vitter as federal judge, despite Democrats' objections over her opposition to abortion," *The Washington Post,* May 16, 2019.

Jacoby, Mary. "There is a house in New Orleans," *Salon,* Oct. 29, 2004.

Kiel, Lauren D. "David Vitter," *Harvard Crimson,* June 1, 2008.

Konigsmark, Anne Rochell. "A Week of Crisis," *Atlanta Journal-Constitution,* Dec. 20, 1998.

MacAoidh, "Video: Jack Vitter Weighs In," TheHayride.com, Nov. 17, 2015.

Moran, Kate. "Wendy Vitter: As a lawyer, mother and now defender of a hounded husband, she had never been shy about standing her ground," *Times-Picayune* (New Orleans) July 22, 2007.

Murray, Shailagh. "Senator's Number on 'Madam' Phone List," *The Washington Post,* July 10, 2007.

Rettig, Jessica. "10 Things You Didn't Know About David Vitter," *U.S. News & World Report,* Aug. 2, 2010.

Senator David Vitter, Facebook, accessed April 27, 2015.

Tapper, Jake. "Senator Vitter Apologizes for His Link to DC Madam," ABC *News,* July 10, 2007.

Text of Senator David Vitter and Wendy Vitter's statements, *Times-Picayune* (New Orleans) July 17, 2007.

Vanderbilt Student Organizations, *Habitat for Humanity Newsletter,* accessed April 27, 2015; and *"Who's Given"* Vanderbilt University, accessed April 27, 2015; and Sophie Vitter, Face- book, accessed April 27, 2015.

Vitter, Airey. Pinterest, accessed April 27, 2015.

Vitter, David. Invitation Flyer, *Politico,* Aug. 1, 2013.

Ward, Vicky. "The Oldest Profession; No Way to Treat a Lady," *Vanity Fair,* May 2008.

Walsh, Joan. "Why David Vitter Matters," *Salon,* July 17, 2007.

"World News with Charles Gibson," ABC *News,* July 10, 2007.

Silda Wall and Eliot Spitzer

Arnold, Laurence. "Bernard Spitzer, Builder, Father of Ex-Governor, Dies at 90," *The Washington Post,* November 3, 2014.

"Becoming his doormat was her sin, her crime and her failing," *New York Post,* March 13, 2008.

Breidenbach, Michelle. "The First Spouse of New York State: Silda Wall Spitzer," *Central New York Magazine — The Good Life ,* July 1, 2007.

Brubach, Holly. "Spitzer's Justice," *Vanity Fair,* March 2006.

Constantine, Lloyd. *Journal of the Plague Year: An Insider's Chronicle of Eliot Spitzer's Short and Tragic Reign* (Kaplan Publishing, 2010).

Darman, Jonathan. "The Confessions of Eliot Spitzer," *Newsweek,* April 17, 2009.

Elkind, Peter. *Client 9: The Rise and Fall of Eliot Spitzer* (New York: Portfolio, 2010).

"Elyssa Spitzer," LinkedIn profile, accessed Feb. 16, 2015.

Estrich, Susan. "What I Couldn't Teach Eliot Spitzer at Harvard Law School," Creators.com, March 12, 2008.

Foderaro, Lisa W. "Why Do the Wives Stand There, Next to Their Men?" *The New York Times,* March 12, 2008.

Fuller, Bonnie. "Eliot Spitzer's Biggest Challenge – Winning Back the Trust of His Daughters," *Huffington Post,* May 25, 2011.

Grynbaum, Michael. "As Spitzer Pursues a Comeback, His Wife Chooses to Stay Offstage," *The New York Times,* July 17, 2013.

Hakim, Danny. "Gilded Path to Political Stardom, With Detours," *The New York Times,* Oct. 12, 2006.

Johnson, Rebecca. "A Fine Balance," *Vogue,* March 2007.

Johnston, David and Stephen Labaton, "The Reports That Drew Federal Eyes to Spitzer," *The New York Times,* March 12, 2008.

Kim, Shinil. "Gapportunities: Taking a Year Off," *Horace Mann Record,* May 29, 2013.

Konigsberg, Eric. "Her Next Job: First Lady of New York," *The New York Times,* Nov. 10, 2006.

Larson, Leslie. "Silda Wall Spitzer gets $7.5 million divorce payout," *Daily News* (New York) April 28, 2014.

Leefeldt, Ed. "Eliot Unzipped," *Leader's Edge,* July/August 2010.

Mabruk, Ahmed N. "Class of 1984: Eliot Spitzer," *Harvard Crimson,* June 2, 2009.

Masters, Brooke A. *Spoiling for a Fight: The Rise of Eliot Spitzer* (New York: Times Books, 2006).

Pappu, Sridhar. "The Crusader," *Atlantic,* October 2004.

Pleasance, Chris. "Eliot Spitzer's tycoon father left the disgraced politician $6 million more than his other two children," *Daily Mail* (London) Nov. 11, 2014.

Rashbaum, William K. "Revelations Began in Routine Tax Inquiry," *The New York Times,* March 11, 2008.

Ridley, Jane and Eloise Parker, "A powerful dad's transgressions can be powerful problem for kids," *Daily News* (New York) March 12, 2008.

Sawyers, Susan. "Silda Wall Spitzer Does the Right Thing," *New York Social Diary,* Sept. 29, 2011.

Schneider-Mayerson, Anna. "Mrs. Spitzer Suits Up,"

Observer (New York) May 1, 2006.

Smith, Chris. "The Governor and the Darkness," *New York Magazine,* March 24, 2008.

"Spitzer's 'Silda shield': Politicians uncouth to use wives as shields," editorial, *Dallas Morning News,* March 14, 2008.

Vielkind, Jimmy. "After divorce, Silda Wall takes Eliot Spitzer's name," *Politico,* Feb. 28, 2017.

Vilensky, Mike. "Silda Wall Spitzer Carves Her Own Path in Politics," *The Wall Street Journal,* April 29, 2016.

Huma Abedin and Anthony Weiner

Abedin, Huma. "Hot Topic: *The Good Wife*," *Harper's Bazaar,* Sept. 1, 2013.

Barbarino, Al. "Unemployed Anthony Weiner moves into fancy Rosen Partners pad," *Real Estate Weekly,* Aug. 15, 2012.

Barrett, Devlin. "Book excerpt: An FBI sex crimes investigator helped trigger 2016's 'October Surprise'," *The Washington Post,* Sept. 22, 2020.

Bollen, Katalien N. L., Alain-Laurent Verbeke and Mar- tin C. Euwema, "Money or children? Power sources in divorce mediation," *Journal of Family Studies,* Aug. 2013.

Bruinius, Harry. "Huma Abedin: Were her consulting jobs proper?" *Christian Science Monitor,* Aug. 21, 2013.

Bruinius, Harry. "Why Anthony Weiner might stay in New York mayor's race," *Christian Science Monitor,* July 26, 2013.

Burnett, James. "Life of the Party," *New York Magazine,* December 2001.

DeFalco, Beth. "Dirty Politics Weiner beat goes on — and on!" *New York Post,* July 31, 2013.

Dowd, Maureen. "Time to Hard-Delete Carlos Danger," *The New York Times,* July 28, 2013.

Draper, Robert. *Do Not Ask What Good We Do: Inside the U.S. House of Representatives* (New York: Free Press, 2012).

Edwards, Breanna. "Weiner's 10 crazy moments," Politico.com, Sept. 10, 2013.

Gaskill, Stephanie and Corky Siemaszko, "Rep. Anthony Weiner may kiss but won't tell about Hillary Clinton Aide," *Daily News* (New York) May 29, 2008.

Goldenberg, Sally and Leonard Greene, "It's Huma's Nature: I Blame Myself," *New York Post,* Aug. 1, 2013.

Grynbaum, Michael M., Michael Barbaro and Amy Chozick, "A Wife with Powerful Ties Is an Unexpected Architect of a New York Comeback," *The New York Times,* May 24, 2013.

Hicks, Jonathan P. "The 1998 campaign: Congress; Weiner Is Victor Over Katz In Bid to Replace Schumer," *The New York Times,* Sept. 16, 1998.

Heilemann, John. "Back From the Death Panel," *New York Magazine,* Oct. 19, 2009.

Johnson, Rebecca. "Hillary's Secret Weapon," *Vogue,* August 2007.

Karni, Annie. "Anthony Weiner recycles himself as a countertop-company executive," *The New York Times,* Sept. 15, 2020.

McCalmont, Lucy. "Weiner: Done with politics, not life," Politico.com, Oct. 21, 2014.

Mechling, Lauren. "Stepping Along With Anthony Weiner," *New York Sun,* May 26, 2005.

Morgan, Spencer. "Hillary's Mystery Woman: Who Is Huma?" *Observer* (New York) April 2, 2007.

Quinn, Sally. "Blaming Huma Abedin," *The Washington Post,* July 29, 2013.

Sideris, Jim. "Letters to the Editor," *Queens Tribune,* April 25, 2013.

Steinberg, Elyse and Josh Kriegman, *Weiner,* documentary released to theaters in June 2016 and subsequently on Showtime.

Tilak, Visi R. "Who is Huma Abedin?" *The Wall Street Journal,* July 26, 2012.

Van Meter, Jonathan. "The Post-Scandal Playbook," *The New York Times Magazine,* April 14, 2013.

"Weiner family income," *US News and World Report,* June 9, 2011.

Melania and Donald Trump

Berselli, Beth. "Names & Faces." *The Washington Post,* Jan. 15, 2000.

Blair, Gwenda. *The Trumps: Three Generations That Built an Empire.* Simon & Schuster, 2000.

Caputo, Michael. Telephone interview with Celeste Katz Marston, April 13, 2019.

Fox, Emily Jane. " 'Melania. Did. Not. Care.': In a Blistering New Book by Stephanie Winston Wolkoff, Melania Trump Sounds a Lot Like Her Husband," *Vanity Fair,* Aug. 28, 2020.

Haney, Stephanie. " 'I will be very traditional like Jackie Kennedy': Melania Trump predicts what kind of first lady she will be while dating then-boyfriend Donald Trump in 1999 interview." *MailOnline* (London), Oct. 14, 2018.

Horowitz, Jason. "Melania Trump: From Small-Town Slovenia to Doorstep of the White House." *The New York Times,* July 18, 2016.

Ioffe, Julia. "Melania Trump on Her Rise, Her Family Secrets, and Her True Political Views: 'Nobody Will Ever Know'." *GQ,* April 27, 2016.

Johnston, David Cay. *The Making of Donald Trump.* Melville House, 2016.

Jordan, Mary. "Questions linger about how Melania Trump, a Slovenian model, scored 'the Einstein visa'." *The Washington Post,* March 2, 2018.

Jordan, Mary. "With a risque past and posh taste, Melania might be a new model for first ladies." *The Washington Post,* Oct. 1, 2015.

Kindelan, Katie. "Ivana Trump says she is 'first lady'." ABC *News,* Oct. 9, 2017.

Kranish, Michael. "Mary Trump once stood up to her uncle Donald. Now her book describes a 'nightmare' of family dysfunction." *The Washington Post,* July 2, 2020.

Kranish, Michael. "In secretly recorded audio, President Trump's sister says he has 'no principles' and 'you can't trust him'," *The Washington Post,* Aug. 22, 2020.

Newman, Omarosa Minigault. *Unhinged: An Insider's Account of the Trump White House.* Gallery Books, 2018.

Nguyen, Tina. "Eric Trump Reportedly Bragged About Access to $100 Million in Russian Money," *Vanity Fair,* May 8, 2017.

Pengelly, Martin. "Melania Trump's photo snub prompts speculation over post-White House path," *The Guardian,* Jan. 22, 2021.

Quinn, Dave. "Donald Trump Reportedly Had 9-Month Affair with Playboy Model While Married to Melania." *People,* Feb. 16, 2018.

Rossi, Bart. Telephone interview with Celeste Katz Marston, April 2, 2019.

Smith, Alex Duval, "Melania who? Trump's wife a forgotten memory in Slovenian home town" *The Guardian* https://www.theguardian.com/us-news/2016/sep/05/melania-trump-slovenia-home-sevnica

Stone, Roger. Telephone interview with Celeste Katz Marston, April 26, 2019.

Taub, Jennifer. "Trump among the kleptocrats," *The Washington Post,* Sept. 3, 2020.

Trump, Ivana, *Raising Trump.* Gallery Books, an imprint of Simon & Schuster, 2017.

Unger, Craig. "Trump's Russian Laundromat: How to use Trump Tower and other luxury high-rises to clean dirty money, run an international crime syndicate, and propel a failed real estate developer into the White House." *The New Republic,* July 13, 2017.

U.S. Office of Government Ethics, Spouse's Employment Assets and Income, 2018 financial disclosure for President Donald J. Trump.

Usborne, David. "An ideal husband?" *The Independent* (UK), Jan. 22, 2005.

Velikonja, Mitja. Email interview with Celeste Katz Marston, April 16, 2019.

Wadler, Joyce. "A Model as First Lady? Think Traditional." *The New York Times,* Dec. 1, 1999.

Woodward, Bob. *Fear: Trump in the White House.* Simon & Schuster, 2018.

Yuan, Jada. "Melania Trump was in no rush to move into the White House. That's when she renegotiated her prenup, a new book says." *The Washington Post,* June. 12, 2020.

Acknowledgements

I would like to thank the people in public life, many of whom I've met during my career as a journalist and who have worked to make our society better. May we voters continue to be mindful to choose worthy representatives who reflect the best in us.

I'm grateful to my husband, Daniel Harman, for his frank opinions, unending enthusiasm and tenderness in the difficult moments. Also to my daughter Isabelle Harman, whose mix of diligence and joy continues to surprise and delight me. And to my daughter Charlotte Harman, who accepts no received wisdom but ventures to see for herself. It's a quality I greatly admire.

I'm indebted to Celeste Katz Marston, a remarkable and resourceful political journalist who interviewed several people for this book. She was generous with her thoughts and insights, and it was a thrill to see her gifted journalistic mind at work.

Thank you to Andrea Burnett, who served as a consistent and passionate cheerleader; Linda Dunn, who teaches me how to keep moving forward; and the YaYa Book Club that read my first book and then invited me into their stimulating midst.

A heartfelt thanks to my editor, Bonnie Britt. I would have no book without Bonnie, and I'm grateful for her sharp editing eye and her command of history and current events.

Finally, I want to thank the Huntington (NY) Public Library, which fed me with resources and gave me space to work outside my home. Thanks, as well, to the women of JAWS, the Journalism and Women's Symposium. Whenever I've needed help, the savvy and skilled JAWS women have come to my aid.

About the author

A veteran political journalist, Anne Michaud is a reporter for the *Wall Street Journal*. She previously wrote a nationally syndicated op-ed column for *Newsday* from 2008 to 2018. She has won more than 25 writing and reporting awards and has twice been named "Columnist of the Year," by the New York News Publishers Association and the New York State Associated Press Association.

Anne covered Bill Clinton's 1996 re-election campaign, Anthony Weiner's 2005 mayoral bid and Eliot Spitzer's rise and fall as New York's governor from 2006 to 2008. Her work has appeared in the *Los Angeles Times, The Boston Globe, Newsweek,* BusinessWeek.com, *Crain's NY Business, Cincinnati Magazine* and more.

Anne has appeared on numerous television and radio programs, including WNYC's *The Brian Lehrer Show,* NY1's *Reporters' Roundtable* and Fox 5 News WNYW. She's a graduate of the Columbia University Graduate School of Journalism and is a wife and mother.

Made in the USA
Middletown, DE
30 June 2021